THE CAULDRON

The Middle East Behind the Headlines

THE CAULDRON

The Middle East Behind the Headlines

AMIR TAHERI

HUTCHINSON
London Sydney Auckland Johannesburg

First published in 1988 by Hutchinson Ltd,
an imprint of Century Hutchinson Ltd,
Brookmount House, 62–65 Chandos Place,
London WC2N 4NW

Century Hutchinson Australia Pty Ltd
89–91 Albion Street, Surrey Hills, NSW 2010,
Australia

Century Hutchinson New Zealand Limited
PO Box 40–086, Glenfield, Auckland 10, New Zealand

Century Hutchinson South Africa (Pty) Ltd
PO Box 337, Bergvlei, 2012 South Africa

British Library Cataloguing Data
Taheri, Amir
  The Cauldron
  1. Middle East. Politics
  I. Title
  320.956

ISBN 009173729X

Set in Linotron Times by Deltatype, Ellesmere Port

Printed and bound by
Mackays, Chatham, Kent

CONTENTS

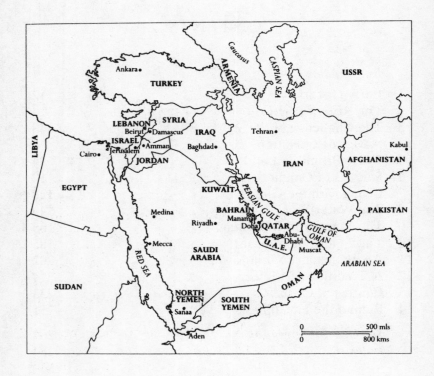

The Middle East

INTRODUCTION

The Middle East, a shorthand military term invented by the British Army in the early years of this century, has, for generations, evoked diverse visions of romantic adventure and terror in the West. Debatable as to its geopolitical accuracy, and endlessly discussed, the term has, nevertheless, become part of the vocabulary of international politics. Attempts to impose substitutes such as 'the Near East', 'the Arab World', 'the Muslim World' and 'Western Asia' have met with only limited success.

A relatively new term, the Middle East describes what is arguably the oldest settled region of the ancient world.

The centuries-long concussion of civilizations that was the clash of the Cross and the Crescent over the control of the Mediterranean established the Middle East as the focal point of contact and conflict between Europe, slowly emerging from its long decadence, and Islam which, heading in the opposite direction, was entering a period of decline that continued well into the twentieth century.

For the Crusaders and their successors, whether travellers or merchants, adventurers or builders of colonial empires, the region was known as the 'Orient' – a fabulous universe of magnificent cities surrounded by desolate deserts. The rich caravans of camels, the poisoned daggers of the Assassins, the harems of the emirs, the slave bazaars, the minarets that pierced the heart of the sky and the blue clouds of opium smoke that shrouded a decaying civilization became the central images of this magnetic and at the same time repulsive 'Orient'.

As a political term, the Middle East had the initial advantage of being free of all such images. To be sure, it was not totally value-free as it underlined the fact that those who coined it contemplated the world from West to East and in relation to Europe's central position. It indicated the rising power and prestige of Europe without being laden with preconceptions and prejudices about the people and history of the geographic region it attempted to describe.

In recent years, however, the term Middle East has lost part of its original innocence, which had never been total in any case. It has become associated with a new set of dramatic images: masked gunmen holding hostages, mutilated corpses thrown out of hijacked jetliners, bloated bodies floating in marshes after a chemical bombardment, ferocious fanatics breathing fire and fury, murderous mullahs pushing child-soldiers into minefields, Arab fat cats roaming French casinos while millions of dispossessed men, women and children waste away in the shanty towns: visions of a land where oil and blood run in parallel streams.

Although everyone agrees that the Middle East exists there is little agreement as to the precise region it covers. During the First World War the Middle East was used as a label to describe a military 'province' covered by the British forces from the Persian Gulf to Tripolitania. Later, some politicians and diplomats as well as scholars used the term to describe the entire region covering Libya, Egypt, the Sudan, the Levant, the Arabian Peninsula, Mesopotamia, Iran, Turkey, Cyprus and Greece. In recent years, however, some scholars have left out Libya, the Sudan and Greece but added Pakistan and Afghanistan to the list of countries covered by the Middle East label.

The intellectual elites of the countries concerned were for long reluctant to use the term 'the Middle East', which they saw as a colonial relic. But once the term was adopted by several nationalist leaders with impeccable credentials, such as Nasser in Egypt and Mussadeq in Iran, its general acceptance became a matter of time. Today there are numerous corporations, newspapers, magazines, news agencies and research institutes throughout the region that use 'the Middle East' as an integral part of their names. Arab, Iranian and Israeli intellectuals have little hesitation in describing their countries as belonging to the Middle East. The Turks, on the other hand, do not seem so sure; they prefer Turkey to be seen as part of an expanded Europe. The opposite is true of Afghan and Pakistani elites who, disregarding the fact that their respective lands were seldom associated with the Middle East, argue that they are an integral part of the region.

Originally intended to serve as a geographical and military expression, 'the Middle East' can now be used to describe far more complex political realities in a wide variety of countries which, despite their diversity, share a common past and must jointly face the challenge of the future.

In deciding where to draw the frontiers of the Middle East, an arbitrary act in all circumstances, I have, nevertheless, taken into account a number of historical, geographic, climatic and cultural factors. But my choice has been primarily determined by political considerations, for the term 'the Middle East' is, above all, descriptive of a certain set of political realities.

The region I propose to study in this book covers the following countries: Egypt, Israel, Lebanon, Syria, Jordan, the Israeli-occupied territories, Turkey, Iran, Iraq, Kuwait, Saudi Arabia, Bahrain, Qatar, the United Arab Emirates, Oman, South Yemen and North Yemen. This is an area of just under 7,300,00 square kilometres with a total population of over 208 million people in 1988.

The Middle East provides a unique meeting point for the three old continents: Europe, Africa and Asia. The Bab al-Mandab and the Suez Canal separate while also bringing together Africa and Asia. And Europe looks at Asia across the Bosphorus. The region as a whole could be described as an isthmus, a *durchsgangland*, between two major bodies of water, the Mediterranean which lies between Africa and Europe to the west and the Indian Ocean to the east. Like a house with many doors the Middle East has been open to cultural influences from regions as far apart as Western Europe and China. It has also served as a route for frequent invasions in all directions – from south to north, from west to east, from east to west and from north to south. In return it has also nurtured civilizations with universal aspirations and capable of influencing the general development of humanity far beyond the Middle East's own geographical limits.

Few regions in the world offer the climatic diversity that characterizes the Middle East. To be sure the desert is the predominant physical feature of the region. It is everywhere. It presses in its deadly embrace the narrow bands of fertile land in the Nile Valley and Mesopotamia and reaches to the gates of the Mediterranean orchards of the Levant. The desert is also almost an ever present companion of the high mountain ranges of the Iranian Plateau and Anatolia and seals off the monsoon-washed Omani province of Dhofar as well as the fertile Yemen, the Arabia Felix of pre-Islamic times. But it is in the Arabian Peninsula that the Middle Eastern desert assumes its full awesome proportions. The seemingly endless nefuds of Arabia amount to a vast no-man's land that extends to the shores of the Persian Gulf and the Arabian Sea. Part of the Arabian desert, the Rub al-Khali (the Empty Quarter) has been justly described as 'the desert of hunger' and recognized as possibly the most barren, the most inhospitable place on earth.

The predominance of desert might seem paradoxical in a region bordered by the Mediterranean and the Indian Ocean and punctuated by other sizeable bodies of water such as the Red Sea, the Black Sea, the Caspian Sea, the Persian Gulf and the Gulf of Oman. The main reason for this is the presence of fairly high mountains that almost invariably seal off the hinterland. Leaving aside the main mountain ranges of

Turkey and Iran, which provide a link between the alpine mountains of Europe and the Himalayas, the rest of the Middle East has an African type relief which almost invariably acts as a barrier to maritime influences. This relief reaches a height of over 2,600 metres in the Sinai Peninsula and soars to 3,000 metres in Lebanon, a stone's throw from the Mediterranean. In Turkey the Taurus seals off the inner Anatolian plateau while the Alburz range of mountains closes the interior of Iran to the climatic influence of the Caspian.

With the exception of Turkey's Black Sea coast, the Iranian coast of the Caspian and parts of North Yemen, the entire region is constantly threatened by drought. The average annual rainfall varies from 1,800 mm on the northern slopes of the Alburz to 720 mm in Jerusalem to almost zero in the interior of the Arabian desert. In some parts of the region rain represents an exceptional event that is witnessed once every twenty years. It was only half in jest that the late Shah of Iran liked to say that he was ready to exchange his country's immense oil reserves with Europe's rainfall.

The problem of water has been at the heart of Middle Eastern preoccupations since the dawn of history. Not surprisingly, the region's most enduring civilizations came into being alongside major rivers that provided a reliable source of water for farming. The organization and management of water resources were quickly established as the most important political issues of Middle Eastern societies and remained so until very recently.

The Middle East represents a veritable mosaic of ethnic groups, religions and languages. Of the region's total population slightly less than half live in countries that belong to the Arab League. The rest are accounted for by three countries: Turkey, Iran and Israel. None of the sixteen states of the region is ethnically or linguistically homogenous and most include within their frontiers many different religious communities.

People speaking one of the several different Arab dialects in the region form some forty-six per cent of the Middle East's total population. Arabic is the national language in Egypt, Jordan, Lebanon, Syria, Saudi Arabia, Kuwait, Bahrain, Qatar, the United Arab Emirates, Oman, South Yemen and North Yemen. But it is also spoken in Israel and the Israeli-occupied territories (1.8 million), Turkey (1.3 million) and Iran (1.1 million).

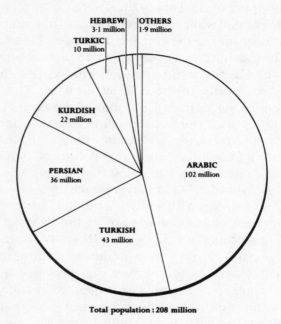

Total population : 208 million

Languages of the Middle East

Turkish, the official language of the Turkish Republic, is spoken by some nineteen per cent of the region's total population. To it one may add the various Turkic dialects (Azari, Turcoman, Tatar and Qashoa'i) which account for a further five per cent. Persian and kindred languages are spoken by nearly seventeen per cent of the region's total population. The official language of Iran, Persian is also spoken in parts of Iraq and several of the Persian Gulf emirates. Kurdish, a language that shares the same roots as Persian, is spoken by some nine per cent of the population of the region. Kurdish speakers are divided among Turkey, the Soviet Republics of Armenia and Azerbaijan, Iran, Iraq and Syria. The remaining four per cent is accounted for by a variety of languages: Hebrew (the official language in Israel), Armenian, Assyrian, Georgian, Tati, Marati and others.

The Middle East, the birthplace of all the four major monotheistic religions, that is to say Zoroastrianism, Judaism, Christianity and Islam, represents the core of the Muslim world. Nearly ninety per cent of the region's total population consists of Muslims. Sunni (traditionalist) Muslims, represented by four major schools – Maleki, Hanafi, Hanbali and Shaf'ei, account for sixty-seven per cent, while shi'ite Muslims – divided into Duodecimains, Nizaris and Zaydis – make up twenty-three per cent of the total. The addition of certain quasi-Islamic groups such as the Nusairis, the Druzes and the Ali-Allahis could bring the shi'ite share up to twenty-five per cent of the total.

Christians – divided into more than thirty different denominations, notably Coptic, Gregorian (Armenian), Jacobite, Chaldean, Maronite, Greek Orthodox and Catholic – account for some five per cent of the population. Jews of all denomination account for a further 1.8 per cent of the population, while the remaining 1.2 per cent is accounted for by followers of a wide variety of other faiths, notably the Baha'is, the Zoroastrians and the Yazidis. The Baha'is are in a particular situation in as much as their faith is not officially recognized by any of the states in the region except Israel. Considered heretical, the Baha'is are persecuted in Iran and Egypt.

Sunni Islam is in a majority in Turkey, Egypt, Syria, Jordan, Saudi Arabia, Kuwait, Qatar, the United Arab Emirates (UAE), Oman and South Yemen. Shi'ites predominate in Iran, Iraq, Bahrain and North Yemen (the Yemen Arab Republic), and also form the largest of many communities in Lebanon. Jews are in a majority only in Israel and form smaller communities in Iran (75,000) and Turkey (65,000). Christians are present in all of the states of the region except Saudi Arabia, Kuwait, the UAE, Bahrain, Qatar, Oman and South Yemen but do not have a demographically dominant position in any of the Middle Eastern states. It is only in Lebanon that Christians, who form some thirty-five per cent of the population, play a leading role in the nation's government. The presidency of Lebanon has been assumed by Maronite Christians since independence.

Only two states, Turkey and South Yemen (the People's Democratic Republic of South Yemen) describe themselves as secular, with no mention of an official religion in their respective constitutions. A third state, Lebanon, does not have a written constitution but leaned towards secularism until the outbreak of its second civil war in 1975 – a conflict that continued into the 1980s. Israel is a Jewish state and treats its non-Jewish citizens on the basis of the 'millet' (religious community) rules inherited from the Ottoman Empire. In practice, however, Israel can be described as more secular than theocratic. Iran, for its part, has been an Islamic Republic since 1979 and could be described as a shi'ite theocracy, although many of the secular laws of the *ancien régime* have remained in force.

In Syria, where sunnis form seventy-eight per cent of the population, the state has been dominated by Nusairi (Alawite) groups since 1970. In Iraq, where shi'ites form a majority, it is the sunni minority that controls the state apparatus. The same is true of Bahrain where a sunni tribe has ruled over the shi'ite majority since the nineteenth century.

The Middle Eastern states represent a wide variety in terms of size, population and economic power. Qatar with 200,000 inhabitants and Bahrain with a population of under 300,000 are among the world's smallest nations. Turkey, Egypt and Iran, however, rank among the twenty most populated countries of the world. Lebanon, with an area of 10,400 square kilometres, and Israel, covering 20,700 square kilometres, are among the world's smallest states, while Saudi Arabia (2.2 million square kilometres) and Iran (1.6 million square kilometres) rank among the world's fifteen largest.

Equally sharp contrasts could be noted in the economic domain. Qatar and the UAE, with per capita GNPs of $17,000 and $15,000 per annum respectively, topped the list of nations with the highest income relative to population in 1988. North Yemen and South Yemen, on the other hand, ranked among the world's poorest nations with annual per capita GNPs of $300 and $320 respectively.

Egypt, with more than $30,000 million in foreign debts, was among the world's most indebted nations in 1988. Iraq, with foreign debts totalling $40,000 million, was in an even weaker position because it faced a higher debt to population ratio. Saudi Arabia, Kuwait, the UAE and Qatar, on the other hand, belonged to the group of twenty or so nations with the highest reserves of foreign currency in the world. While Turkey, Egypt and Iran had already completed the early phases of industrialization, most other countries of the region had virtually no industrial base. Israel remained the sole exception as the only country with a strong industrial and export-oriented economy that was not dependent on oil. Nevertheless, even the Israeli economy could not be said to count on a global scale because of its very limited size.

The Middle Eastern countries, accounting for some 4.5 per cent of the world's total estimated population, claimed just over 3.5 per cent of international trade or almost as much as Italy's share of the same. In the 1960s and 1970s almost all the Middle Eastern countries experienced above average economic growth rates. Iran with ten per cent and Saudi Arabia with 8.9 per cent led the way. Much of this unusual growth was due to sharp increases in the price of crude oil in 1971, 1973 and 1979. From 1983 onwards, however, lower growth rates, averaging under four per cent per annum, were registered by the more buoyant of the region's economies. In the case of Iran and possibly Egypt there was no real growth after 1980 in the sense that whatever growth was achieved was offset by population increases.

The region's immense oil and natural gas reserves provided it with a unique asset in planning long-term economic development. Estimates made by the Organisation of Petroleum Exporting Countries (OPEC) in 1988 showed that more than 70 per cent of the world's proven crude oil reserves belonged to the Middle East. Iran's reserves of natural gas were estimated to be the second largest in the world after the USSR. Oil production in the Middle East could continue at 1988 levels for a total of 120 years a full 87 years after the last oil-wells anywhere else in the world have run completely dry. From the year 2021, unless other oil deposits are discovered in the meantime, the Middle East will become the world's only oil-exporting region.

To the outside world the Middle East appears as a region of exceptional political instability. The very term 'the Middle East' is often synonymous with crisis. But the crisis in the Middle East is not confined to the Arab-Israeli conflict which, because of its exceptional nature, has attracted the attention of world public opinion for more than forty years. The region's instability is illustrated by the fact that it has experienced no fewer than seven major wars and more than twenty smaller conflicts since 1941. During the same period the Middle East was shaken by a major revolution and more than 240 successful or abortive *coups d'état*.

The Middle East as we know it today is the product of a very long history that dates from the dawn of civilization. The region's political structures, and most of its present-day political problems, however, were by-products of the First World War which completed the process of establishing western hegemony over the region – a process that had begun in earnest with the French expedition to Egypt under Bonaparte.

Many of the long-term problems of the region almost never hit the headlines. And yet it is by studying these problems that one can try to understand the major political undercurrents that shape the future of every country in the Middle East and determine the region's role in the world of tomorrow.

The present study seeks to evoke and analyse some of the basic issues of Middle Eastern society in their proper historical context in the hope of a better understanding of future developments in the region. This I have tried to do in the form of a guided tour of the Middle East's history and politics. Because it is the present state of the region and its future developments that interests me most in this study I have devoted only one chapter to the pre-Islamic period.

Until the Nineteenth Century Islam dominated the region politically. Since then, however, nationalism, offering modernization, has established itself as an attractive alternative to Islam in some countries of the Middle East. The fact that Islam and nationalism have at times joined forces, especially in the struggle against foreign domination and colonialism, does not mean that either might be prepared to abandon its quest for the exclusive domination of the region's political life. The complex history of tense relations between Islam and nationalism provides a major part of the present study.

Some students of Middle Eastern politics have been tempted by the idea of discovering a predetermined pattern of development that could explain the many unexpected twists and turns of events in the region. Climate, geopolitics and religion are all factors that must be taken into account in any attempt at understanding the course of events. But even then one must be prepared for countless other factors which, often in most improbable ways, affect developments in the Middle East. Many of these factors are external and cannot be explained in regional terms alone. The politics of the Middle East is the result of the interaction of diverse and divergent forces some of which remain totally alien to the region.

1

EARLY HISTORY

The Middle East has been the birthplace as well as the graveyard of a number of civilizations which, through more than 10,000 years of almost cyclical rise and decline, have left their imprint on all aspects of life in the region.

Most scholars agree that the change from a life of hunting and food gathering, which implied a nomadic pattern of existence, to one of more or less fixed settlements supported by agriculture is the first stage in the development of the earliest civilizations. Archaeological research undertaken during the past 150 years shows that agriculture was first discovered in the Middle East. Some sites in Palestine (the West Bank of Jordan), Turkey and northern Iran have been identified as what could be described as the world's earliest villages where cultivation, accompanied by the domestication of certain animals, began to be practised between 8,000 and 5,000 years before the birth of Christ.

The fact that the Middle East was among the first regions to emerge from the glacial period made it an almost natural venue for the discovery and practice of the art of cultivation. The region's temperate climate and fertile oases soon attracted whole new populations moving into Egypt from the Sudan and Ethiopia and into the Iranian Plateau and Asia Minor from Central Asia and the Caucasus.

Although small settled communities existed in parts of Iran and Anatolia before either the Nile Valley or Mesopotamia, it was in these two well-watered parts of the Middle East that the first large-scale civilizations came into being. The Nile, because it receives no tributaries along the entire course of its passage through Egypt, favoured the development of a centralized state and discouraged attempts at creating small-scale and self-contained communities of the kind prevalent in other parts of the region. It is possible to suggest that the Nile was Egypt's first Pharaoh. The pattern of development in Mesopotamia was different. The Tigris, which provides some sixty per cent of Mesopotamia's surface water, receives numerous tributaries from the Zagross mountain range and offered ample opportunities for the emergence of a number of autonomous communities. Some of these communities soon developed into city states and then went on to become mini-empires in their time.

The first of these city states was Sumer in lower Meso-potamia which reached its zenith in *circa* 3,500 BC. The Sumerians, a non-Semitic people, were, nevertheless, not related to the Aryans who had conquered the Iranian Plateau some five centuries earlier. Many legends have come into being about Sumer and its achievements. These include one that wheat-farming in the ancient city state was as productive as it is in North America today and another that would have us believe that the Sumerians invented solar batteries. What is certain, however, is that Sumer mastered the use of some metals, especially bronze and copper, and used timber and carved stone in its buildings. It was also in Sumer that man first discovered that trade could be more profitable than marauding raids on one's neighbours. Sumerian merchants covered a vast area from present day Khuzestan to the Mediterranean coast of Syria.

Pharaonic Egypt had meanwhile developed into a well-organized state covering the whole of the Nile Valley and spreading its trade and cultural influence to Nubia and Ethiopia in the south and to Palestine and Syria in the north. The rising Egyptian civilization was prosperous enough to undertake vast public works projects and to finance an ever-growing elite of intellectuals, civil servants and priests as well as a standing army which was the first in human history.

Around the second millenium BC a series of climatic catastrophes in the Arabian Peninsula and in Central Asia provoked mass migrations towards the more fertile and better watered parts of the region. These migrations often assumed the form of full-scale invasions. The Hittites and the Mitani, for example, captured Anatolia and parts of northwest Iran through a series of invasions that lasted over more than two centuries. Almost at the same time the Kassites moved into Mesopotamia and eventually brought about the destruction of Sumer. The confederation of Aramean tribes that consisted of the Canaanites, Philistines, Israelites and Phoenicians spread into the Levant while the Hyksos established themselves in parts of Egypt.

The Phoenicians, who established a number of port cities on the Mediterranean, created a powerful trading civilization and also developed the first alphabet which quickly replaced the Mesopotamian cuneiform and the Egyptian hieroglyphics. This in turn helped the spread of Aramaic languages throughout the Middle East.

With Sumer wiped off the map of the Middle East it was the turn of other parts of Mesopotamia to develop their original civilizations. Babylon, on the lower Tigris, emerged as the ancient world's largest and most prosperous city where immense fortunes made out of farming and trade were partly invested in the advancement of arts, sciences and technology. In *circa* 1,200–1,000 BC Mesopotamia produced its first 'imperial' power in the shape of Assyria based on the fertile lands of upper Tigris. Assyria was more of a war machine than a state and spent most of its undoubted energies in invading neighbouring lands from Khuzestan to Palestine. Assyrian kings became known as symbols of death and destruction throughout the ancient Middle East and were probably the first in history to practise a policy of the enforced eviction of whole peoples from their traditional homelands.

The Assyrian Empire was, in its turn, overthrown by the

Medes, an Aryan people who had entered the Iranian Plateau in *circa* 1,000 BC at the same time as the kindred tribes of the Persians who settled on the southern slopes of the Zagross. The Medes created an empire of their own, the first in the Iranian Plateau, based on their capital city of Hagmatanah (modern Hamadan) and controlled much of present-day Azerbaijan, Kurdistan and parts of Mesopotamia and Syria.

The power of the Medes was broken by the Persians who had, in the meantime, subjugated the kingdom of Anshan, in southwest Iran, and also established control over the eastern shores of the Persian Gulf. The Persian dynasty of Achaemenids quickly developed into the first world empire that extended from present-day Afghanistan to Libya and from Greece to the Arabian Sea. In the process of its formation, the Persian Empire absorbed a variety of civilizations ranging from the Assyro-Babylonian to the Egyptian. Aramaic was adopted as the lingua franca of the empire and a unified civil service, controlled from Susa and Persepolis, administered the empire on the basis of full religious and cultural autonomy for more than twenty subject nations. The first metal coinage and the first regular postal services in history helped boost trade and cultural intercourse between Asia, Europe and Africa.

The Persian conquest was the culminating point of nearly 2,000 years of invasions from the east. This trend was reversed in 331 BC when a Macedonian army, led by Alexander the Great, defeated the Achaemenid king Darius and ended the Persian Empire. Persepolis was set on fire and a new empire, extending from the Aegean to India and including Mesopotamia, the Levant and Egypt, came into being. Alexander's empire, larger than that created by Cyrus the Great two centuries earlier, proved short-lived. The conqueror died soon after an unsuccessful attempt at penetrating into India. Two of Alexander's generals, Seleucus and Ptolemy, divided the empire between them. Seleucus established a dynasty that controlled Mesopotamia, parts of Syria and the Iranian Plateau while Ptolemy's descendants continued to rule Palestine and Egypt.

The Seleucid Empire was eventually overthrown by a new Iranian dynasty, the Arsacids, based on Hyrcania, east of the Caspian Sea. The Arsacids re-conquered the whole of the Iranian Plateau as well as Mesopotamia and also gained control of the southern Caucasian kingdom of Armenia. Known as the Parthian Empire, the new Arsacid power soon found itself confronted with another energetic empire that had, in the meantime, destroyed the Ptolemaic state and established control over Egypt, the Levant and Syria. This new power from the west, the Roman Empire, later also captured much of Anatolia and imposed a monopoly over navigation in both the Aegean and the Mediterranean.

For nearly four centuries rivalry between the Roman and the Parthian empires provided the core of the region's geopolitics. Numerous costly wars produced no decisive outcome: Armenia changed hands a few times and the Syrian frontiers were nibbled at on occasions but neither side was able to alter the map of the region as had been possible during the conquests of Cyrus the Great and Alexander the Great.

The duel between Rome and Iran did not prevent both empires from undertaking major development projects. Under Roman rule Egypt achieved a degree of prosperity unique in its history, while Alexandria emerged as the ancient world's largest metropolis. Syria and Palestine also experienced a sustained economic boom. In Parthian Iran, which at the time included much of Central Asia, cities such as Damghan, Rey, Gorgan, Khojand, Marv and Bokhara became important centres of civilization. Part of the prosperity experienced by both sides was due to an unprecedented expansion in world trade in which Rome and Parthia had the lion's share. The two empires were, in fact, each other's main trading partners. The famous Silk Route, which began at Sian in China and linked Asia with Europe via Iran, was first developed under the Parthians. Rome imported a variety of goods from Asia, especially textiles and spices, and paid for them in gold and silver.

In AD 224 the Parthian Empire was overthrown by a Persian dynasty from the south, the Sassanids, who claimed legitimacy by pretending to be the descendants of the ancient Achaemenians. The Parthians had tried to maintain a good part of the Greek influence which had been established in Iran during the Seleucid era and some of their kings even described themselves as 'Hellenophiles'. This attitude reflected the fact that a good part of the population of many major cities in the empire were Greek 'colons' whose presence had led to the development of a mixed Graeco-Persian culture. The Sassanids, however, were determined to re-Persianize the country and in their propaganda described the Arsacids as virtual traitors. More importantly, they wanted to impose their own rigid version of Zoroastrianism as the sole religion of the empire. The tradition of religious tolerance, established by Cyrus the Great and continued under the Seleucids and the Parthians, was gradually abandoned.

The end of the Parthian Empire did not lead to peace between Iran and Rome and the Sassanids pursued their campaign against the imperial power from the west with greater vigour. The adoption of Christianity as the state religion by Rome in the fourth century added a new religious dimension to the old duel between the Roman Empire and Iran. The Sassanids exploited divisions within Christianity and offered safe haven to numerous heretical sects persecuted by the official Roman church.

In the meantime the Roman Empire had been divided into an eastern and a western half. The eastern half came to be known as the Byzantine Empire with Constantinople (present day Istanbul) as its capital. An essentially Middle Eastern power now that its umbilical cord to Rome was cut, the Byzantine Empire proved an even more aggressive adversary for the Iranian power which continued to seek domination over the entire region.

Endless conflicts between the two empires, combined with a series of civil wars and peasant revolts experienced by both, meant that they had little fighting energy left when a new force, this time from the south, began to seek domination in the Middle East. This new force was Islam which I shall discuss later.

This brief survey of the history of the Middle East from the earliest times to the eve of the Muslim conquests reveals the main features of the region's politics over nearly 2,000 years. The first of these features is the extent to which colonial rule was imposed on much of the region for centuries. Egypt, for example, did not have an ethnic Egyptian ruler from the time it was incorporated into the Achaemenid Empire in the 5th century BC until 1952. Syria, the Levant and Mesopotamia also had similar experiences. The Persians, the Greeks, the Romans and the Byzantines who ruled the region were all Indo-European peoples, while a majority of the region's population, outside the Iranian Plateau and Anatolia, were of Semitic or Hamitic origin. The Persian, Greek and Roman 'colons' who established themselves throughout the region were never numerous enough to alter seriously the racial and ethnic composition of the native populations.

The fact that governmental power was in the hands of alien minorities had one important consequence: the development of large cities where groups of diverse ethnic identities could live and work together. These cities, in turn, encouraged the expansion of trade which quickly developed into an instrument of power in the hands of the ruling minorities. The tradition of rule by minorities, whether ethnic or religious, has continued to the present day and oversized cities remain important bases of political power in many countries of the region. Trade, which is easy to tax and control, facilitated the emergence of the *rentier* state, a state which depends on indirect taxation and foreign revenues rather than income gained from taxes paid by people engaged in agriculture and industry. This factor is of crucial importance insofar as it reduces, or totally removes, the influence that a majority of subject peoples could exert on the policies of their government.

Although the Middle East had developed a number of major cities such as Thebes, Hagmatanah, Nineva and Susa long before the Macedonian invasion, it was during the Seleucid and Ptolemaic eras that the construction of cities reached its apogee. Alexandria has already been mentioned. Antioch, Baalbek, Alexandretta, Latakiah and Damghan were also put on the map during the Macedonian domination. The tradition was continued by the Romans who expanded the old cities and constructed new ones. Constantinople eventually emerged as the most splendid achievement of man in urban planning and development, a position it retained until modern times.

The fact that many towns were created on the basis of military calculations or for the purpose of serving trade routes meant that little or no organic link initially existed between the new urban centres and the surrounding rural areas. Many Middle Eastern towns and cities did not come into being in response to the specific needs of the farming communities around them but served the interests of an often distant and powerful state. Such towns and cities could rise or fall together with the dynasties that had ordered their creation.

The dominant political position of the cities also meant that international trade was tailored to the needs of the urban populations only. Even the Egyptian wheat exports to the European portions of the Roman Empire did not alter the fact that rural populations benefited only incidentally and marginally from the expansion of international trade. Differences in standards of living between rural and urban areas in the Middle East became a permanent and striking feature of life in the region and continue to this day.

The 'alien' nature of the state in the Middle East was often reinforced by the fact that the military, who ensured conquest and protected the ruling elites against foreign threats as well as domestic revolts, were seldom recruited from among local populations. Persian, Greek and Roman garrisons guarded their respective empires with the help of mercenary forces drawn from regions as far apart as Gaul and Central Asia. Throughout the centuries the presence of mercenary forces as protectors of the state became an important feature of Middle Eastern politics. In later times these mercenary forces moved against their masters and established imperial states of their own.

During Achaemenid, Macedonian and early Roman rule in the region religion played little or no role. To be sure, the successive ruling dynasties had their own respective religious beliefs. But at no point did they try to impose their own beliefs on others or prevent other religious traditions from thriving. Cyrus the Great, for example, singled out religious freedom as the most important principle in his 'universal declaration of human rights' and allowed the Jews, who had become captives in Mesopotamia, to return to Palestine and rebuild their temple in Jerusalem.

Neither Zoroastrianism nor Judaism, the first two of the region's four monotheistic religions, had any proselytizing ambitions. As a result neither was developed into an instrument of empire-building. But once Rome had adopted Christianity as its official religion it was no longer possible for religious feuds to be kept out of the region's political life. The advent of Islam, the fourth and last major monotheistic faith to be born in the Middle East, reinforced the link between religion and state power in the region by simply removing all distinction between secular and temporal matters. An important consequence of the emergence of religion as a political force in Rome, a development paralleled in Sassanid Iran, was increased pressure on the rural populations who now had to pay two sets of taxes to the state and the organized religious hierarchy alongside it.

The history of the Middle East from the earliest times to the advent of Islam is, in fact, a history of countless wars waged by rival empires created by, and destroyed by, invading forces who were conscious of their 'roots' in lands beyond the confines of the region itself. This pattern of invasion, halted for but a brief moment by Islam, was quickly resumed and has continued into the twentieth century.

Wars of conquest were by no means the only form of conflict in the region. Religious wars and peasant uprisings were also frequent. The Byzantine Empire saw it as its own divine mission to root out all heresy and at times treated parts of its own territory inhabited by heretical sects as enemy country. In Sassanid Iran a number of religious revolts, the most important of which was organized by the Mazadakites, were mercilessly crushed while the empire spent much money and propaganda energy on fomenting religious feuds in Byzantine territories.

Religious persecution did not, however, achieve its object-ive of eliminating the countless creeds that had developed among various communities over thousands of years. Even today, and despite Islam's zeal to convert all subject popu-lations, the Middle East remains a veritable museum of very ancient religious beliefs. The development of religion as a common denominator, the principal element in communal identity, was encouraged by the fact that the many com-munities of the region seldom saw the state as an expression of their own culture. One could be a subject of the Achaemenid, the Seleucid, the Roman or the Byzantine empires without being Persian, Greek or Roman. The religious bond, however, was unmistakable and fully defined whole communities.

The transient nature of Middle Eastern empires is illust-rated in the tels of Mesopotamia and Syria and the tepehs of Iran and Anatolia. These are fairly high mounds constituted by layer after layer of debris left by falling civilizations. In the tepehs at Hasanlu in northern Iran, for example, archaeo-logists have discovered the remains of half a dozen civiliz-ations spanning a period of some 3,000 years. The tradition of razing whole cities to the ground meant that many of the region's large cities were either totally wiped off the map or reduced to but a shadow of their past grandeur. Damghan's population in 1980, for example, was less than fifteen per cent of what it had been in the second century BC. Only the charred skeleton of the royal palace now remains of Persepolis, while Alexandria, Antioch and Aleppo are shadows of their great past. Thebes, Babylon, Nineveh and Lydia exist only in the form of ancient ruins.

The destructive tradition has continued to this day. The Iraqis made sure that not a single building stood in the Iranian port-city of Khorramshahr when they were forced to evacuate it in 1982. The Iranians repaid the compliment by razing the Iraqi port-city of Fao to the ground before they left it in 1988. The so-called war of the cities in which Iran and Iraq fired more than 400 missiles at each other's cities in the spring of 1988 was a modern version of the deadly combats of the past in which the turning of populated areas into desert featured as a major military objective. In a stele, found near Susa, the Assyrian king Assurbanipal boasts of how he turned the cities of Ilam into 'wasteland fit for wolves only'.

The successive waves of invasion and the rise and fall of empires did not radically alter the structural divisions of the region's communities. The most important of these divisions distinguished the settled populations (hadharis) from the nomads and both of them from urban communities. For thousands of years settled peasant communities formed more than seventy per cent of the population with nomads representing around ten per cent. The remaining twenty per cent was accounted for by urban populations – a very high percentage not surpassed anywhere in the world until the industrial revolution in Western Europe. The relative size of the hadharis, the nomads and the city-dwellers remained virtually unchanged until the 1960s when almost all of the Middle East's towns and cities began to grow at a rate faster than the growth rate of the population of the region as a whole. In 1988 towns and cities of more than 5,000 inhabitants accounted for some forty per cent of the region's population, while nomads accounted for no more than two per cent.

The village communities as well as towns and cities

developed class structures of their own. Landless peasants, artisans, landlords, priests, professional soldiers, clerks and aristocrats represented distinctive socio-economic groups which, as was the case in Sassanid Iran, degenerated into virtual castes allowing for little or no social mobility. Slavery, virtually non-existent in the Iranian Plateau, was widely practised in other parts of the Middle East and greatly expanded under the Roman and Byzantine empires.

Racial distinctions, on the other hand, counted for little in most parts of the region. Egyptian, Assyrian and Achaemenid stone carvings and figurines distinguish between the dominant races of their respective empires and the subject populations. And Darius the Great makes much of the fact that he is a Persian and an Aryan. But there is no evidence that race ever served as a barrier to social advancement of individuals and communities or was used as an ideological instrument of domination. If anything, the Middle East has been a veritable melting pot of different races and ethnic groups throughout the past 6,000 years. It was not until the twentieth century that racist, ethnocentric and nationalist ideas, largely imported from Europe, captured the imagination of certain intellectual elites in Turkey, Iran and a number of Arab countries.

2

THE RISE OF ISLAM

At the start of the seventh century the Middle East's two 'super powers', the Byzantine and Sassanid empires, were already on their way to a long and painful decline. The Sassanid Empire had fought a series of ruinous wars against wave after wave of invaders from Central Asia while holding its own in periodical clashes with the forces of the Emperor of Constantinople. On one occasion, and in what was to be Persia's last outburst of conquering energy, Sassanid forces even reached the Mediterranean for the first time in more than five centuries.

The Byzantines were in no better shape. The growing pressure of the 'barbarians' from the north and the west and frequent palace revolutions and civil wars had loosened Constantinople's hold on the outlying provinces of the empire.

Neither the Sassanids nor the Byzantines had ever considered the Arabian Peninsula as a source of serious threat to the balance of power in the region. Arabia was a vast but poor and sparsely populated chunk of desert where nomadic tribes engaged in endless wars among themselves. To be sure small-scale Arab incursions into both Sassanid and Byzantine territories did occur every now and then. But each time an efficient punitive mission proved sufficient to restore order and calm. The task of watching over the restless tribes of the peninsula was entrusted to two Christian Arab states that acted as vassals of the Byzantine and Sassanid empires. On at least two occasions the Sassanids were forced to intervene directly in order to bring the situation in Arabia under some control. And Yemen was for a while turned into a Persian satrapy under the Sassanid general Vahraz.

A series of events contributed to instability in Arabia. The destruction of an ancient dam at Marib together with irrigation systems in Ibb and Saadah over a number of years had turned Yemen, Arabia's most fertile region, into a scene of desolation and famine. An Abyssinian invasion had aggravated the effects of the region's economic decline and led to the migration of tribes from both Yemen and Hadhramaut towards the north.

It was against this background of crisis that Muhammad, a forty-year-old merchant belonging to a poor branch of the aristocratic Qureish clan in Mecca, began to preach a new religion. Mecca was at the time the most prosperous of all Arabian cities and an important station on the caravan routes to Syria. The city also enjoyed a certain religious distinction as the site of the ka'abah, a black stone venerated by generations of bedouin (nomadic) tribesmen as well as merchant families from many parts of Arabia.

Muhammad's religion, soon known under the title of Islam which means surrender to the will of the Creator, advocated three principles. The first of these was towheed or the oneness of God, a belief which ran counter to pantheist cults prevalent in Mecca at the time. The second principle was nubuwwah (prophecy), which meant that God had dispatched many prophets to various nations in order to show them the Right Path. Muhammad was to be the last of these rasuls, or envoys from Allah, the One and Only God. Finally, Muhammad spoke of Ma'ad or Resurrection on the Day of Reckoning, when good and evil deeds will be measured and rewarded or punished on an individual basis.

The practice of the new religion was organized on the basis of five 'pillars' (arkan). They were: the act of adherence to Islam (shihadah) by bearing testimony to the unity of God and the fact that Muhammad is His messenger; prayers five times daily; fasting (sowm) during the months of Ramadan; the giving of alms (zakat) and performing the pilgrimage to Mecca (haj) provided certain conditions were present.

The new faith at first failed to attract much attention in Mecca and Muhammad's assertions that he was a messenger provoked derision at first and hostility later. Only a handful of people, among them Khadijah, Muhammad's wife, and his cousin Ali took the Prophet's message seriously and converted to Islam. Pressure from the Meccans eventually became so unbearable that Muhammad and his followers decided to leave the city. This they did in September 622 when they left for the city of Yathrib further to the north. The move, conducted at night and in great secrecy, came to be known as the 'hijrah' or migration and marks the beginning of the Islamic era.

In Yathrib, which was re-named Madinat al-Nabi (the City of the Messenger), Muhammad achieved the success that had eluded him in his native Mecca. There he quickly became the political as well as spiritual head of a dynamic community determined to expand its power and influence in Arabia. Muhammad's rule in Medina, considered by many Muslims as the perfect model for government anywhere in the world and at any time, had a number of important features. All distinctions based on class or tribal affiliations were declared non-existent as the entire population was organized into a single 'ummah' or community of believers. Men were all equal in the eyes of Allah and could distinguish themselves only through piety.

Muhammad won his first military victory over the Meccans two years after establishing his power in Medina. He led a party of Muslim fighters on a raid on a Meccan caravan from Syria. This was the famous battle of Badr (full moon) which was, in fact, little more than a brief armed encounter in which forty-nine Meccans were killed. The proceeds of the plunder were equally shared among the believers in Medina and Muhammad's prestige as a general was established among his followers.

The angry Meccans returned a few months later and soundly defeated the army of the Prophet. This was the battle of Ohod named after a hill just outside the city. Muhammad himself was wounded and his uncle, Hamzah, killed in the fighting.

Not satisfied with this limited success the Meccans returned a third time with a view to seizing Medina and putting an end to what they saw as a growing threat to the security of their caravans. This time the Prophet had the help of a Persian adventurer, Salman, who had converted to Islam. Salman taught the Muslims the art of digging ditches all around Medina, thus preventing the Meccan army from entering the city. This was the battle of Khandaq (the ditch) which ended with a Meccan retreat after a brief siege.

The presence of the Jews, a numerous and prosperous minority in Medina, posed a number of serious problems for the Prophet. Having tried and failed to convert them to Islam by presenting his new faith as the continuation of the teachings of Abraham and Moses, the Prophet soon decided that the Jews of Medina represented a threat to the future of Islam. The Jewish Banu-Qainoqua clan was accused of having collaborated with the Meccans and had its assets seized on the orders of the Prophet. The clan was allowed to emigrate to Syria. The Banu-Nadhir clan of Jews were also expelled from Medina and later crushed in an armed encounter at Khaybar. Finally, the Banu-Quriza, the last of the Jewish clans in the city, were declared enemies of Allah and severely punished. All the males of the clan, aged sixteen years or more, were put to the sword while the women and children were sold as slaves.

With Medina under his uncontested control the Prophet began planning for the conquest of Mecca. He tested the will of the Meccans in 628 when, accompanied by a few close followers, he attempted to enter his native city to perform the traditional pre-Islamic pilgrimage rites at the ka'abah. The Meccans refused to let Muhammad enter the city but signed an agreement with him under which he was to be admitted to the ka'abah the following year.

This was Muhammad's first significant victory against the Meccans. He failed to persuade the Meccans to describe him as 'Prophet of Allah' in the agreement reached but had enough cause for rejoicing in the fact that he had been taken seriously and treated as an equal.

Meanwhile, Muhammad's simple message of faith in Allah and his preaching of equality and fraternity regardless of tribal and class backgrounds continued to find new converts. Even a number of leading Quraishites crossed over to the new Prophet while the number of converts among the poor in Mecca itself continued to grow.

By 630 Muhammad felt strong enough to march on Mecca. The gates of the city were opened for him without a fight. The fall of Mecca had a domino effect on virtually the whole of Arabia: tribe after tribe and city after city pledged allegiance to the new prophet and his irresistible message of mono-theism. Within less than two years the new Islamic power, as yet not organized into a state, dominated a vast area from Hadhramaut and Yemen to the frontiers of Syria.

Islam, initially addressed to the Meccans who had refused to adopt it, had by 631 developed a universal ambition which recognized no political frontiers. It was, therefore, only natural that Muhammad, once he had established his hold on Arabia, should begin thinking of further conquests. It was in his capacity as the general of the Muslim armies that the Prophet led an expedition to Syria. This proved to be something of a failure as the Prophet decided to retreat even before facing a Byzantine border force dispatched to protect the frontier. Back in Medina the Prophet contented himself with writing letters to the Byzantine Emperor Heraclius and the Sassanid King of Kings Khosrow Parviz inviting them to convert to Islam. He received no replies and in 632 died of a violent fever in Medina, almost twenty-three years after the first surahs (psalms) of the Qur'an, Islam's holy book, had been revealed to him after an encounter with Archangel Gabriel in a cave near Mecca.

Muhammad had not had the time or the wish to work out

his theory of the universal Islamic state in any detail. But his rule involved major innovations. First, the traditional separation of religion and state, practised in the Middle East since the early Sumerian and Egyptian civilizations, and continued by the Babylonians, Assyrians, Persians, Greeks and Romans, was ended with consequences that are still with us. Different dynasties in the Middle East had often claimed divine missions or even pretended to have divine origins. But they had all supported, or at least tolerated, a distinct priesthood that enjoyed specific rights and duties alongside the machinery of the state. Even the Pharaohs and Roman emperors who introduced themselves as earthly gods allowed one or more independent religious structures to exist in parallel with the regular organs of government such as the bureaucracy and the army.

The system of rule developed by Muhammad in Medina has often been described as a theocracy. But this was, in fact, not so. Muhammad certainly did not see himself as a religious 'supreme guide' or a high priest of any church. Nor did he allow for the emergence of a professional priesthood. It can be argued that under him it was the state which, in fact, annexed religion rather than the other way round. The Prophet could not have known that Islam would end up having its own clerical classes and that the mosque would gradually escape state control and would then try to re-organize Muslim societies under theocratic rule.

Muhammad's second innovation as a ruler was that he declared religion to be a matter of here and now, a guide for managing the affairs of this world and not dreaming about the fears and joys of the hereafter. His kingdom was very much of this world. More importantly, he asserted that the perfect society could be created on this earth provided men obeyed a set of simple rules laid down by their Creator. Right from the start Islam was labelled 'the easy religion' by those who welcomed it as a relief from the complicated and sterile theological wranglings of Judaism, Christianity and Zoroastrianism in the seventh century. Once again it was not politics that was redefined in religious terms but the other way round. His was not religious politics but a political religion.

Finally, the Prophet introduced a totally new and revolutionary political concept virtually unknown in the Middle East. This was the concept of equality. To be sure, Muhammad divided mankind into believers and non-believers and certainly reserved more rights and privileges for men rather than women. But apart from this he declared all believers to be equal. Clan and tribal distinctions were pushed aside, although they were to return later, and class distinctions abolished. Middle Eastern societies had never degenerated into caste-ridden communities of the type that existed in the Indian sub-continent. But the social stratification of Sassanid society came very close to a simplified version of the Indian castes. As for the Byzantine Empire all the traditional racial, ethnic and class distinctions that had developed over thousands of years continued to be accepted as unchangeable facts of socio-political life.

Some scholars have seen in Muhammad's rule in Medina features of the Mazdakite movement half a century earlier. Others have tried to explain it in terms of historical materialism and seen in it an early version of the classless communist society. Such speculations are totally misleading. Mazdak had advocated, and put into practice within the small communities that he created, a total abolition of private property to the point of denying men and women the right to contract monogamous marriages. Echoes of Mazdak's teachings might have reached Muhammad through Salman Farsi, the Persian exile who had left Iran in the wake of the massacre of Mazdak's followers by the Sassanid kings. But Islam strictly respected private property and the right of inheritance. Muhammad himself had been a merchant: 'businessmen are friends of God,' he declared. The twenty per cent tax he fixed on income and wealth was lower than rates prevalent in most parts of the region at the time and certainly not higher than those in force in most modern societies.

The equality that Muhammad preached with burning

passion was political and not economic. Islam did not foresee or desire any withering away of the state. On the contrary it saw the state as the expression of divine will on earth and gave it authority undreamed of before. The traditional Middle Eastern states had all recognized some measure of separation of the private and public domains that left large sections of life free of state intervention and jurisdiction. The Islamic system, however, gave the state moral and political authority over all aspects of individual private life. The Islamic state considered it a duty to propagate the good and combat evil everywhere and at all times.

Islam has, at times, been described as a 'derivative' or 'second degree' civilization. Muhammad did not claim to have a totally new message. He made it clear that his message was the same as God had sent to mankind through other prophets, notably Abraham and Jesus. The Qur'an takes up all the main themes of the Old and New Testaments with slight variations and develops them with greater passion. The Prophet did not ignore the religious customs of the Arab tribes either. The haj pilgrimage, for example, was a modified version of annual rites performed by bedouin tribes and Meccan clans long before Muhammad was born. Prayers and fasting as well as alms-giving were borrowed from both Judaism and Christianity, while the system of Qissass (retribution) was in force throughout Arabia and simply adopted by Islam with certain important modifications.

All this, however, does not make of Islam a poor imitation of other monotheistic religions that had taken shape in the Middle East. Like all movements aimed at a radical transformation of society, Islam had to portray itself as the revived version of a golden past while also promising to achieve an even better future for mankind. It parted ways with Judaism on one crucial issue. Islam presented itself as a religion for the whole of mankind and for all times and not just as a message addressed by God to a chosen few. Islam's very earthliness also distinguished it from Christianity. Muhammad never claimed any supernatural distinctions and went out of his way to emphasize the role that Islam intended to play in re-ordering human societies.

Muhammad had dreamed of a well-ordered and peaceful society based on respect for unalterable divine laws. But the reality that followed his death was quite different. His first successor, the old and pious Abu-Bakr, died after only two years of indifferent rule during which the seeds of future discords among Muslims were sown. Omar, who succeeded Abu-Bakr as Caliph (Regent of God on earth) in 634, became the architect of Islam's early and greatest victories. Syria was conquered in the same year and Egypt fell five years later. The Sassanid Empire was defeated in 642 and Muslim armies reached the frontiers of India and Central Asia. Less than two years after the fall of Persia, Omar was assassinated by Firuz, a Persian who had pretended to have converted to Islam in order to enter Arabia and meet the Caliph. This was the first political murder in Islam and was to mark the start of a long tradition that has continued into the twentieth century.

Omar's successor, Othman, was also assassinated (656), this time by a group of Arab conspirators apparently in support of Ali, the Prophet's cousin and son-in-law. Ali, declared Caliph in a moment of confusion, was immediately challenged by Muawyyah, the powerful governor of Syria and a close relative of the murdered Othman. The confrontation between the armies of Ali and of Muawyyah started a long tradition of civil war that was to become part of Islam's political tradition.

Ali had to deal with yet another revolt: that of Talha and Zubayr, two Arab generals, supported by one of the Prophet's widows Aiyshah who bore the title of 'the Mother of the Believers'.

These civil wars created a deep *malaise* within the Muslim community and encouraged the creation of a terrorist-cum-military movement known as the khawarej (literally, the outsiders). The khawarej believed that peace could be restored to Islam through a series of selective assassinations. Ali's attempts at extinguishing the revolt of the khawarej proved fruitless and in 661 he was assassinated by a member of that seditious sect.

Ali's death left Muawyyah unchallenged as the new Caliph. He persuaded Hassan, Ali's eldest son, to forswear all claims to rule in the name of the Prophet and transferred the capital of Islam from Medina to Damascus. He introduced two further innovations. He named his son Yazid as the next Caliph and thus established a dynasty. More importantly he launched a plan aimed at the Arabization of Syria within the life-span of two or three generations. Under Muawyyah and his immediate successors the inhabitants of newly conquered lands were described as 'mawali' (clients) and given every incentive to take their conversion to Islam a step further by adopting Arabic as their language. In the absence of an Arab elite capable of administering an expanding empire, Muawyyah and other members of the Umayyid dynasty that he established, invited many of the 'mawali' to play an important role in the government.

This policy did not only contribute to stability in the empire but also encouraged a new intellectual movement that led to the creation of an Islamic civilization. Under the Umayyids Islam extended its conquests from the frontiers of China to southern Spain. Muawyyah and his successor initiated a policy that was to become part of Islamic traditions of government. They used newly converted peoples as the advance guard of new conquests. Persians and Syrians were used in the conquest of North Africa while the North African Berbers spearheaded Islam's expansion into southwestern Europe. In later centuries other newly converted peoples, most notably Mongols, Tatars and Turks, were used as mercenaries by Arab caliphs before ending up as rulers in their own right.

The rapid expansion of Islam has often been described as a result of the forcible conversion of conquered peoples. But the conquerors of the desert, in fact, made little or no attempt at winning converts by force. In a sense it was not even in their interest to have all the conquered peoples convert to Islam as this meant the loss of 'jezieh', the poll tax imposed on non-Muslims throughout the empire. In Persia, for example, the task of mass conversion to Islam did not begin until after the Arabs had been expelled and native Muslim dynasties installed in various parts of the country.

The Umayyids achieved something unique: they united under their rule virtually the whole of the Middle East plus all of its peripheries. This had never happened before and was not to be repeated after the fall of the Umayyids in Damascus. The Umayyid state had another original feature: it was the first state in the history of the Middle East to claim legitimacy not only on the basis of force and conquest but in the name of an ideology.

It was precisely on the grounds of ideology that the Umayyid state finally came to grief. The aristocracies of Mecca and Medina had backed Muawyyah against Ali but had never reconciled themselves to the transfer of the capital of the empire to Damascus. Supporters of the House of Ali, on the other hand, refused the 'bey'aa' (act of allegiance) towards the Umayyids and considered Hussein, Ali's second son, as the rightful Caliph. The seeds of schism sown by the murder of Othman soon grew out of all control. Yazid, Muawyyah's son, was strong enough to defeat a rebellion led by Hussein in Mesopotamia.

Hussein was killed on 10 October 680, a date that was to become a rallying point for shi'ites who gradually emerged as a distinct sect. The word shi'ah means partisan and originally designated those Muslims who had supported Ali's claim to the caliphate against that of Othman and, later, of Muawyyah. But shi'ism, over time, developed into a complete theological system that went far beyond a mere political quarrel over who should be caliph. At the centre of shi'ite theology stood the concept of 'ismah' or infallibility which was recognized as the central condition for rule over the 'ummah' or community of believers. Only the Prophet Muhammad, his daughter Fatimah, her husband Ali and the male descendants of Fatimah and Ali were said to have been endowed by the quality of 'ismah' as a result of divine favour. Thus only they would have legitimacy as rulers of Islam. All other rulers would be illegitimate and tyrannic.

Many Muslims saw in the shi'ite theory of the state little more than the revival of Persian and Byzantine monarchist traditions. They argued that Muhammad himself had never claimed to enjoy any special status over other believers and that the rulers of Islam should be chosen from among the most pious and competent of Muslims regardless of their lineage. The traditionalists, known as the sunnis, were, in turn, divided into four schools or 'madh'hab' (path), offering different interpretations of Islamic rules chiefly by commenting on the text of the Qur'an or citing anecdotes related to the life of the Prophet.

The traditions attributed to the Prophet were known as 'hadith' and developed into a continuous cascade of anecdotes that did not stop until the last decades of the nineteenth century. More than two million such anecdotes have been collected and commented upon by both the sunnis and the shi'ites during the past fourteen centuries. The authenticity of many, if not all of them, is difficult to prove.

The Qur'an itself was first compiled and written down in 632, shortly after Muhammad's death, on Omar's orders. But the text thus prepared was not considered as official and exclusive. At least nine other versions, written down by the various secretaries of the Prophet, existed until after Omar's death.

The Caliph Othman appointed a special committee to prepare a single official version of the holy book. The new version, largely based on that prepared under Omar but taking into account alternative texts, was declared official and final and reproduced in more than twenty copies and dispatched to the major cities of the empire. The oldest calligraphed copy of that version dates back to 776.

The Umayyid Empire tried, in vain, to steer clear of the theological schisms that divided Islam and thus lost the very basis for its legitimacy. Weakened by tribal uprisings in

Arabia and growing secessionist movements in Persia, the dynasty of Damascus was, by the middle of the eighth century, no longer strong enough to defend itself. In 750 an army raised in Khorassan and commanded by Abu-Muslim, a Persian general, entered Mesopotamia and installed Abul-Abbas, a distant relation of the Prophet, as the new Caliph. Baghdad was chosen as the new capital of the Islamic state and all but one member of the Umayyid clan were put to the sword. The sole survivor managed to reach Spain where he founded a new dynasty that was to have a brilliant career of its own.

The Bani-Abbas clan, who now ruled over almost the whole of the Middle East, repaid their debt to the Persians by giving them a central role in the administration. The Barmakis, a Persian family, established themselves as a parallel dynasty as the caliph's grand viziers.

The Abbasids, as the new ruling dynasty came to be known, ignored their early promises of reverting to a system of selecting the caliph through consensus and firmly established a form of hereditary monarchy. The ruler did not call himself king and retained the titles of Caliph and Emir al-Momeneen (Commander of the Faithful). But in reality he was a traditional Middle Eastern monarch in every respect.

The economic and cultural development of the region that had begun under the Umayyids was speeded up under the Abbasid dynasty. The Caliph Harun ar-Rashid and his son Ma'amun presided over a state that was, without a doubt, the 'super power' of its time. The progress achieved was not limited to theology or philosophy, which was revived largely thanks to the translation of ancient Greek texts into Syriac and Arabic, but also covered industry and commerce. Important manufacturing units were created, often under state ownership, in Baghdad, Ray and Samarkand while trade with both China and India to the east and Egypt and Europe to the west reached unprecedented proportions.

This 'golden age of Islam' began to draw to a close from the ninth century onwards. The Abbasids, having lost their tribal source of support in Arabia itself, became increasingly dependent on Iranian bureaucrats and merchants as well as Turkic mercenaries. The Caliph and his vast entourage lived in luxury and could hardly claim to represent Islam's austere and egalitarian message.

Shi'ite revolts in Hejaz in 762 and 786 had already shaken the Caliphate before the rebellion extended to Mesopotamia and the gates of Baghdad itself in 814. In 877 it was the turn of the negro slaves of the empire to raise the banner of revolt. A highly lucrative trade in African slaves had brought tens of thousands of negroes into the empire over the preceding half century. Now these slaves and their descendants were joined by other disaffected groups in a massive uprising that came to be known as 'thawrat al-zanj' (the Revolution of the Black). The 'zanj', as the rebels were known, sacked Basra in 882 and established a brief period of rule over parts of southern Mesopotamia and Khuzestan.

By 900 the flame of revolt had been passed on to the followers of Hamdan Ibn Qarmat, a charismatic shi'ite leader, who succeeded in creating an Islamic state of 'workers and peasants' in the Bahrain archipelago. His successor, Abu-Sa'id, captured Basra and Kufah in 913. Later, in 930, Mecca itself was conquered by another descendant of Qarmat, one Abu-Taher, who came close to conquering Baghdad itself.

These conflicts led to a sharp rise in taxes, needed to finance the mercenary forces of the Caliph. Many fertile regions of the empire were laid waste and important trade and caravan routes closed because of insecurity. The Abbasid state, like almost all other Middle Eastern empires before it, was seen as an 'alien' force by many of its subjects who saw no reason to defend it or even to finance its many wars.

With the caliphate weakened by successive revolts and its legitimacy questioned because of widespread corruption within the administration, the road was open for secessionist movements to seize control of large provinces in the farther corners of the empire. By 756 both Andalusia and

the Maghreb (present-day Morocco and Tunisia) were well
on their way to becoming independent emirates. Later, it was
the turn of Egypt to break away under the Fatimids who
created a shi'ite caliphate in Cairo. In Iran, Taher Zul-
Yaminayn (Ambidextrous) who had been a commander of
the Caliph's army in Khorassan, declared his independence
and founded the Taherid dynasty in 820. In 873 it was the turn
of the Saffarids to emerge as an independent dynasty in the
Iranian provinces of Sistan, Kerman and Ray. A Saffarid
army then marched on Mesopotamia with the aim of captur-
ing Baghdad and putting the Caliph to death. But this
operation ended in Khuzestan when Yaqub Laith, the
charismatic leader of the Saffarids, died a sudden death.

By the end of the ninth century the authority of the Caliph
had all but vanished in most parts of the Iranian Plateau. The
Samanid dynasty, founded in 902, controlled much of
Khorassan and Central Asia and actively encouraged a
Persian renaissance that included concerted efforts to reduce
Arab influence to a minimum.

Another Persian dynasty, the Buyids, established in the
Caspian region of Tabarestan, openly claimed descent from
the Sassanids and revived many of Iran's ancient Zoroastrian
traditions in the name of shi'ism. Ahmad, the leader of the
Buyids, gave himself the title of Shahanshah (King of Kings),
and marched on Baghdad where a captive Caliph was all too
willing to recognize the legitimacy of the new power in
exchange for purely formal allegiance to the caliphate as a
religious and not a political institution. From then on the
Caliph of Baghdad exercised little or no power over the
administration and survived as no more than a religious relic.
A separation of the mosque and the state had become a
reality although few people on either side cared to admit it
openly.

Meanwhile, Egypt and Syria had also broken away from
the authority of the Caliph. The Toulounid dynasty, founded
by a freed Turkish slave in Fostat in 879, and the Hamdanid
dynasty, created by Sayf ad-Dawlah in Syria in 944, made

sure that all territories west of the Euphrates escaped the authority of the Caliph in Baghdad.

Towards the end of the tenth century the Middle East witnessed the full emergence of a new power, that of the Turkic tribes, which was to dominate the region for many centuries to come.

The first Turkic state established in the Middle East was created by Mahmoud, the son of a mercenary slave who had distinguished himself as a brilliant military commander in Central Asia. Mahmoud's new Ghaznavid dynasty, named after the city of Ghaznah in present-day Afghanistan which became the capital of the new empire in 999, turned its back on the Middle East and focused its attention on the forcible spread of Islam in the Indian subcontinent.

At the other end of the region, in Egypt, the Fatimid dynasty had already established itself as a major power extending from North Africa to the Levant. The dynasty was founded by one Ubaid-Allah who claimed direct descent from the Prophet through Muhammad's daughter Fatima – hence the term Fatimid. The adventurer turned caliph called himself the Mahdi (the Well-Guided One), the Messiah of the shi'ites. Ubaid-Allah's stormy and brutal rule never extended into Egypt itself, which was not annexed by the Fatimids until 969 under the Caliph Al-Mu'ezz who founded the city of Cairo and later conquered Syria.

The Fatimids, using shi'ism as the ideological basis of their rule, created a strong and prosperous society which attracted many writers, poets, theologians, artists and architects from the whole of the Muslim world. The Fatimids enjoyed the support of a vast network of secret organizations throughout the Middle East, thus establishing a shi'ite political tradition that was to be revived by Ayatollah Khomeini in the 1980s. Hundreds of well-trained propagandists, known as 'da'ee' (he who makes the call), visited virtually every town and village of some size in Levant, Mesopotamia, Iran and Central Asia to preach the gospel of Fatimid shi'ism. They claimed that all governments of the day had to be overthrown and replaced by rulers appointed by the Caliph of Cairo who alone enjoyed divine legitimacy. The propaganda of the da'ee was further strengthened by the activities of the 'hashasheen' (the assassins) who formed a secret military society dedicated to the physical elimination of the enemies of the Fatimid faith.

The Fatimids emphasized Islam's central political feature which is the creation of an ideology-based society. To achieve this they combined a fairly liberal economic policy, which encouraged free enterprise, with the services of an efficient system of propaganda and repression that discouraged political dissent.

The power of the Fatimids began to decline in the Levant at the start of the eleventh century. The more cosmopolitan nature of the population in Syria and Palestine, where Christians formed important minorities even then, made it more difficult for the Fatimids to impose their particular brand of Islam. In 1070 the Seljuk, a new Turkic dynasty established in parts of Iran and Anatolia, detached Syria and parts of Palestine, including Jerusalem, from the Fatimid Empire. Just over one hundred years later Egypt itself was conquered by the Kurdish commander Saladin who brought Fatimid rule to a definitive end.

The rise of the Seljuks in the eleventh century marked the decline of shi'ism which had, in its different Fatimid and Buyid versions, dominated practically the whole of the Middle East for more than a hundred years.

Military officers in the service of the Ghaznavids, the Seljuks were sunni Muslims and regarded all brands of shi'ism as heretical. Inspired by the Persian erudite Nezam Al-Molk, who served as Grand Vizir to the first three Seljuk kings, the new dynasty launched a massive anti-shi'ite campaign which combined energetic repression with a theological onslaught waged at the level of Islamic schools. Scores of 'madrasseh' (theological schools) were created in Iran and Mesopotamia and numerous books and pamphlets were written and published with a view to proving the heretical nature of shi'ism. The mass of the people who had been forcibly converted to shi'ism in the previous century were reconverted to sunni Islam, again by force. The 'assassins' reacted with a series of political murders. Nezam Al-Molk who had been designated as the number one enemy of the faith was among their victims.

The Seljuk rulers recognized the legitimacy of the Caliph in Baghdad and pretended that they ruled on his behalf. They adopted the title of the 'Sultan' (literally, the Controller), which implied that their role was limited to one of ordering the affairs of the community as appointees of the Caliph. Over time, however, the title of the Sultan achieved far greater authority, reflecting the decline in the power and prestige of the caliphate.

The Seljuks broke the tacit truce observed between Islam and the Byzantine Empire in Anatolia for over two centuries and launched a series of successful campaigns in Asia Minor. Alep Arsalan, the second of the Seljuk sultans, won a famous victory against the Byzantines forces at Malazgard in 1070, marking the end of European rule in Anatolia.

The establishment of the Seljuk state marked a definite break between the Middle East and North Africa exactly at a time when Europe was preparing for its first counter-attack against Islam in nearly five centuries. The arrival of the Crusaders and the establishment of Frankish principalities in the Levant (1099) introduced a totally new factor in the politics of the region which was to affect the overall development of Islam for the following two centuries.

The success of the Crusaders was, in part, due to the weakening of the Seljuk power. The death of Malekshah, the third Seljuk Sultan, led to a break-up of the Turkic empire among various warlords known as the Ata-Begs (literally, Father-Chiefs). Ata-Beg dynasties were established in Armenia, Azerbaijan, Mesopotamia, Fars and Kerman. One of the Ata-Begs, Nur-Addin (1146–73), captured Syria and distinguished himself in the fight against the Crusaders. Another, Saladin (Salah Addin), succeeded in retaking Jerusalem, Islam's third holiest city, from the Franks in 1187 and extended his domain into Egypt where he founded the Ayyubid dynasty. A small branch of the Seljuks survived in Asia Minor with Konya as its capital until 1327, when it was destroyed by the Ottomans. It called itself the Sultanate of Roum (Rome).

The Crusaders, who established feudal-style principalities on the Mediterranean coast of the Levant, did not succeed in extending their power beyond the mountain ranges that seal off the Middle Eastern hinterland. Their domination of the kingdom of Armenia proved short-lived and none of the major centres of population fell into their hands. Nevertheless, they re-opened the west-to-east invasion route that had been taken by the Greeks and the Romans from the sixth century BC until the advent of Islam.

This new invasion from the west was different from all previous ones in one important domain. The Crusaders fought in the name of an ideology with a fervour that equalled that of their Muslim adversaries. To be sure, the Crusaders were not solely motivated by a desire to control the Holy Land and extend the frontiers of Christendom. The prospect of making large profits from trade and plunder was also important in helping them mobilize the forces needed for the invasion of the east.

The century-long presence of the Crusaders in the Levant did not lead to any appreciable increase in the size of Christian communities in the region. But it facilitated the resumption of extensive cultural exchanges for the first time in nearly four centuries.

On balance, the Muslim Middle East had much more to offer in terms of cultural and scientific achievements than did Europe at the time. Islam had discovered the heritage of ancient Greece and continued much of the progress that Rome had achieved in such fields as trade, engineering and construction. Europe, slowly emerging from the Dark Ages, came to learn about its own roots partly thanks to its encounter with Islam in the Middle East and Andalusia.

By 1299 the last Crusader principality, at Acre, had been

recaptured by Muslim forces and its European ruling elite expelled to Cyprus. But the trading factories created during the Crusades survived and continued to grow in importance. The Syrian coastal cities, as well as the island state of Cyprus, experienced an unprecedented economic boom as a result of a steady increase in east-west trade.

Europe had been only one of the two major sources of invasion in the history of the Middle East, and the arrival of the Crusaders on the scene marked the return of only one of the two arms of a pincer that had threatened the region since ancient times. The other arm was represented by successive invasions from the east, mostly through the steppes of Central Asia and northern Khorassan. That invasion route had been blocked by Islam as early as the eighth century and, later, even turned into an avenue for the spread of the new faith as far as Sogdiana and China.

By the start of the thirteenth century the invasion route to and from the heart of Asia began to be trodden in the direction of the Middle East. The new invaders were the Tatars (known as Mongols in the West) who had established a considerable empire under Chengiz Khan (1167–1227). This was no ordinary invasion and the Tatars unleashed their energies against Muslim Tansoxiana and Khorassan like a tornado. Within a very short time almost the whole of Iran and parts of Mesopotamia fell under Tatar rule. In 1257 another Tatar ruler, Halaku Khan, captured Baghdad and ordered the massacre of the last Caliph and all his family. A year later, Halaku's armies conquered Syria.

The Tatars' total disregard for Islamic theories of the state pushed all ideological considerations into the background for a while and restored force as the true and essential source of power in the region. Since then, the Tatar invasion has been blamed by Muslim writers for almost all of the Middle East's ills until the emergence of European colonialism. The invaders from the steppes have been portrayed as barbarous killers with no culture or tradition and steeped in wayward paganism.

Although the new invaders certainly massacred a great many people in the earlier stages of their progress, it would be difficult to hold them solely responsible for the decline of the region. As is almost always the case, the Middle East was invaded because it was already weak and in decline. The Tatars, mostly Bhuddist until their gradual conversion to Islam over the two centuries that followed their first invasion, proved extremely tolerant as far as religion was concerned. Halaku, whose mother had been a Christian slave, was married to a Christian from Anatolia and did not seem to have any definitely set religious views. His rule saw the perennial, and often bloody, sunni-shi'ite disputes pushed into the background and confined to the theological seminaries. Had Halaku and his successors been determined partisans of an alternative religious ideology, which they were not, they might well have imposed their own faith on the inhabitants of the countries they conquered. Islam's hold on large parts of the region, especially in the Iranian country-side, remained tenuous at best until the rise of the Safavids, who established a new theological state, in the sixteenth century.

One major country of the Middle East that escaped domination by the Tatars was Egypt, where the Turkic state of the Mameluks was established from 1250 onwards. The Bahrid dynasty, which ruled from Cairo, offered refuge to the last survivors of the Caliph's family and thus kept the fiction of legitimacy based on the caliphate alive. The Bahrids were in turn overthrown and massacred by the Borjid dynasty of Circassian mercenaries in 1382. Once again, the new rulers of Cairo kept the principle of the caliphate alive without, however, allowing religion to play more than an essentially ceremonial role in the running of the state. The Borjids remained in power until 1517 and the conquest of Egypt by the Ottomans.

Halaku's empire had, meanwhile, divided into three separate kingdoms based on Mesopotamia, Isfahan and Khorassan. A fresh Tatar invasion, led by Teymur-e-Lang

(Teymur the Lame or Tamerlane), led to the creation of a vast new empire extending from Central Asia to Iran, Anatolia and Mesopotamia. Teymur's armies also raided and devastated much of the Levant, reviving the terrible memories of the first Tatar invasion of the region. Teymur died in 1405. Most people believed that he had converted to Islam and he did nothing to contradict this. What is certain, however, is that he maintained the Tatar tradition of keeping religion out of politics as far as possible. The Teymurid Empire did not survive the death of its founder and soon divided into a number of principalities. Shahrokh and Ulug-Beg, two of Teymur's successors, ruled in Khorassan and helped rebuild some of the towns and villages destroyed by Chengiz Khan and Halaku. The cities of Samarkand and Herat became important centres of trade and intellectual activity and remained in that position until the eighteenth century. The fact that numerous Islamic seminaries came into being under Teymur's successors, especially in Samarkand which at one point boasted more than 12,000 students of theology, must be seen as an indication of the Tatars' gradual but sincere conversion to the faith of Muhammad. Another indication of the Teymurids' new Islamic zeal was the massive campaign of persecution they conducted against both Zoroastrians and Nestorian Christians who had continued to play important roles in the life of Iran. These religious minorities were either put to the sword or forced to convert to Islam. Many of them chose to emigrate either to India or to the Levant.

The last Tatar rulers were chased out of Iran and into Central Asia by the Safavids who founded a shi'ite dynasty and soon turned their new empire into a major power in the Middle East (1501–1736). The Safavids had to fight on two fronts: in the east against the Uzbeks, who continued the tradition of invading the Middle East from Central Asia, and against the Ottomans who had established themselves in Anatolia, Mesopotamia and the Levant as well as Egypt and parts of North Africa. It was under Shah Abbas the Great that the Safavids reached the summit of their success. Isfahan, the Safavid capital, became one of the most populous and refined cities of the world in the seventeenth century.

The Safavid duel with the Ottomans was an important factor in facilitating the growth of European influence in the region. The two neighbouring empires fought each other in the name of their respective brands of Islam and considered each other as heretics. The Safavids turned the issue of control over the shi'ite holy cities of Mesopotamia, annexed by the Ottomans during their southward expansion, into one of the most important political issues in the region up to present times.

Despite their undoubted zeal which prompted them to import scores of shi'ite preachers from Lebanon, the Safavids did not succeed in imposing their faith on all Iranians. The dynasty was overthrown by an Afghan rebel army that consisted mainly of sunni Muslims and Uzbek mercenaries and adventurers. Later, another sunni general, Nader Afshar, was declared king and succeeded in reuniting Iran for a brief period. Nader Shah even felt strong enough to lead a profitable raid on India in the name of Islam.

The Afshar dynasty, however, proved ephemeral and Iran was plunged into anarchy until the emergence of a new ruling clan, the Qajars, who were shi'ite Turcomans and claimed direct descent from Chengiz Khan. The Qajars soon came face to face with a totally new source of danger: the rise of the Russian power to the north. After initial successes that took the Qajar standards into Georgia and Armenia at the end of the eighteenth century the tide turned irrevocably against Iran in its confrontation with the Tsars.

The Ottoman Empire, meanwhile, had established itself as something of a super-power from the middle of the fifteenth century onwards. The empire was founded by Osman Beg, a Seljuk military commander who broke with his masters, and led his clan into conquests in Anatolia. The Ottoman power was momentarily stopped by Teymur who captured the Turkish Sultan, Bayazid (Bajazet) and held him prisoner in a cage. But once the Tatars had faded away the Ottomans resumed their career as conquerors. In 1453 Constantinople fell to the armies of Muhammad II, known as the Fat'eh (Conqueror), and the Byzantine Empire, which had been the region's oldest state, came to an end.

The conquest of Egypt and Syria by Sultan Selim I (1512–20), and probing raids into the Balkans, gave the Ottomans a momentum that was not to be broken for more than four centuries. Under Suleyman the Magnificent (1520–66) the Ottoman Empire extended from the gates of Vienna to the Nile and from Baghdad to Algeria.

The success of Ottoman arms, especially in Europe, helped mask the socio-cultural decline that Islam had begun to experience in the Middle East. There are sharply divergent views as to the causes and the starting point of this decline which was to lead to an almost total domination of the region by European colonial powers from the nineteenth century onwards. What is certain, however, is that the balance of chances between the Middle East and Western Europe had radically altered in favour of the latter long before Bonaparte entered Egypt.

3

THE CHALLENGE OF THE WEST

The war booty that Sultan Selim I had brought back with him from Egypt in 1517 had included the then largely irrelevant title of the Caliph of All Muslims. But it was not until 1774 that the Ottoman sultans began to use the title and attach to it growing political significance. By that time, however, Islam was more divided than ever and Islamic civilization in general had begun to experience the crisis which continues to this day.

Ottoman military victories had for long masked the empire's decadence which was to make it the 'sick man of Europe' in the nineteenth century. The Ottomans disdained commerce and industry as somewhat unmanly pursuits for a race of warriors destined to take the message of Islam to the remotest parts of the civilized world. By the end of the sixteenth century the vast commerce of the empire had fallen almost entirely into the hands of European merchants as well as Armenian and Jewish communities in Anatolia, Levant and Egypt. Between 1536 and 1740 the various European powers persuaded the Ottoman authorities, either by using the threat of war or by offering large bribes, to conclude a series of capitulatory accords in favour of western merchants and their agents. These accords, collectively known as Capitulation, were in time extended to cover very large non-Muslim communities within the empire. This was a major concession on the part of Islam, a religion which insists that its hold on society should be total and exclusive.

Safavid Iran, always anxious not to fall behind its mortal enemy the Ottoman Empire, soon followed suit and signed its own capitulatory agreements with half a dozen European states. In time almost the whole of the foreign trade of both Iran and the Ottoman Empire fell into the hands of western merchants supported by local religious minorities.

As economic power gradually slipped out of the hands of the state in the Middle East, the exercise of political power also became a subject of subtle rivalries. Here, it was the turn of the religious authorities to chip away at the prerogatives of the shah and the sultan. In shi'ite Iran the mullahs or religious leaders developed their own power structures in parallel with the state apparatus. Through control over huge areas of endowed land they dominated the economy of several important provinces. They also perpetuated the idea that they alone represented divine legitimacy and that the shah's rule depended on their express consent. Through the mosques and thousands of religious shrines almost all over Iran they enjoyed an organization that the Safavid state often lacked. Another permanent threat to the authority of the state in Iran came from the tribes, often nomadic, who often recognized no law but their own.

The situation might have been different in the Ottoman part of the Middle East. There a majority of the inhabitants were sunni Muslims and were theoretically not supposed to have a cadre of professional and full-time clerics. In reality, however, the empire developed a veritable army of theologians who administered tens of thousands of mosques, shrines, madrassehs (seminaries) and maktabs (Qur'anic schools). These professional clerics used a variety of titles including mufti, mevlevi and shaikh. Their political power was less pronounced than that of their counterparts in Iran but not necessarily less significant when it came to major issues.

Both the Ottomans and the Safavids had initiated and continued to help the expansion of a network of professional clerics as part of the dispositions they needed for fighting their

theological duel. Both states did not hesitate to massacre
those of their subjects who subscribed to what they saw as
heretical brands of Islam. In the end, however, both knew
that theological propaganda represented a more effective
means of promoting religious uniformity.

From the sixteenth century onwards the Middle East was,
in effect, in a state of civil war between shi'ism and sunnism.
Islam, which might have served as a powerful unifying factor,
was established as the main cause of deep divisions in the
region. The European powers were quick to realize this and
soon began doing their best to exploit it to their own
advantage. The shi'ite-sunni war was not confined to the duel
between the two neighbouring empires and extended well
into many of the territories each controlled.

An inevitable result of the theological rift was a mood of
intolerance that gradually set in throughout the region. In a
manner worthy of the totalitarian states of the twentieth
century, both the Ottoman and the Safavid state machines set
out to discourage all free thought. Philosophy, which had
been the passion of Muslim intellectuals until the thirteenth
century, was now considered as akin to heresy and strongly
discouraged. People interested in speculative thought were
forced virtually to go underground and constitute semi-
secret, often initiation-oriented, fraternities, which came to
be known as tariqats (paths). But free thought requires fresh
air and openness and the tariqats soon degenerated into
exclusive clubs with their own esoteric dogmas. The impressive movement of translation of hellenic texts that had
been begun by Muslim and Nestorian scholars in the Middle
East in the earliest decades of Islam came to a virtual halt.
Many books were burned and entire libraries disappeared.
Prose writing became a preserve either of state bureaucrats or
dogmatic theologians.

While philosophy was anathema, science was considered a
dangerous realm in which to venture. Poetry was tolerated
and at times even encouraged. But this consisted of poor
imitations of past models and sterile exercises in form.

Humour was strictly forbidden for Muslims and all satirical works that were produced, nonetheless, were presented under the label of 'Israeliat', meaning 'the work of the Jews'.

Between the sixteenth and the final decades of the nineteenth centuries the Middle East produced virtually no original thinker or poet of note comparable with those who had turned Islam into the world's most dynamic civilization in the first five hundred years of its existence.

Some Muslim scholars have attributed the rise of religious bigotry in the Middle East to the devastations caused by the Tatar invasions. They argue that Islam, frightened that it might be destroyed by barbarous hordes from Central Asia, withdrew into itself and sought protection behind the walls of strict orthodoxy. Whatever the value of this analysis, there is no doubt that Islam had lost a good part of its self-confidence and inherent optimism as a result of the humiliation it had suffered at the hands of the Tatars.

The principal cause of decadence was, nevertheless, the rise of fundamentalism in both its shi'ite and sunni versions. Islam had spread throughout the Middle East like a bush fire largely thanks to its openness, simplicity and closeness to the day-to-day concerns of mortal men. In its different fundamentalist versions, however, it became complicated, cruel and far removed from the sufferings of the poorer people. It was a frightened Islam that became frightening.

While the Muslim Middle East was embarked on a course of historical decline, Western Europe was beginning to move in the opposite direction. The so-called Dark Ages were drawing to a close and the Age of Enlightenment promised freedom of thought unprecedented in Europe since the fourth century. Between the end of the Crusades and the period described as the Industrial Revolution, the economy of Europe experienced a high rate of growth sustained by a rising population and the expansion of trade with both the East and the new American colonies of Spain, Portugal, Britain and France. The immense wealth of the Americas gave Europe virtually inexhaustible reserves at exactly the time that the development of new sea routes gradually severed the Middle East's trade and economic links with India and the Far East.

The Crusaders had failed to secure permanent conquests on land but ended up winning a far greater prize for Europe: the control of the Mediterranean. This reversed a situation that had enabled Islam to dominate world trade and finance its conquests on the European continent itself. During over a century of Muslim control over the Mediterranean routes, the Europeans had had no role in that crucial region except as pirates. After the Crusades the roles were reversed: Europeans became rich merchants using the sea while Muslims organized as bands of corsairs. Attempts by the Ottomans to regain control of at least the eastern part of the Mediterranean reached a peak with their victory at Prevesa (1538). But the defeat of the sultan's navy at Lepanto in 1571 ended all hopes for the return of Muslim domination of the sea routes.

The Mediterranean had not been the only source of wealth for the Muslim Middle East. Of potentially greater importance as a trade link was the Indian Ocean, which remained secure from European incursions until 1498 when the Portuguese discovered the Cape route. Within a few decades the Indian Ocean, too, had been turned into a European lake with Muslims playing only a marginal role as small traders or pirates.

Islam had developed as a civilization of movement, transit, trade and cultural intercourse. The Middle East had been the throbbing heart of that civilization. By the early seventeenth century, however, the Middle East was virtually blocked on all sides. The Mediterranean and the Indian Ocean had become remote bodies of water controlled by outside powers, while the emergence of Russia began to seal off the Middle East to the north. The spectacular development of sea trade also meant the gradual decline of Middle Eastern caravan movements. The famous Silk Route disappeared from the map and major caravan entrepôts declined into a shadow of their glorious past.

A high level of urbanization had always been an important feature of life in the Middle East. Cities were, indeed, essential for the survival and growth of a civilization based on movement and trade. The loss of sea and land trade routes led to a hecatomb of Middle Eastern cities: Damghan, Rey, Hamadan, Mossul, Konya, Aleppo and Cairo all suffered substantial losses of population and a marked decline in their economic power. Many other cities were left in ruins or reverted to the position of large, sleepy villages on roads leading from nowhere to nowhere. The decline of cities with their cosmopolitan populations further encouraged religious bigotry and intolerance which, in turn, prevented the progress of arts and sciences.

The only field in which the Middle East had tried to keep pace with Europe was that of war. Both the Ottoman and Safavid states enlisted the services of European adventurers and merchants for the purpose of setting up armament factories, mainly cannon foundries, and revising their traditional methods of warfare. Both states ignored the fact that military power could not exist in isolation and that a strong army alone could not discourage and defeat foreign aggression. By the time these facts were recognized by part of the ruling elites in Iran and the Ottoman Empire, the Middle East had already fallen two centuries behind Europe in terms of political and scientific progress.

The Middle East was dragged into modern times as a result of a series of military defeats suffered at the hands of European armies. The first of these took the form of Bonaparte's Egyptian expeditions (1798–1801) which marked the start of the western colonialist movement directed against the region. Bonaparte not only demonstrated the superiority of European arms but also underlined the role that the new western art of psychological warfare could play in a conflict. The French general circulated a rumour that he had secretly converted to Islam and that his real motive in invading Egypt was the creation of a powerful Islamic state that would then spread the Only True Faith to the whole of the globe.

The French expedition included a number of researchers and scholars who undertook major studies of Egyptian history, culture, architecture and ancient beliefs. The appearance of the first Orientalists on the scene meant that the Middle East was now seen by the West as an object of history, the accumulated debris of successive civilizations that could be studied not as a living fact but as a universe of dead fossils. What study was made of the Middle Eastern way of life focused on the exotic and began a whole tradition of portraying the Orient in strong romantic colours.

The encounter with the West provoked two diametrically opposed reactions in the Middle East. Part of the ruling elites, inspired by the clerics, advocated the erection of even stronger cultural walls as a means of keeping Islam safe from any possible harm. Others, however, began to observe the way the invaders lived, worked and fought and soon recognized the superiority of European methods and techniques. Over time they became the first advocates of 'westernization' or 'modernization' in the region. It was no accident that Egypt, only a few years after the French expedition, became the venue for the first modernizing experiments in the Middle East.

The break-up of the Ottoman Empire, rendered inevitable by the weakening of the state and the decline of a heavily-indebted economy, was hastened by a series of Christian revolts in the European possessions of the sultan. In 1829 Greece won its independence, while Romania and Serbia achieved autonomy. Bulgaria became an independent state in 1878 and Bosnia and Herzegovina broke away from the empire shortly afterwards. In 1913, on the eve of the First World War, Albania won its freedom. The fact that such predominantly Muslim parts of the empire as Albania, Bosnia, Herzegovina and parts of Macedonia also took up arms against the Ottoman 'Sublime Port' reflected the rising tide of European-style nationalism which transcended the limits of religious faith.

Meanwhile, Egypt had become all but independent under

Muhammad-Ali (1811–49) who became Pasha and the un-disputed master of the country after massacring the last of the Mameluks. Paying only formal allegiance to the Sublime Port, Muhammad-Ali Pasha established his own dynasty supported by a cosmopolitan elite of Circassians, Greeks, Albanians and Armenians. By 1847 the Pasha had added the Sudan to his Egyptian possessions and was planning the conquest of the Arabian Peninsula, Mesopotamia and the Persian Gulf.

Convinced westernizers, Muhammad-Ali and his success-ors established a more or less European-style court and adopted some of the outward aspects of life in Europe. But what they were not prepared to do was to allow Egyptian society to assume its responsibilities in a context of individual and collective freedoms. The structure of society remained 'oriental' while French was becoming the lingua franca of the court and the rich classes associated with it.

The opening of the Suez Canal had been seen by Khediv Ismail, Muhammad-Ali's successor, as a first step towards restoring to Egypt its ancient role as an important link in world trade. Instead, the canal was to prove a source of new problems for Egypt – problems which resulted in the virtual loss of the country's independence.

The Egyptian state took almost exactly the same path to perdition as had been trodden by the Ottomans a generation earlier. The Pasha was tempted into borrowing huge sums of money against his hoped-for income from the canal. When this did not materialize in the volumes expected he became technically bankrupt. A Franco-British condominium was imposed on Egypt in 1878, followed by the status of a British protectorate four years later. In 1899 a joint British-Egyptian condominium was imposed on the Sudan.

The dismemberment of the Ottoman Empire did not stop with the loss of Egypt and the Balkans. Between 1830 and 1912 France imposed its rule on Algeria, Tunisia and Morocco while Italy turned Tripolitania into a colony.

Iran, weakened by nearly a century of civil war and chaos,

was in no better position to protect itself against the new European colonial powers. In the eighteenth century a number of British merchants and adventurers had been invited by the shah to help Iran expel the Portuguese from a stronghold they had established in Gameroun (present day Bandar Abbas), which dominated the entrance to the Persian Gulf. The eviction of the Portuguese, however, had been followed by the establishment of British and Dutch 'factories' in various key ports of the waterway which served as a vital link with India.

Iran's situation, however, did not become desperate until it became involved in a number of disastrous wars against Tsarist Russia between 1814 and 1832. The Qajar dynasty, steeped in corruption and enjoying no popular base of support, had entered the campaign against Russia under the influence of the shi'ite mullahs who had declared jihad or holy war against the infidels from the north. The pretext used by the mullahs was the mistreatment of Muslim minorities in Georgia and parts of Armenia which had already fallen under Russian suzerainty.

By the middle of the nineteenth century Iran had already lost the whole of the Caucasus to Russia while Britain annexed more than half of Baluchistan as part of the Indian Empire. The Central Asian khanats also severed their traditional links with Iran and ended up as either colonies or protectorates of the Tsarist Empire. Afghanistan, for its part, snatched Herat away from Iran with British military and diplomatic support. The areas lost by Iran in that short time accounted for more than a third of the population of the kingdom.

The speed with which the Middle East, the home of world powers since the dawn of history, became a patchwork of colonies or semi-colonies within less than a century might at first appear surprising. But a closer examination of the balance of power between Europe on the one hand and Egypt, the Ottoman Empire and Iran on the other shows that the unprecedented technological and economic progress of the former was more than matched by the decline of the latter from the end of the sixteenth century onwards. The rise of Europe had changed all the rules of the international game. These rules few people in the Middle East were able to understand until it was practically too late to try and seize the initiative. The challenge of the West, however, became the central issue in Middle Eastern politics and remains so to this day.

Egypt's attempts at westernization had been copied by both the Ottoman Empire and Qajar Iran during the nineteenth century. In 1826 Sultan Mahmud II abolished the corps of the janissaries and replaced it with a standing army organized on a European model and composed of recruits rather than professional soldiers. His successor Sultan Abdul-Majid pushed the reform movement a step further and presided over a reorganization of the state apparatus. Known as the tanzimat (re-ordering) the reforms included an abolition of the poll tax imposed on non-Muslims and established the full legal equality of the sultan's subjects regardless of their religious faith. Six years later a new law providing for free compulsory education at the primary level was promulgated. But in the absence of an adequate number of teachers and faced with strong opposition from the ulema (the Muslim religious leaders) it was only partially applied.

Many Ottoman intellectuals realized that Europe's success was, at least in part, due to the growing participation of the people in the political process. These intellectuals became the advocates of meshrutiyat or constitutional rule. It was under their influence that Sultan Abdul-Hamid promulgated a constitution in 1876 and accepted certain limits on his own absolute power as sovereign and Caliph. The constitution was, however, suspended by the Sultan himself after only two years and remained a dead letter until its revival by the Young Turks' movement in 1908. In 1909 Abdul-Hamid himself was deposed as Sultan and Caliph.

The reforms undertaken by the Qajar kings, notably Nasser-Eddin Shah from the middle of the nineteenth century onwards, were not as extensive or as ambitious as the Turkish 'tanzimat'. Nevertheless, certain symbols of westernization such as a standing army, a few newspapers, a short railway line, a telegraph network and a bank made their appearance in Iranian life. In 1906 a group of intellectuals, liberal mullahs and tribal chiefs led a successful constitutional movement which forced the Shah to accept such western concepts as parliamentary rule and an independent judiciary.

Nevertheless, in both the Ottoman Empire and Iran, attempts at westernization stopped far short of providing a mechanism for meaningful popular participation in the political process. The aim of the reformists was to strengthen the administration and protect the vested interests of the dominant classes rather than enlarging the basis of government. Muslim clerics, both shi'ite and sunni, remained strongly hostile to all serious reform programmes that might undermine their own hold on much of society, especially in the rural areas.

More importantly, the westernizing intellectuals did not even try to develop a constituency for European-style political reforms. The masses remained totally outside the debate on whether or not the Middle East had anything to learn from Europe. This absence of the masses was of crucial importance: it meant that any reform achieved thanks to the favours of the ruler or pressures from foreign colonial powers could easily be undone. Even the Iranian constitutional movement, which mobilized a genuine popular following in Tehran, Isfahan and Azerbaijan, did not, in the end, succeed in creating mass parties that could have defended its achievements at times of adversity.

The westernizers tried to circumvent one crucial issue: what to do with the mosque? Almost all of them were resolutely opposed to the influence of the ulema and many of them might have even become free-thinkers in private. But none dared openly raise such dangerous topics as the role of Islam in society and the possibility of a secular form of government. Even today most of the Middle East's modernizers shy away from these topics or dismiss them as irrelevant to the task of reshaping their societies.

The timidity of the modernizers, combined with the tenacity of the ruling classes and the ulema, meant that no significant transformation of life-styles took place until after the First World War. A new middle class based on state functionaries and merchants came into being in Turkey, Egypt and Iran. But its influence in society at large remained strictly limited.

Both Russia and Britain, which had emerged as rivals in their quest for domination in the Middle East, allied themselves with the most reactionary forces in the region and did all they could to stifle attempts at serious political reform. Britain's limited and half-hearted support for the Iranian constitutionalists was something of an exception to this rule.

The two colonial empires had created their respective networks of influence in the region by financing some of the ulema as well as a number of tribal chiefs, princes and influential merchants. The fact that Britain and Russia dominated the region's trade gave them an additional instrument for extending their influence in the fragile societies with which they dealt. The Capitulation accords were in time given a broader interpretation to enable many local dignitaries to claim Russian or British protection while remaining the subjects of either the sultan or the shah.

On the eve of the First World War Britain was already established as the principal power in the Middle East, a position it was to maintain until the 1950s. Cyprus had already been annexed from the Ottoman Empire (1878), while the port of Aden, which controls the entrance to the Red Sea, had become a British colony in 1839. Hadhramaut, Oman, Muscat, the Trucial Coast, the Qatar Peninsula, the Bahrain archipelago and the shaikhdom of Kuwait had all been forced to become British protectorates. Britain controlled the Suez Canal, Bab al-Mandab and the Strait of Hormuz, three 'choke points' in East-West trade and three important military positions in a sensitive region. Britain's principal aim at the time was to prevent Russia, or any other European colonial power for that matter, from gaining a foothold in the Middle East and thus posing a threat to British possessions in the Indian subcontinent. In other words, the Middle East was cast into an entirely new role: that of a buffer zone between rival European empires.

The discovery of substantial reserves of oil in the Middle East in 1908 increased the region's strategic value for the European colonial powers especially after the British Royal Navy was converted to the use of petroleum from 1911 onwards.

When the First World War began in Europe the Ottoman state was under the control of the Young Turks whose pro-German leaders, Enver Paha and Talat Pasha, dreamed of the creation of a turkic empire extending from Europe to Central Asia. Considered moribund if not already dead, the 'sick man of Europe' appeared in unexpectedly good health in the early phases of the war. Ottoman troops launched a series of major attacks against both Russian and British positions in the Middle East. A daring dash for the seizure of the Suez Canal did not succeed but helped put the empire back on the military map of the Middle East. The campaign against Russia, that included an invasion of northern Iran, also got off to a good start but ended in disaster. The Russians soon turned the tide and pushed the Ottoman troops back into Anatolia before launching their own invasion of Turkish territories.

Right from the start of the hostilities Britain had established contact with the various Arab tribes of the region with a view to inciting them to rebellion against Ottoman rule. By 1916 the Arab revolt which took the form of a series of guerrilla operations against isolated Ottoman garrisons had emerged as an effective weapon in the hands of the British commanders in the Middle East. Between 1915 and 1917 British troops, at times supported by Arab guerrillas, captured Iraq, the region of Trans-Jordan, parts of Syria and the whole of Palestine. Jerusalem fell to British troops on 9 December 1917, the first time in more than 800 years that Islam had lost control of its third holiest city.

The end of the war provided the victorious Entente – Britain, France and Italy – with an opportunity to expand their colonial empires at the expense of the badly mauled Ottoman state. The Bolshevik Revolution which toppled the Tsar and removed Russia from the colonial chess-board in 1917 did little to temper the appetite of the western triumvirate. The United States, which had joined the Entente not as a full ally but as an 'associate', played only a marginal role in the process of redrawing the map of the Middle East. The peace treaty drafted by the Entente and imposed on the Sultan was truly humiliating. It ceded the whole of Thrace to Greece and northeastern Anatolia to Armenia which had become an independent republic in 1918. The southeastern provinces of Anatolia, mainly inhabited by the Kurds, were to become an autonomous region with a right to secession. As for the Izmir (Smyrna) region, a strange formula was imposed enabling Greece to annex it within five years. The city of Istanbul (Constantinople) was to remain the capital of a truncated state but put under international control together with the Bosphorus and the Dardanelles. The Sultan was to be allowed an army of no more than 50,000 men and was expressly forbidden from creating either a navy or an air force. Finally, the finances of the defeated power were to be controlled by France, Italy and Britain who also decided to divide the remaining Ottoman territories into three distinct 'zones of influence' under a separate accord.

The Sultan's representatives signed the unequal treaty at Sèvres, near Paris, in August 1920. Unknowingly, they also sealed the fate of the Ottoman empire and the caliphate as well.

4

A MOSAIC OF NATIONS

The semi-colonial system that was imposed on the Middle East as a result of European victories in the First World War might have been expected to be an encouragement to the forces of religious reaction who preached xenophobia and bigotry as the best means of preserving the identity and interests of the region. Instead, it was an age of Western-style nationalism that was ushered in from Egypt to Afghanistan.

The three main 'nations' that lived in the Middle East – the Arabs, the Turks and the Iranians – had not experienced the First World War in the same way. The Arabs, or at least some of them, had sided with the British and could, therefore, claim to be among the victors – at least theoretically. The Iranians might have lost a great deal but were saved by the collapse of the Tsarist Empire to their north. Iran's territorial integrity remained secure although it fell under exclusive political control by Britain. The Turks, however, appeared as big losers on all counts. They had lost most of their territory and been left with only nominal independence under the Treaty of Sèvres.

By 1919 the fate of Turkey seemed to have been determined for at least a generation. Having lost some 1.5 million dead, mostly as a result of epidemic diseases and massacres rather than in the war itself, the Turks were not expected to have any energy left for resisting the colonial diktats of the European powers.

The passionate resolve of one charismatic leader was to change that situation. He was Mustafa Kemal Pasha, a young general of the Sultan and the architect of the Ottoman army's sole major military victory in the war. A member of the society of 'Young Turks', Kemal had taken an active part in the constitutional revolution of 1908 and forged close links with Jemal Pasha's reformist 'Unity and Progress' movement.

In May 1919 Kemal was named by the Sultan as Inspector-General of the army with the task of supervising a speedy disarmament of the Ottoman forces in accordance with the wishes of Britain and France. But when Kemal arrived at Samsun at the start of his new mission he did exactly the opposite of what he was supposed to do. He called on local commanders to stockpile arms, recruit new soldiers and co-ordinate their activities with the defence committees already set up in many towns and villages. The Turkish Army of the East, the country's only military force still in fighting mood, was promptly put under Kemal's command. In June Kemal was recalled to Istanbul but refused to obey orders and instead went to Erzerum where a national congress elected him as president. The congress ratified a National Pact. The pact rejected most of the concessions that the various colonial powers had imposed on the moribund empire and emphasized Turkey's political independence and territorial integrity within its frontiers of 1914.

In September 1919 a second national congress, this time including representatives from virtually all parts of Anatolia, confirmed the National Pact and named Kemal President of the state and chief of the executive. The Sultan reacted by forming a new government and called for general elections with a view to forming a democratic parliament which began work in January 1920. Kemal who had established his 'capital' at Ankara, midway between Istanbul and Erzerum, seemed well on the way to final victory. The Sultan, however, did not give up without a fight. Encouraged by the ulema who feared Kemal's secular nationalism, the Sultan exercised his powers as the Caliph of Islam and decreed jihad (holy war) against the kemalists who were described as 'infidels' and 'miscreants'.

The nationalists, who enjoyed the support of a majority of army officers, bureaucrats and intellectuals, might have been quickly isolated by the rising tide of religious fanaticism. The ulema blamed the officers for the country's defeat and assured the illiterate masses that only the Caliph could lead them into recovering the past grandeur of Islam. The Sultan's forces, however, proved no fighting match for the nationalists, while public opinion began to find in Kemal the providential man that the nation's dangerous position required at that time.

In June 1920 a Greek army, with at least moral support from Britain, invaded Bursa and succeeded in evicting the kemalist troops from Izmir. The Greco-Turkish War had begun. A series of battles and skirmishes in which the Greeks enjoyed superiority in both numbers and armaments enabled the invaders to move deep into Anatolia by the spring of 1921. Kemal had organized his advance defence lines on the River Sakraya some 100 kilometres to the west of Ankara. And it was there that the battle of destiny was fought between 23 August and 13 September. The Greek army was defeated and forced to retreat to Izmir where it managed to hang on for another year. On 9 September 1922 the kemalist forces captured Izmir and set it on fire. The Greeks escaped by the sea, taking with them some of the city's Greek-speaking families.

On 1 November 1922 the Turkish parliament, known as the Great Assembly of the People, announced the abolition of the monarchy. Two weeks later Sultan Mehmet VI left Istanbul on board a British boat for permanent exile. The Assembly, no doubt anxious not to further antagonize the ulema on the eve of delicate negotiations with Greece and the Western imperial powers in Lausanne, named the deposed Sultan's cousin, Abdul-Majid, as Caliph, limiting his powers to strictly religious matters.

The Lausanne Treaty, signed in July 1923, represented a

major diplomatic coup for the new kemalist state. It reflected almost all of the aspirations of the National Pact that had become the cornerstone of Kemal Pasha's policy. Apart from giving Turkey a much fairer territorial deal, the treaty unequivocally recognized the full independence of the new state.

The success achieved by the kemalist movement in its struggle against the foreign domination of Turkey established nationalism as a credible alternative to Islamic fundamentalism in the eyes of the educated elites of the Middle East. This was an example to be emulated. Kemal, soon given the title of Atatürk (Father of the Turks) and referred to as 'the Eternal Chief', based his system on three basic principles. The first was national sovereignty. This was a revolutionary concept in the Middle East for it rejected the Islamic belief that all power belongs to the Creator. Secondly, Atatürk established the principle of secularism. The caliphate abolished, religion became a purely individual concern. Finally, Atatürk sincerely believed that only democracy and the rule of law could ensure Turkey's modernization in the long run. A democrat by conviction but a dictator by temperament, Atatürk exempted himself from the rules of democracy and exercised almost absolute power. He was a benevolent dictator, if any such breed can be imagined to exist. He made of Turkey the first truly modern nation state of the Middle East.

The system developed by Atatürk largely depended on one crucial assumption – that a Turkish nation did, indeed, exist. Atatürk rejected both pan-Islamism, which had become fashionable in the nineteenth century, and pan-Turkism, which had captured the imagination of some young officers and intellectuals in the early decades of the twentieth century. Convinced that he needed a Turkish nation, Atatürk simply decided to invent one. A number of books, mixing myths and history, were commissioned with the aim of proving the existence of a Turkish nation throughout history. Some French ethnologists were invited to Istanbul and given all the encouragement needed for 'proving' that the Turks were, in fact, related to the Celts and thus a European nation. Mythological Greek, Tatar, Kurdish and Persian heroes were 'turkicized' and presented as the ancestors of the modern Turkish nation.

Like all other nationalisms, the new Turkish nationalism needed to admire some nations and hate others. Germany, with its Prussian military traditions, was held up as an object of admiration and the Arabs as peoples one could safely hate. A massive campaign of de-Arabization was launched. The Arabic alphabet was abandoned in favour of one based on Latin and many Arabic and Persian words were purged from the vernacular. The transliteration of those Arabic and Persian words that had to be retained was carefully modified to disguise their origins as much as possible and make them sound truly Turkish. In any case thousands of new Turkish words were coined, often borrowed from French or German, and the share of Arabic and Persian words in the Turkish vocabulary was reduced from approximately seventy per cent to less than fifty per cent over a period of two decades.

Inciting the people into a dislike of the Arabs was no difficult task. Most Turks saw the Arabs as traitors to Islam who had sided with an infidel enemy and stabbed the caliphate in the back. The memory of that Arab 'betrayal' did not fade from the Turkish political mind until the 1970s and was a factor in persuading the government of Ankara to extend full diplomatic relations to the state of Israel. Turkey was the first Muslim nation to do so and remained the only one until 1980.

The Arabs had joined forces with Britain in the First World War with very high hopes. They were soon to be disappointed. Their fate was decided not with any reference to their aspirations but on the basis of big power calculations. The San Remo Accords (1920–22) gave Britain mandates over Iraq, Trans-Jordan and Palestine while France became mandatory power for Syria and Lebanon. Syria was divided into three portions: an Alawite state, a Druze state and a Syrian sunni-state.

Meanwhile, the seeds of one of the most important conflicts in the region's history had been sown by Britain even before the end of the war. The Balfour Declaration of 1917, designed to mobilize international Jewish support for the Entente, pledged British support for the creation of a 'national home' for Jews in Palestine.

While the Arabic-speaking peoples of the region no doubt became more conscious of their specific identity as a result of the war, this did not lead to the emergence of a distinct nationalist movement. Few thought of all Arab-speaking peoples as one nation, a concept that became popular in the 1960s. Egyptians, for example, were seldom, if ever, described as Arabs, a term largely used to single out the inhabitants of the Arabian Peninsula, Trans-Jordan and parts of Mesopotamia. Tribal, regional and sectarian sentiments and traditions were too strong to allow the idea of nationhood to dominate political thinking even in the larger cities where the shock of the West was felt more strongly. The various Arab peoples resembled the Latin nations of Europe in the sense that they shared a common culture and spoke languages derived from the same stem. Had it not been for the unprecedented development of the means of communication and the rapid growth of compulsory education between the 1920s and the 1980s, the Arabic of Yemen, for example, might have become as distinct from the Arabic of Egypt as is French from Romanian. In any case, speaking the same language and even sharing the same religion and cultural background, crucial though they are in inspiring nationalist sentiments, cannot complete the process of nationhood without the help of numerous other factors. Any list of such factors would always leave out elements that cannot be defined and described with scientific exactitude.

The tremors caused by the First World War in the region led to the emergence of new ruling elites in both Turkey and Iran. In the Arab countries of the region, however, power remained in the hands of traditional groups, often of tribal background or related to old Ottoman families, who ruled under the close supervision of British and French colonial officials. The various Arab countries still had a long period of struggle before they achieved their full independence between the 1930s and the 1960s.

The first Arab country to embark upon the fight for independence was Egypt, which had become a British protectorate in 1914. With the war over, Britain's legal status in Egypt quickly came under attack from sections of the urban middle class that wanted to reorganize the country on the lines of a European-style nation state. In 1918 the Umma (nation) Party, led by the lawyer Sa'ad Zaghlul, passed a resolution demanding full independence for Egypt. Zaghlul's attempts at achieving a negotiated settlement with the British, however, proved a total failure as the Colonial Office in London toyed with the idea of turning Egypt into a full colony of the empire.

Zaghlul and members of his delegation in talks with the British High Commissioner Wingate in Cairo announced the formation of a new political party in December 1918. The new party was aptly named Wafd (Delegation) and quickly attracted support from virtually the whole of the Egyptian intelligentsia and a number of powerful merchants. More importantly, it was endorsed by King Fu'ad who had succeeded to the throne in 1917 and shared the dream of an independent and westernized Egypt.

The king's move forced the pro-British prime minister to resign. This led to scenes of jubilation in the streets that soon degenerated into riots. A general strike, ordered by the Wafd Party, brought the country to a virtual standstill in the spring of 1919. The initial British response to these events was to arrest Zaghlul and deport him to Malta. But the move incited further riots that were suppressed by British troops. More than 2,000 people were killed but the strikes continued. London finally agreed to set up a commission of enquiry. The commission, led by Lord Milner, recommended the end of the protectorate and the safeguarding of British interests through the conclusion of a series of treaties with Egypt.

Zaghlul, allowed to return from exile, led an Egyptian delegation to London in June 1920. The official Egyptian government, dominated by ethnic Turks, however, was suspicious of Wafd's motives and offered greater concessions to the British.

The new British High Commisioner, Lord Allenby, believed that a mixture of firmness and concessions offered to the formal governmental authorities in Cairo would undermine the position of the Wafd. Accordingly, Zaghlul was sent into exile once again, this time to the Seychelles. A few months later, however, London unilaterally cancelled the protectorate accord between Britain and Egypt (28 February 1922).

This was by no means an end to the British domination of Egypt. Britain claimed four major rights for itself: to control Egypt's defences, to directly protect Britain's communications links in Egypt, to control the administration of the Sudan and to protect foreign minorities in Egyptian territory.

The British declaration included the proviso that all four major rights reserved for Britain would revert to the Egyptian government on the basis of treaties to be signed at an unspecified date. No treaties were signed until 1936 and Egypt's independence remained largely a matter of form. The most immediate result of this formal independence was King Fuad's decision to drop the Turkish title of Sultan in favour of the Arabic Malek. And it was in his new capacity as 'constitutional monarch' that Fuad ordered parliamentary elections in 1924. The Wafd won a majority and Zaghlul was named Prime Minister. The stage was set for a triangular power struggle involving the royal court, the Wafd and the British High Commission.

The political crisis caused by the power struggle was to last for nearly thirteen years, at the end of which Egypt was able to reassert its political unity and face Britain with new demands for full independence. A series of accords signed in 1936 established an Anglo-Egyptian condominium over the Sudan and ended the British domination of the Egyptian armed forces. In exchange, Britain was allowed to maintain troops in the Suez Canal zone and given the right to use Egyptian air space and the port facilities of Alexandria at times of war. These accords were facilitated in part by the removal of Zaghlul from the scene – he was murdered by Islamic gunmen – and the growing concern of the Egyptian middle classes about Italian colonial expansion in neighbouring Libya. With fresh clouds gathering in the skies of Europe the Egyptians felt that they might need British support in case a new war broke out.

Throughout the struggle for full independence Egypt's politics were dominated by the Wafd, a liberal, mildly nationalistic movement. The nationalism espoused by Wafd was strictly Egyptian and not Arab. There was, in fact, no recognizable constituency for pan-Arab nationalism. Even the ultra-nationalist Watan (Fatherland) Party defined itself in essentially Egyptian terms and traced its cultural roots to the pharaonic civilizations of the Nile Valley.

Egyptian nationalism, while opposed to foreign domination of the country, was neither xenophobic nor specifically anti-western. On the contrary, it aspired towards a western-style parliamentary system and dreamed of the day that Egypt would take the same path to progress that had led Western Europe to strength and prosperity. Egyptian nationalism represented the continuation of a political tradition established by Muhammad-Ali Pasha.

By the time Egypt joined the League of Nations in 1937 another newly-created Arab country, Iraq, had also emerged as a more or less independent actor on the Middle Eastern scene. At first glance, Iraq, carved out of the Ottoman Empire by Britain, appeared an untenable state. Just over half of the population in 1918 were Arab-speaking, many of them nomadic tribes in southern Mesopotamia. Of these, over seventy per cent were shi'ites and the rest sunnis belonging to two different sects. The remaining half of the population consisted of Kurds, Turks, Turcomans, Assyrians, Nestorians, Sabeans, Persians, Yazidis and Jews. Almost the entire ruling class consisted of sunnis with an Ottoman ethnic background.

Demands for full independence from British rule were first launched in the holy cities of lower Mesopotamia as well as Baghdad in 1918 shortly after the end of the war. But when it became clear, in 1920, that Britain had no intention of allowing its creature to become independent, a series of riots were organized throughout the country. Unlike the Egyptian revolt of the preceding year the Iraqi uprising was openly anti-west and strongly influenced by the shi'ite mullahs of Najaf and Karbala. The uprising was also far more difficult to quell and calm was not restored until more than 3,000 people had died in clashes with British forces. One thing had become clear as a result of the revolt: Britain could not hope to turn Iraq into a straight colony of the crown. Iran, which did not relish the idea of finding the British to its west, strongly supported demands for Iraqi independence.

The British decided to kill two birds with one stone: Iraq would receive its independence while Britain would pay some of the moral and political debt it owed to its war-time Arab allies. These allies, grouped around the family of Sharif Hussein, the Custodian of the Ka'aba at Mecca and the Governor of Hejaz under the Ottomans, had originally been promised the control of the entire region from Mesopotamia and the Levant to the frontiers of the Yemen. But this was not to be. The French, who occupied Syria, dethroned one of Sharif Hussein's sons, Faisal, who had been declared king by the British. At the same time the family was threatened in its home-base in the Hejaz by the rising power of a new Wahhabi force led by the energetic Abdul-Aziz Ibn Saud. The British had originally thought of making Abdallah, another son of Sharif Hussein, King of Iraq. But they were forced to change their plans once Faisal had been thrown out of Damascus. The solution found was simple: Faisal would become King of Iraq while a new kingdom would be carved out for Abdallah in Trans-Jordan.

In August 1921 the British organized a referendum aimed

at inviting Faisal to become King of Iraq. Needless to say no opposition to the idea was allowed and few scruples were shown in arranging the results in accordance with the wishes of the British high command in Baghdad. The very idea of putting an 'outsider' on the throne in Baghdad was repulsive to many inhabitants of the new states, especially the shi'ites and the Kurds.

In 1933 Faisal died and was succeeded by his son Ghazi who was killed in a car accident in 1939. In the meantime, Britain imposed a series of accords on Iraq. These accords recognized the new country's formal independence but made sure that Britain maintained a strong hold on all aspects of Iraqi politics.

Iraq's strategic importance at the heart of the Middle East had been appreciated by all the colonial powers during the war. The discovery of oil in the Kurdish regions of the new country in 1918 dramatically increased the value of Britain's new possession. Nevertheless, Iraq appeared an unusually fragile state right from the start. The new Turkey of the kemalists did not relinquish Ottoman territorial claims on the Mossul region, while Iran continued to dream of gaining control over the shi'ite holy shrines of southern Mesopotamia. The presence of the French in neighbouring Syria was a potential threat, while the rising Saudi power in the peninsula quickly found itself in conflict with the shi'ite tribes of the Bani-Ka'ab confederation in the Basra region.

To face these threats Britain, unable to provide indefinite military protection, financed and organized the creation of a strong Iraqi army led by a sunni military elite. Very quickly, the army emerged as the most important player on the Iraqi political scene. It fought the Kurds in the north and shi'ite tribes in the south and protected the increasingly valuable oil installations. More importantly, it served as an instrument for turning the Iraqis into a single, unified nation – a process that has continued into the 1980s.

Iraq quickly became the linchpin of British policy in the Middle East. It was from its military bases in Iraq that Britain launched an invasion of Iran in 1941 and later put military pressure on the government in Tehran during the oil national-ization crisis of the early 1950s.

In 1932 Iraq, with a total population of just under four million, was already beginning to aspire after the leadership of the Arab world. Its growing wealth from oil, its close ties with Britain and the presence of a strong ruling elite capable of pursuing an active diplomacy gave Iraq assets that other Arab states, with the sole exception of Egypt, lacked. The fact that Iraq also had a larger population than any Arab country east of Suez further strengthened the country's claim to leadership. The ancient rivalry between the Nile Valley and Mesopotamia over the domination of the region was revived. The creation of the Saadabad Pact, bringing together Iran, Turkey and Iraq in 1932, reinforced Britain's position in the Middle East.

While Iraq was ideally designed to serve as Britain's watchdog in the Persian Gulf and the Levant, another newly-created country, Trans-Jordan, quickly emerged as London's control post for the Arabian Peninsula and the strategic Gulf of Aqaba. Trans-Jordan, which was renamed the Hashemite Kingdom of Jordan after the Second World War, was, in fact, a garrison disguised as a country. There, the British created an army, the Arab Legion, which they entirely financed and commanded. Most of the 6,000 soldiers that made up the Legion were recruited from among bedouin tribesmen. The Legion, although numerically small, soon became the most efficient fighting force between Egypt and Iran.

Devoid of natural resources and without a sizeable settled population capable of developing an agriculture, Jordan had for long to depend on British stipends for economic survival. Politically, the new state's relative success was largely due to the wisdom and decisiveness of King Abdallah who, having missed the chance to become monarch in Baghdad, had been put on the throne in Amman.

The fall of the Ottoman Empire, meanwhile, had also led to the emergence of five more or less independent states in the

Arabian Peninsula itself: the Yemen, the Hejaz, Assir, Najd and Shammar.

Right from the start of the First World War Britain had allied itself with the rulers of Hejaz, and Colonel T.E. Lawrence, the British intelligence officer who coordinated the Arab revolt against the Ottomans, had dreamed of giving the whole of Arabia to his friend, Sharif Hussein of Mecca. The force of the future in Arabia, however, was the emirate of Najd where an energetic Abdul-Aziz Ibn Saud had acceded to power in 1902. Ibn Saud's ambition was first to unite the whole of the Peninsula under his own rule and then aim at creating a unified Islamic state covering the Middle East and beyond.

As a religious and political leader of the Wahhabi sect of Muslims Ibn Saud created a fraternity of holy warriors known as the Ikhwan (brethren) in 1912 and strengthened his control over the bedouin tribes of central Arabia. A few years later he conquered the emirate of Shammar to the north and by 1920 was preparing for an invasion of Hejaz. Ibn Saud made no secret of his plans for seizing control of Mecca as well as the holy city of Medina which together made Hejaz the most highly coveted prize in the whole of Islam.

Sharif Hussein's response to the challenge from Najd, was to seek a military alliance with Britain. But negotiations on the subject failed as a result of disagreements concerning the future of Palestine. In 1924 Hussein, encouraged by his British friends, declared himself the Caliph of Islam. The move, designed to discourage an attack from Najd, produced the opposite result. Ibn Saud's bedouins entered Hejaz and, meeting little resistance, captured Mecca just six months after Sharif Hussein had named himself the Caliph. In January 1926 Ibn Saud proclaimed himself the King of Hejaz. His new conquests were all recognized by the British under the Jeddah Treaty signed in 1927. The British agreed to deal with Ibn Saud only after the Soviet Union had formally recognized the Kingdom of Hejaz early in 1927. The USSR was also one of the first countries to establish diplomatic relations with the

Kingdom of Saudi Arabia in 1932. These relations, however, were severed by Saudi Arabia in 1938, presumably on the advice of the United States. In 1930 Assir was virtually annexed by the new state which took the title of the Kingdom of Saudi Arabia in 1932. In 1934 Prince Faisal, one of Ibn Saud's sons, led a successful campaign against the Imamate of Yemen and further exended the frontiers of the new kingdom. The Saudi state, despite the small size of the population it controlled – under two million in 1930 – and its relative remoteness, could claim a major role in the region thanks to its control of the Haj pilgrimage and, from the late 1930s onwards, its important oil production.

The Imamate of Yemen, although never fully controlled by Ottomans, declared its full independence in 1919. Known as Arabia Felix to the Romans, Yemen had suffered steady decline as a result of a gradual breakdown of its ancient systems of irrigation. Dominated by the Zaidi sect of shi'ites under an Imam, this was a medieval-style theocracy where time seemed to have come to a standstill. Even the shock of the defeat suffered in the war against the Saudi invaders did not jolt the Imamate out of its torpor.

The Imam's vague hopes of gaining control of the port of Aden and the shaikhdoms of Beihan and Hadhramaut to the south were dashed in 1935 when Britain formalized its control of the entire region. Aden became a crown colony and British protection was imposed on the sultanate of Lahej and a string of other mini-states between the Red Sea and the Omani province of Dhofar.

The two principal colonial powers in the Middle East, Britain and France, have been criticized for what is described as 'the division of the Arab nation into several states'. The belief that, had it not been for European colonialists, the Arab-speaking peoples of the region might have been united within a single state is so strongly held by Arab nationalists that it is difficult to challenge. But Arab nationalism, as it emerged in the 1960s, did not exist as a serious political force in the Middle East in the earlier decades of this century. In

some cases, it could even be argued that the colonial powers
created larger states than might have otherwise been the case.
Iraq, for example, was a multinational state where the Kurds,
to cite only the largest of the various minorities, might well
have had a state of their own. The Treaty of Sèvres had, in
fact, promised the Kurds precisely such an expression for
their national aspirations.

Syria and Lebanon, which gained their independence after
the Second World War, might have been divided into several
smaller units based on ethnic or sectarian differences. In
southern Arabia, British rule eventually led to the unification
of more than a dozen shaikhdoms and emirates into a single
state. The seven shaikhdoms of the Trucial Coast, in the
Persian Gulf, also ended up as a federation, and if Qatar and

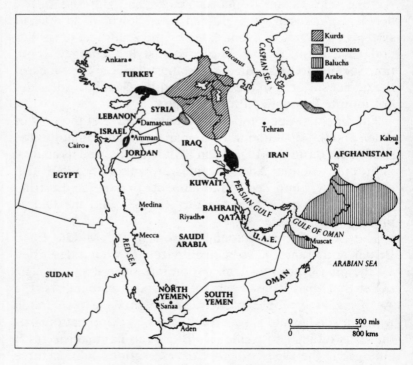

Ethnic Minorities in The Middle East

Bahrain chose to go their own separate ways it was because their respective ruling families refused membership of the United Arab Emirates in 1971.

Vague aspirations towards unity had always played a part in the politics of the Middle East. But these were essentially pan-Islamic and not nationalistic in the narrower sense of the term.

The first manifestation of a pan-Arab nationalism dates back to 1904–1908 when a group of exiled Arab Christians in Paris created 'The League of the Arab Fatherland' under the leadership of Neguib 'Azouri. The programme of the league cited as its number one priority the separation of 'the civil and religious power in the interest of Islam and the Arab nation'. It was obviously aimed against the Islamic theocratic rule under which Christian and Jewish Arabs could never become full citizens of the state. Further, the league defined the 'Arab empire' it wished to create as a state covering only parts of Mesopotamia, the Levant and the Arabian Peninsula. The Yemen, the emirate of Najd, Lebanon – where Christians formed the largest community an Iraqi principality based on Baghdad and, last but not least, Egypt were to be excluded from the 'empire'.

The league's view of Egypt's position was significant. It 'rejected the idea of unifying Egypt and the Arab Empire under the same monarchy, because Egyptians do not belong to the Arab race; they are of the African Berber family (sic) and the language which they spoke before Islam bears no similarity to Arabic.' Needless to say the league did not even dream of including North Africa in its concept of an Arab nation and would have been surprised by the extension of Arab identity to Mauritania, Somalia and Jibouti in the 1960s and 1970s.

At any rate, pan-Arab nationalism remained a minority interest, mainly for Syrian and Lebanese Christians, until the 1940s when the emergence of Israel as a state furnished it with the adversary that, like other nationalistic movements, it needed in order to survive and develop.

The idea of creating a Jewish state in Palestine was first raised by Theodor Herzl (1860–1904) who has been recognized as the founder of modern political Zionism. In his preface to *Der Judenstaat (The Jewish State)*, published in 1896, Herzl analysed the causes of anti-Semitism and concluded that the notorious Berlin slogan 'Juden Raus' (out with the Jews) pointed the way to the solution. What Europe was confronted with was a 'Jewish national question' that could not be settled until and unless the Jews were recognized as a distinct nation and given the chance to have a state of their own.

Herzl's analysis was in full conformity with the mood of his time; he was a product of the age of nationalism. What was significant, however, was that he did not advocate the creation of a Jewish state where most Jews lived – that is to say in central and eastern Europe. He described his idea as 'a very old one: the restoration of the Jewish State'. That meant the occupation of at least part of Palestine by European Jews.

The Zionist movement, financed by Jewish communities in various European countries as well as the United States, began purchasing land in Palestine soon after Herzl published his manifesto. Most of the land thus acquired came from the possessions of the Ottoman Sultan who, deeply in debt as he was, welcomed the opportunity for making some money by selling largely barren land to people who did not appear to pose any danger to his rule.

The first Jewish colonies in Palestine had been established in 1878 and 1883 before the Zionist conference of 1897 in Basle inaugurated a continuous flow of new Jewish immigrants towards the 'promised land'. At the start of the First World War the Jews in Palestine, including the natives, numbered around 25,000 from a total population of more than 600,000.

In 1917 the British government, anxious to mobilize international Jewish support for its war efforts, declared itself in 'favour' of the principal aim of the Zionist movement. The Foreign Secretary, Lord Balfour, in a letter to Lord

Rothschild, said: 'His Majesty's Government view with favour the establishment in Palestine of a national home for the Jewish people, and will use their best endeavours to facilitate the achievement of this object, it being clearly understood that nothing shall be done which may prejudice the civil and religious rights of existing non-Jewish communities in Palestine or the rights and political status enjoyed by Jews in any other country.'

The letter, which was quickly dubbed 'The Balfour Declaration', amounted to a British commitment to the realization of the aims of the Basle conference without any prior consultations with the Arabs. By 1919 the number of Jewish colonists in Palestine had risen to 65,000 or nearly one-tenth of the population. The Zionist leaders made no secret of their intention to create a separate state of their own regardless of the fact that the Balfour letter had used the rather vague term of a 'national home' for the Jews. It was under British pressure that Emir Faisal, the son of Sharif Hussein, met with the Zionist leader Dr Chaim Weizmann, who had succeeded Herzl, in 1919 to discuss future relations. At the end of a series of talks the two men signed an agreement in which Weizmann was presented as a representative of Palestine, as yet not a legal entity, while Faisal spoke on behalf of an equally non-existent 'Arab state'.

Faisal also conducted an exchange of letters with another Zionist leader, Felix Frankfurter. In a letter dated 3 March 1919 Faisal referred to his talks with Weizmann in both Europe and Arabia and wrote: 'we feel that the Arabs and Jews are cousins in race, having suffered similar oppressions at the hands of powers stronger than themselves, and by a happy coincidence have been able to take the first step towards the attainment of their national ideals together.' Faisal, who headed the Arab delegation at the Versailles peace conference, expressed 'deepest sympathy' for the Zionist cause and announced that the Arabs 'will wish the Jews a most hearty welcome home'.

The situation on the ground, however, was quite different

from what Faisal believed it to be. The Palestinians were beginning to realize the threat posed to their own existence by the rising tide of Jewish immigration from Europe. Palestinian protest demonstrations had already taken place in Jerusalem and Jaffa before the publication of the Balfour Declaration and a series of clashes had posed Arab peasants against Jewish settlers in a number of localities. Faisal, who was trying to become King of Syria with suzerainty over Palestine, was fully aware of the Palestinian grievances but dismissed them as the results of some 'misunderstandings' fomented by 'less educated and fanatical elements' among the Arabs.

Three factors helped dramatically to increase the number of European, especially Russian and Polish, Jews who came to settle in Palestine. The first of these factors was the security that Britain offered thanks to its military presence in the Levant. The second was the rapidly expanding financial and organizational powers of the Zionist movement which enabled it to help an increasing number of Jewish families to settle in the Middle East. Finally, a decision by the United States Government to impose strict limits to Jewish immigration between 1921 and 1924 forced many Jews from central and eastern Europe to forget about the New World and head for the 'promised land'.

The Jewish colonial movement in Palestine was different from other European experiments in colonialism in one vital domain: the Zionists did not wish to exploit the local Arab population. Their aim was to create a parallel society of their own alongside the indigenous Arab communities who did not, as yet, feel that they belonged to a 'Palestinian' nation. The number of new Jewish arrivals rose to more than 10,000 a year between 1921 and 1933 when it jumped to an annual average of more than 50,000. In 1939, at the start of the Second World War, Jews numbered just over 425,000 or a third of the total population.

Under the terms of the British mandate in Palestine the Jews were authorized to create an 'agency' to represent their interests and ensure contact with the mandatory authorities. By 1920 the 'agency' was well on its way to becoming a fully-fledged state apparatus. It organized the election of a national council, which served as parliament, and created a militia, Haganah, based on conscription. An independent educational system and the direct taxation of Jewish income further emphasized the development of the agency towards full statehood. In 1924 a Jewish university was inaugurated in Jerusalem, the first modern centre of higher education in the Levant.

The new Jewish community that grew in Palestine had a number of distinct advantages over the native Arab population. Strong organization and dedicated leadership gave the Jewish settlers a sense of purpose and a means of mobilizing their energies that the Arabs lacked. Co-operative villages (mochavs) and collective farms (kibbutzim) gave the settlers an intimate relationship with the soil of the new homeland and created a shared sentiment of solidarity and equality. Mochav and kibbutzim members played a key role in the Histadrut, the central labour organization, as well as the Haganah.

The Histadrut, led by David Ben Gurion who was to become the first prime minister of independent Israel, emerged as something more than a traditional European-style trade union. The absence of any significant capitalist enterprise in Palestine meant that the Histadrut itself often acted as the locomotive needed for the country's new industries.

The Jewish settlers developed a lively political system in which a variety of political parties, ranging from the extreme left to the religious-conservative, competed for votes. A dynamic press and a rich intellectual life gave the nascent community further cause for pride and self-confidence. The Arabs, in contrast, remained under the influence of the ulema and the traditional tribal and clan elders, many of whom had unwittingly helped the emergence of the new settlers' community by selling land to the Jews.

By 1920 some wealthy Palestinians had become fully aware of the damage they had done to their own community by selling land to immigrants from Europe. They wanted to buy back the land but this was no longer possible as the system of collective ownership established by the Jewish agency made any private transactions impossible.

In 1921 the seething hostility between Arabs and Jews degenerated into a series of riots in Palestinian towns. The British authorities had to use military force to restore calm. A year later Britain published a White Paper on Palestine offering a number of concessions to the Arabs. The most important of these was a decision to limit Jewish immigration in future to Palestine's economic capacity for absorbing new arrivals. The Arabs received assurances that the Jews would not be allowed to become a majority in the areas under the mandate.

In practice, however, the various organizations that handled Jewish immigration quickly developed new ways of bypassing the controls imposed by the British authorities. Illegal Jewish immigration continued to increase right up to 1947 and the end of the mandate. More extremist Zionist groups, ironically influenced by certain aspects of the burgeoning fascist movements in Europe, created secret para-military organizations to fight both the British and any future Arab force that might stand in their way. In time such groups as Irgun and Stern degenerated into terrorist organizations and used cold-blooded murder as a means of furthering political aims.

Hostility between Arab and Jew has often been presented as a confrontation between Islam and Judaism. But the real reasons for the crisis were, in fact, political. To be sure, most Muslims could not reconcile themselves to a dramatic change in the status of Jews who had always been regarded as a respected, but certainly not equal, community in Islamic lands. And the ulema certainly played a part in inciting hatred against the Jews in Palestine. Haj Amin al-Hussaini, the Chief Mufti of Jerusalem, made no secret of his pro-Hitler sentiments right from the early 1930s. Nevertheless, religion played only a secondary role in promoting the crisis. Many leaders of the Arabs in Palestine were Christians and espoused the aim of secular nationalism. They might have suffered from the traditional Christian prejudices against Jews. But they certainly did not think in terms of religious conflict in determining their stance *vis-à-vis* the Jewish community in Palestine.

The real core of the conflict consisted of the rivalry between two communities for the control of the future of the same country. The Palestinians witnessed the emergence of new Arab states all around them and could not understand why they alone should be forced to share their country with another, totally alien, community brought in from Europe. Some Jews understood the Palestinian viewpoint and even sympathized with it. But the majority of the settlers aspired to full statehood. Zionist leaders at times spoke of a bi-national state in which Arabs and Jews would enjoy joint sovereignty. But by 1931 it had become clear that Arab and Jew would be unlikely to live together without one being dominated by the other. In 1930 an Arab strike, led by the Mufti of Jerusalem, had turned into bloody riots with armed gangs attacking Jewish settlements and killing a number of people, including women and children. Once again Britain had to use force to restore calm.

By 1937 the failure of the British authorities to stop illegal Jewish immigration had become all too apparent. Once again the Arabs decided to take up arms. This time, however, they were confronted with a stronger and much better armed Haganah. The Zionist terrorist groups, for their part, launched a campaign of violence against Arab villages. This was to culminate in the Deir-Yassin massacre in which the Irgun and Stern gangs killed hundreds of Arab women, children and old men.

Meanwhile, the Palestinian leadership had become deeply divided. One group continued to follow the Mufti while another belonged to the Nashashibi clan which maintained

close links with King Abdallah in Amman. The Mufti had by
then decided to pin his hope on the results of a European war
which seemed inevitable. Convinced that Hitler's Germany
would win, he thought he could afford to wait for the British
mandate to come to an end before moving to push the Jewish
settlers out of Palestine.

In May 1939 another White Paper was published in
London. This one suggested strict limits to Jewish immigration so that the Jewish population of Palestine would
never exceed one-third of the total. This, however, did not
end Arab guerrilla activities which continued for several
more months. The British forces were, in fact, under attack
from both sides as Jewish terrorist groups also began to hit
against what they saw as a long-term threat to their plans for
independence. The partition of Palestine became increasingly inevitable as the leadership on both sides of the conflict
passed into the hands of more extremist elements.

On the eve of the Second World War a direct clash between
Zionism and pan-Arab nationalism had emerged as a long-
term threat to peace in the Middle East as a whole.

The rise of new nationalistic sentiments throughout the
Middle East eventually affected Iran also. The Bolshevik
Revolution in Russia in 1917 had removed from the Iranian
scene one of the two colonial powers that had dominated
Iranian politics for some sixty years. The other power, Great
Britain, tried to seize the occasion for imposing its exclusive
hold on the process of decision-making in Tehran. A secret
treaty, signed by both sides in 1919, envisaged the turning of
Iran into a British protectorate in all but name.

The country's difficulties, however, went beyond the
problem of how to cope with the sharply whetted British
appetite for domination in the Middle East. The badly
weakened government in Tehran had to cope with a situation
in which the very existence of Iran as a nation state was at
stake. The Bakhtiari and Luri tribesmen in the south were
under virtual British control through their chiefs who received
stipends from the Anglo-Persian Oil Company which had by

then emerged as a state within a state. In the southwestern province of Khuzestan, where most of the oilfields were located, the British financed and generally supported an Arab dominated shaikhdom under Shaikh Khaz'al.

The situation was no better in other parts of the country. In Kurdistan a rebel leader, Isma'il Simatquo (Simko), led a full-scale uprising that was to continue for several years. In the Caspian Province of Gilan, Mirza Kuchak Khan, a former mullah turned revolutionary, was in control of the forest regions as well as the port of Enzeli. In May 1920 a detachment of Soviet troops landed at Enzeli to support Kuchak Khan's Soviet Republic of Gilan. Almost at the same time Tabriz, the capital of Azerbaijan, and the holy city of Mashad in the northeast were also the scenes of much agitation. Iran seemed destined for dismemberment.

In February 1921, however, the situation changed dramatically. A nationalist group, led by the liberal journalist Sayyed Ziaeddin Tabataba'i, organized a successful *coup d'état* that forced the government to resign. Tabataba'i was named prime minister by the ineffectual Qajar monarch, Ahmad Shah. Reza Khan Mir-Panj, who had led the seizure of Tehran at the head of the Cossack Brigade, the country's only regular military unit, was named war minister and quickly emerged as the new government's strong man.

Tabataba'i, before he was forced to go into exile less than four months after his successful coup, had time to abrogate the 1919 treaty with Britain and negotiate the cancellation of Russian colonial privileges in Iran. An Irano-Soviet treaty, signed on 26 February 1921 in Moscow, ended capitulation, Russian control over Iran's customs in the north and the huge debts that Tehran had accumulated over more than five decades of unequal relations with the Tsarist Empire. In exchange, Iran undertook not to allow any foreign power to station troops on its soil or to use it as a base for aggression against the Soviet Union.

By 1925 Reza Khan, who had become prime minister in 1923, had been proclaimed the new Shahanshah (King of

Kings) by a constituent assembly that deposed the Qajar dynasty. The Qajar Ahmad Shah was already in exile in southern France and rejected appeals by his partisans to return home and challenge the decision of the assembly. As the new shah, Reza took the family name of Pahlavi (heroic) and emphasized the fact that he was the first ethnic Persian in a long time to ascend the throne of Cyrus the Great.

Strongly influenced by Atatürk's reforms in neighbouring Turkey, Reza Shah launched his own plans for the modernization of Iran. The powers of the mullahs were sharply reduced as Islamic courts were replaced by a new system of secular justice. Government financed and controlled schools were created throughout the country and offered a non-religious curriculum in which emphasis was put on the teaching of the Persian language and history. Most of the Qur'anic schools, run by the mullahs, were either ordered to close or forced to do so for lack of financial support from the government. The wearing of traditional tribal and provincial clothes was restricted in favour of European-style wear. Turbans were banned and replaced by a specially designed kepi known as the Pahlavi hat. The wearing of beards was also discouraged with forcible shaving sessions carried out by army units in the central bazaars of many cities. More importantly, the wearing of the chador, the 'purdah' of Iranian women, was also declared illegal. The unveiling movement, as this measure came to be known, sent shock waves through traditional Iran and was seen by the mullahs as a clear indication of Pahlavi's desire to de-Islamicize the nation.

In subsequent years the mullahs claimed that Reza Shah had secretly converted to Zoroastrianism, Iran's ancient religious faith. This was certainly untrue for Reza never abandoned his vague attachment to shi'ite Islam. What he was convinced of, however, was that in order to modernize Iranian society he needed to mobilize the people's energies. At that time only Islam could have mobilized the Iranian masses. But Islam had, at least since the seventeenth century, become a force against all modernization which it saw as westernization and the loss of Islamic values. Reza Shah hoped that Iranian nationalism could provide the mobilizing force needed. And like Atatürk in neighbouring Turkey he set out to create a nation that could play the part he had envisaged for it.

A great admirer of Atatürk, Reza Shah paid a state visit to Turkey, the only foreign country he had ever travelled to, and returned more than ever convinced that nationalism was the force of the future. Having ordered a thorough reform of the judiciary, which led to the creation of a western-style legal system, Reza Shah adopted another of Atatürk's ideas: the use of the state as the principal means of regulating the nation's economy. A number of state enterprises, ranging from Iran's first railway system to a small armament factory, came into being while the government exercised full monopoly on all foreign trade.

Reza Shah's base of support in Iran was not much different from that of Atatürk in Turkey. A vastly expanded civil service, the armed forces whose strength had been multiplied twenty times between 1921 and 1940, the new intelligentsia centred on Tehran University from 1935 onwards, and the urban middle classes generally supported the shah's reforms and shared most of his ambitions. The peasants, forming more than seventy per cent of the population until the 1940s, admired Reza Shah for his courage as a soldier and his success in quelling the numerous armed bands that had plunged the countryside into anarchy.

Reform of the Persian language was a top priority for Reza Shah. A Persian Academy was created with the task of purging the language of as many Arabic and Turkic words as possible. The Academy coined thousands of new words and promoted research into Iran's pre-Islamic languages and modes of life.

Reza Shah's modernization differed in one important aspect from Atatürk's experiment in Turkey. Reza Shah, despite his early fascination with republican ideas, became an absolute monarch and reduced the parliament and the press to largely ceremonial functions. He did not create a political party and did not allow others to do so either. From 1930 onwards he developed an unhealthy appetite for amassing a personal fortune – a fact that sharply reduced his popularity among the middle classes and undermined his credibility as a man capable of leading Iran into the modern world.

When Atatürk died in 1938, at the age of fifty-seven, his legacy remained secure. Three of his lieutenants, Celal Bayar, Ismet Inonu and Fevzi Cakmak, were immediately able to assume command while the Republican People's Party (RPP), the political machine he had created, proved capable of mobilizing the urban areas for the purpose of continuing the task of modernization.

Reza Shah's rule came to an end in entirely different circumstances. He was forced into exile in September 1941 after British and Soviet forces had invaded Iran in spite of its declared neutrality in the Second World War. Reza Shah's departure from the scene not only brought the continuity of his attempts at modernization into question but immediately reawakened almost all of Iran's old demons, ranging from fanatical mullahs to secessionist movements. The beard, the turban and the chador, all symbols of resistance to the shah's westernization programme, were almost instantly restored as the mosques and the tribal institutions regained their influence.

The period 1918–48 that witnessed the full emergence of Turkish, Arab, Iranian and Zionist nationalisms as major players in Middle Eastern politics also witnessed the brutal repression of a number of other national movements in the region. The Palestinians did not get a state of their own largely because the already existing Arab states refused the United Nations-sponsored partition of the mandate territory. The reasons for which other nations, such as the Kurds and the Armenians, did not achieve statehood in the region were more complex.

The idea of self-determination, promoted as a slogan by the

US President Woodrow Wilson, captured the imagination of almost all the elites in the Middle East. Maronites, Druzes, Alawites and shi'ites in Syria and Lebanon began dreaming of their own mini-states as did the Assyrians and the Yazidis in Mesopotamia. Some enthusiasts of the idea of self-determination even chose Wilson as a first name for their offspring. But by 1921 it had become clear that none would get what they wanted, at least not in the foreseeable future.

Only two groups, or nations, came close to winning statehood: the Kurds and the Armenians. Both were very ancient peoples with histories going back to *circa* 1,000 BC. Both had a sufficiently large and potentially viable territorial base on which to build a new nation state.

The Armenians formed a majority of the population in the extreme east and northeast of Anatolia, as well as in the mountainous regions of Yerevan, Shiravan, Nakhjevan and Qarabagh to the north of the River Aras. A strong Armenian community also lived within the frontiers of Iran, notably in the city of Isfahan.

A non-semitic people, the Armenians were racially close to Iranians but had emphasized their ethnic and cultural identity by converting to Christianity in 301. A strong national church (Gregorian) supervised the task of preserving the national language, complete with an alphabet of its own, and encouraging an impressive literary production. Because of their passion for further education and their detachment from clan and tribal rivalries in the region the Armenians succeeded in achieving an important role in both the administration and the economy of the Ottoman Empire and Iran.

As the Ottoman Empire began to crumble under pressure from the western powers the Armenians, along with other Christian minorities, were increasingly regarded as potential allies for the infidel enemies of the Sultan-Caliph. In 1894–95 a series of pogroms was carried out against the Armenians in eastern Anatolia. Sanctioned by Sultan Abdul-Hamid in his capacity as the Caliph, these pogroms led to the destruction of scores of Armenian villages and the death of thousands of peasant families. In 1909 it was the turn of Muslim militants to seize the opportunity offered by the decline in the authority of the Sublime Port to organize a series of new pogroms against Armenians. Six years later, the Young Turks' government in Istanbul ordered a wholesale expulsion of the Armenians from the eastern provinces of the empire. This led to the massacre of an estimated one million men, women and children and the expulsion of a further 500,000. In 1918 the Armenians managed to set up a republic in the Caucasus and began pursuing an expansionist policy against the moribund Ottoman Empire to the west. But the Armenian Republic was itself swallowed up by the USSR under Stalin and lost all hopes of uniting the estimated 2.5 million Armenians scattered all over the world.

In 1918 the Kurds numbered between three and six million people and were scattered in Turkey, the Caucasus, Iran, Iraq and Syria. More than half of the Kurds lived in eastern Anatolia and it was there that the idea of a national state for the Kurdish people began to take shape in the first decades of the twentieth century. The Ottoman authorities, always wary of Kurdish intentions, prevented educated Kurds from returning to their native villages. As a result, the Kurdish educated elite was almost always in exile, in Cairo, Alexandria, Beirut and Paris.

Between 1916 and 1918 some attempts were made by Britain to foment an anti-Turkish revolt among the Kurds. But these attempts met with little success. The Kurds had at the time allied themselves with the Turks, in the name of Islamic solidarity and under the authority of the Caliph, and waged holy war against the infidels. Part of that holy war had consisted of the massacre of Armenians throughout eastern Anatolia. In many cases the Kurds appropriated the farms and houses of the Armenian families they had put to death.

The Treaty of Sèvres gave the Kurds a fleeting chance to achieve at least some measure of autonomy. But all their hopes were dashed when the new kemalist government signed the Lausanne Treaty in 1923. No mention was made of the Kurdish right to self-determination. A year later the Kurds of Anatolia were preparing for revolt. The revolt that finally came in February 1925 was not provoked by the setback suffered at Lausanne. It had more immediate and tangible causes. The abolition of the caliphate by the kemalist power removed the legitimacy of Turkish rule in the eyes of the Kurds. At the same time the Kurds regarded Mustafa Kemal as an enemy of Islam and resented his policy of imposed westernization. It was no accident that the rebellion was led by a prominent Muslim shaikh and called for the restoration of the caliphate and the reimposition of Qur'anic laws that had been abolished by Kemal.

The Kurdish revolt, which had included an attempt at seizing the town of Diyarbakir, was ruthlessly suppressed by the Turkish Army which destroyed scores of villages and organized countless political executions. A precarious calm was restored in the Kurdish provinces which remained under martial law until 1940. The very words 'Kurd' and 'Kurdish' were banned from the Turkish vocabulary and their use made punishable by fines and terms of imprisonment. It was not until March 1988 that a Turkish newspaper (*Cumhuriyet* of Istanbul) felt confident enough to use the forbidden words in a news story.

At least nine other revolts, mostly of a local nature, shook the Turkish authorities in eastern and southern Anatolia between 1926 and 1940. In most cases the leadership of the revolt rested with local religious dignitaries. But in at least two of the revolts in 1936–37 in the region of Dersin and the foothills of Mount Ararat the idea of a separate Kurdish state assumed more prominence in comparison with religious demands made by the shaikhs.

The Kurdish problem has continued to haunt the Turkish authorities for more than sixty years now. The policy of 'turkicization' through compulsory education, propaganda and material incentives was first launched in 1928 and has continued into the 1980s. At the same time the government has created hundreds of new villages for the purpose of concentrating the Kurdish population and thus facilitating the physical control of a difficult terrain. Finally, an estimated two million ethnic Turks have been settled, often under threat of force, in Kurdish areas as part of a policy of turning the Kurds into a minority in their own ancestral land. But judging by the continued instability in eastern and south-eastern Turkey none of these policies has succeeded in persuading the more militant Kurds to abandon their dream of an independent state.

The development of Kurdish nationalism in Iraq was a much slower process. The new state did not pursue the type of revolutionary and anti-Islamic policies that characterized Atatürk's rule in Turkey. The Baghdad government's hold on Kurdish regions remained largely symbolic until the late 1930s and the development of oilfields gave the Kurds an opportunity to improve their living standards. Nevertheless, Iraq did not succeed in its attempts at the Arabization of the Kurds and the Kurdish problem continues as a major threat to Iraqi political stability.

The Kurdish revolt of 1921 in Iran was basically motivated by a number of local grievances and the personal ambitions of certain chiefs rather than any sense of particularism. It was only after 1945 that secessionist sentiments manifested themselves among Iranian Kurds.

Unlike the Armenians, who dreamed of a single unitary state, the Kurds aimed at the creation of separate autonomous republics in Iran, Turkey and Iraq in the hope that these would, in time, be brought together within a pan-Kurdish federation. This strategy enabled the various governments that faced Kurdish revolts to incite one tribe against another and prevent the Kurds from mobilizing all of their national energies at any given time. The Kurds often became mercenaries in the service of the various states under whose authority they lived. From the 1920s onwards Turkey, the USSR, Iran and Iraq, and later even Israel and the United States, played the Kurdish card in a variety of different situations.

The Kurds have also provided a fertile field for radical, especially left wing political movements in the Middle East. The various communist groups that came into being in Syria, Iraq, Iran and Turkey recruited many of their militant cadres from among the Kurds.

5

TWICE PROMISED LAND

The Second World War, which dramatically altered the political map of Europe, had, in its immediate aftermath, little impact on the overall situation in the Middle East. The war had been mostly fought outside the region and only Iran had suffered direct military occupation after its territory was invaded by Soviet and British forces in 1941. Turkey had managed to stay out of the war in spite of some Armenian-sponsored pressure on Moscow to annex the cities of Kars and Ardahan and their environs. As for Egypt the battle of El-Alamein had ended all possibility of the war spreading into the Nile Valley.

France's defeat in the early stages of the war made it possible for Syria and Lebanon to declare their independence, partly with British encouragement. But the emergence of these two new states had been a foregone conclusion for many years and would in no way alter the general balance of power in the region. Although Syria refused to recognize the 'separation' of Lebanon, there was no fear at the time that the ambitions of the ruling elites in Damascus might lead to a serious crisis in the near future. Lebanon, for its part, was hailed as the 'Switzerland of the Middle East' and cited as a successful example of how different ethnic and religious groups could live and work together within a single state.

The end of the war left the position of Britain as a paramount power in the region apparently strengthened. The

British hold on Egypt and Iraq remained intact despite growing nationalist agitation in both countries. Britain also controlled southern Arabia and virtually dictated the policies of the sultanate of Muscat and Oman, the Trucial Coast and the emirates of Qatar, Bahrain and Kuwait. Trans-Jordan remained a British army bastion while the Imamate of Yemen also looked to Britain for advice and support. Only Saudi Arabia had already decided to tie its future to the United States as the most powerful of western nations. In Iran, British influence was under growing pressure, especially while Soviet troops occupied the country's most fertile and populated provinces.

In 1945 when the war came to an end few people expected the Middle East to be destined for one of the longest and most complex of crises in its history – a crisis provoked by the creation of a new Jewish state in Palestine right in the heart of the Arab world.

The British Labour Party's success in the general election in July 1945 was quickly hailed by nationalist forces throughout the region as the beginning of a new era of decolonization. The Jews in Palestine were fully aware of Labour's pro-Zionist sympathies and were encouraged in their hopes for an independent state.

The Labour prime minister, Clement Attlee, and his foreign secretary, Ernest Bevin, however, were quickly divested of their decolonizing illusions and reverted to Britain's traditional hegemonistic policies in the region. They became fairly enthusiastic Atlanticists and played a crucial role in extending the Cold War to the Middle East. By 1946 both Turkey and Iran had been forced to take sides in the Cold War and adopt a militant anti-Soviet foreign policy. The fact that the two countries had had a long history of conflict with Russia made them the West's natural partners in the new 'crusade' against Soviet Communism.

The Arab countries, however, did not feel threatened either by the USSR or by the worldwide communist movement it inspired. The Soviet Union appeared remote to most

Arabs and not a single communist party existed anywhere in the Arab world until 1948. The Arabs saw the new British discourse regarding the East-West confrontation as just another excuse by the traditional colonial power for maintaining its positions in the region.

A few months after the end of the war Egyptian nationalists launched a mass movement calling for the cancellation of all colonial accords with Britain and an immediate withdrawal of British troops from Egypt. They also wanted the formal union of Egypt and the Sudan to be announced and recognized by Britain. The Labour government, no doubt influenced by powerful officials within the Foreign and Colonial Office in London, tried to adopt a tough stance and arranged for the Anglophile Ismail Sidky Pasha to become prime minister in Egypt. The old pasha lost little time in negotiating and signing a new accord under which Britain would retain most of its prerogatives. The Egyptian parliament, however, refused to ratify the treaty and the pasha resigned. His successor Mahmud Nokrachi Pasha took the conflict to the United Nations where the Soviet Union, acting as a member of the Security Council with the right of veto, appeared as a defender of the Arab cause for the first time.

Britain's attempts at dragging Iraq into new and closer treaty relations fared no better. The signature of a new pact in January 1948 between the two countries led to nationwide demonstrations in Iraq and forced the Regent Prince Abdul Ilah to announce its cancellation. But Iraq's treaty relations with Turkey and Jordan remained intact.

The Labour government scored a successs in Trans-Jordan by imposing a treaty on the desert emirate in 1948. Under the treaty, Prince Abdullah was recognized as the king of a fully independent state which took the title of the Hashemite Kingdom of Jordan.

The Labour government's policy regarding Palestine consisted of strict adherence to the terms of the 1939 White Paper under which Britain had undertaken to hand over its mandate to an independent state within a decade. The paper also limited Jewish immigration to 75,000 a year, a fact which persuaded the Zionists that unless they acted quickly they would never be able to have a population base strong enough to support an independent Jewish state. With the war over in Europe, Palestine was seen by the survivors of the Nazi holocaust as the true promised land. Jewish immigration to Palestine was strongly encouraged by the United States and financed by American Jews. The reasons for Washington's support were not entirely altruistic. The Truman administration did not wish to see tens of thousands of new Jewish immigrants coming to the United States for fear of an anti-semitic backlash. At the same time Truman himself was anxious to secure Jewish votes and political support in general for the difficult presidential elections ahead. Washington, therefore, pressured London to lift its restrictions on Jewish arrivals in Palestine. Britain, however, preferred to listen to its traditional Arab friends rather than to the United States on this particular issue. The 1939 quotas were applied wherever possible.

Faced with British intransigence the Zionists launched a terror campaign. The Haganah, which up to 1946 had acted as a police force, was led into a guerrilla struggle against the British forces. Taking orders from David Ben Gurion the Haganah commanders carried out a series of sabotage operations and fully cooperated with outright terrorist groups such as Irgun and Stern. One of the most spectacular operations carried out by the Zionist terror groups was against the British military headquarters at Jerusalem's King David Hotel. Scores of British soldiers were killed or wounded in an attack that heralded a full Jewish revolt in the mandate territory.

By 1947 Britain had just under 100,000 troops in Palestine and yet was unable to control the situation. The Jews fought with the force of desperation against an enemy who was determined not to use all of its might against a people which had already suffered unprecedented violence in Europe. Illegal Jewish immigration remained the most important cause of conflict. While the Arabs continued to blame Britain for not doing enough to stem the tide of European Jews into Palestine, the Zionists attacked camps where illegal immigrants were kept pending a review of their cases. One incident concerning illegal immigrants was to become part of Zionist mythology. A ship called *Exodus*, with some 4,500 Jews aboard, had left for Palestine from France in the summer of 1947. It was intercepted by the Royal Navy and turned back, first to France and eventually to Hamburg which was occupied by British troops.

As early as July 1946 Britain had proposed a partition of Palestine into two Jewish and Arab provinces in the vain hope that the two could later form a single federal state. The Zionists, however, pushed this British plan a step further and proposed the creation of two independent states in Palestine. Under this plan the Jews would gain control over the desert of Negev (Negueb), the coastal strip, Galilee and the western boroughs of Jerusalem. The Arabs, controlling the Gaza Strip, the West Bank of Jordan and eastern Jerusalem, would gain access to the sea through a corridor linking the hilly terrrain of the interior to Jaffa.

The Zionist plan, designed to be rejected by the Arabs, led to greater tension in Palestine and persuaded London that this was a quintessential colonial hornet's nest that was best avoided. The rising cost of policing a land claimed by two equally determined groups was an important element in dictating Britain's next move. Also important from Britain's point of view was the fact that the future of Palestine was well on the way to becoming a major source of friction between London and Washington. Accordingly, Bevin announced that the whole of the Palestine dossier had been referred to the newly created United Nations for arbitration.

In May 1947 the UN General Assembly, meeting in an extraordinary session, appointed an eleven-member committee to come up with a plan for the future of Palestine. Only one Muslim country, Iran, was a member of the committee in which Holland, Canada, Sweden and Czechoslovakia formed a strong pro-Zionist group. India and Yugoslavia tended to support the Arab side while Guatemala, Uruguay and Peru backed the Jewish cause under pressure from Washington. Australia, though more hostile to the Zionists, remained neutral.

In the end the commission came up with two reports. The majority proposed the partition of Palestine into seven territorial units. Of these, three would go to a Jewish state while an Arab state would get another three. The seventh, consisting of Jerusalem, would have an international status under UN control and supervision. The plan envisaged the handover of more than fifty-five per cent of Palestine to Jews who formed under thirty per cent of the total population at the time. More importantly, over forty-eight per cent of the population in areas allocated to the future Jewish state were Arabs who would, by definition, not be allowed to exercise their right to self-determination. The majority plan also proposed an economic union between the two states, a move interpreted by Arabs as an attempt at giving the Jews full control of all trade and industry in Palestine.

The minority report, largely made up by Iran with support from India and Yugoslavia, was even more unacceptable to both the Zionists and the Arabs. It was based on the earlier British plans for a bi-national state in which Arab and Jew would live together and jointly exercise sovereignty.

A rare consensus among the major powers at the United Nations enabled them to back the majority report and have it adopted by the UN without much difficulty. The partition plan was slightly modified under British pressure in favour of the Arabs who were to receive control of the cities of Beersheva and Jaffa deep inside the territories allocated to the Jews. The partition plan was soon adopted by a majority of the Zionist leaders as the least of all evils. But opinion among them was by no means unanimous. Some of the Zionist visionaries still hoped for a bi-national state while the more radical groups demanded the whole of Palestine plus parts of Mesopotamia and Egypt in their quest for a Jewish empire.

The partition plan was approved by the General Assembly on 29 November 1947. All thirteen Muslim states independent at that time voted against the plan while ten other countries abstained. The plan attracted the support of the United States and the USSR plus 31 other European, Latin American and Asian countries. Britain, the mandate power, abstained. It was evident that a new Jewish state was being imposed on its would-be geopolitical habitat by force: not one of the Middle Eastern nations would agree to recognize the legitimacy of the new country. Even Iran, which often prided itself on the fact that Cyrus the Great had liberated the Jews from bondage and allowed them to rebuild their temple in Jerusalem, was unable to consent to what appeared to be an arbitrary construct imposed by the big powers.

The Arabs, for their part, saw the creation of a Jewish state as a direct challenge to their own existence as independent countries. Some Arab leaders, notably in Iraq and Egypt, were prepared to accept a special status for Jews within an independent Palestinian Arab state. Some radical groups in Syria and Saudi Arabia, however, openly talked of forcing all of the non-native Jews out of Palestine.

Deeply divided on most vital issues, almost all the Arab elites were united in their resentment of what they described as 'the tragedy of Palestine'. The secular nationalistic leaders saw the proposed Jewish state as a sequel to colonialism. The more traditionalist Islamic leaders, for their part, could not tolerate the fact that part of the land of Islam was being turned over to non-Muslims by 'infidel' powers meeting in New York. Ethnic, nationalistic and religious factors in the brewing conflict were further complicated by economic considerations. The Palestinian merchant classes were quick to realize that they would have no chance against Jewish competitors who were supported by powerful communities in Western Europe and North America.

The Arab failure to come up with a coherent strategy for facing the challenge of the new Jewish power, however, meant that the Zionist leaders could proceed with their plans without any great hindrance. The Arabs were not even able to help create a credible Palestinian leadership. The Grand Mufti of Jerusalem, Haj Amin al-Hussaini, who had spent most of the war years in Nazi Germany, returned to Palestine in 1946 and was instantly recognized by the Arab League as the representative of his country. The Mufti, enjoying support from Egypt and Syria, was, nevertheless, looked upon with some suspicion by Iraq and Jordan who continued to pursue pro-British policies. King Abdallah's agents in Jerusalem succeeded in creating an alternative leadership of their own and propagated the idea of attaching Palestine to the Hashemite kingdom as early as 1947.

The United Nations' inability to impose its decisions, a fact subsequently recognized as a matter of course in numerous other instances, had become all but apparent by the autumn of 1947. A war between the Arabs and the Zionists thus became inevitable. The British announcement that they would withdraw all their forces by 14 May 1948 had the expected effect of accelerating both sides' preparation for armed conflict. By December 1947 the sporadic encounters that had continued for more than a year developed into a full-scale war between Arabs and Jews with British forces being attacked by both belligerents whenever this became possible.

The Arabs attacked Jewish kibbutzim, communication centres and districts within the larger cities. The Arab 'volunteer' force, grouping together Palestinians, Egyptians, Syrians and members of the Muslim Brotherhood from various other countries together with elements from the Arab Legion in Jordan, proved so successful at first as to cause serious concern in Washington. The Arabs enjoyed the initial advantage of being in a defensive position while attacking the enemy's logistics and communication lines. The Jewish forces, on the other hand, had to conquer much of the land, and some of the cities, allocated to them by the UN.

Faced with pressure from the Jewish lobby to send American troops to help defeat the Arabs in Palestine,

Truman reversed his original support for partition and began preaching a UN trusteeship to be installed in place of the British mandate. The most immediate effect of this major shift in American policy was to strengthen the resolve of the Zionists to win as much land as possible. From the spring of 1948 the pace of the war quickened and the tide turned against the Arabs. By the end of April 1948, just two days before the end of the British mandate, the Jewish national council, which had constituted itself into a provisional government for an as yet non-existent state, decided by six votes against four to reject a proposal for postponing the declaration of independence. More importantly, the council decided not to recognize the frontiers delineated in the UN partitions plan. On May 14, hours before the departure of the last of the British mandate officials, the birth of the state of Israel was proclaimed by Ben Gurion. The Soviet Union and the United States immediately recognized the new state, thus ending all efforts aimed at cancelling the partition plan and working for other formulae for the future of Palestine.

On 15 May 1948 the members of the Arab League declared war on Israel and announced that they would be sending their troops to help Palestinian forces win the civil war that continued in most parts of the territory. The various Arab states entered what was the first of their wars against Israel with different, and at times even conflicting, motives, and in dispersed order. Their decision to enter the war was at least in part promoted by inter-Arab rivalries and the personal ambitions of the various leaders.

Hashemite Jordan, which at the time enjoyed the most effective fighting force in the Arab world, played a crucial role. King Abdallah, no Arab nationalist, had no particular objection to the presence of an immigrant Jewish colony in Palestine. All he was interested in was to profit from a confused situation and expand his own realm. For long he had maintained secret contacts with Zionist leaders and promised them full autonomy and protection if and when he attached mandate Palestine to his own desert kingdom. The British,

who financed Abdallah and commanded his army, must have
known about and encouraged those plans. Abdallah's far
from hostile attitude towards the Jews soon turned him into
the *bête-noire* of Arab nationalists who began to refer to him
as 'Rabbi Abdallah'. The Jordanian Arab Legion, under
British command, scored early victories and captured the
whole of the West Bank plus the eastern half of Jerusalem.
Then it came to a halt while Israeli forces dealt with a Syrian
incursion to the north. An Eygptian attack, meanwhile,
reached the cities of Hebron, in the West Bank, and Ashdod
on the Mediterranean.

These early victories, however, failed to give the Arabs a
strategic advantage. Unable or unwilling to co-ordinate their
efforts the various Arab governments involved in the war
agreed to a UN sponsored cease-fire which gave the Israelis a
golden opportunity for mobilizing and training fresh forces
and securing new weapons, mostly from Czechoslovakia. In
June the UN appointed a Swedish diplomat, Count Bernadotte, as mediator in charge of negotiating a peace settlement. Bernadotte proposed a new partition plan which would
divide Palestine between Jordan and Israel. Less than a
month later, however, hostilities were resumed on all fronts.
Bernadotte was murdered by Zionist gunmen in September
1948.

By the autumn of 1948 the tide of war had turned in favour
of the Israelis who had virtually encircled the Egyptian forces
in the Sinai and halted a Syro-Iraqi attack in the north. Only
the Jordanians managed to hang on to most of their early
gains. By 1949 the Israelis were in control of the whole of the
Negev down to the Gulf of Aqaba and also occupied parts of
the Egyptian Sinai. In February Egypt agreed to sign an
armistice with Israel enabling the encircled Egyptian forces to
return home. Egypt remained in control of the Gaza Strip
with a population of more than 65,000 Palestinians. A few
weeks later a truce accord was signed with Lebanon under
which Israeli forces evacuated parts of Lebanese territory
they had occupied in a bid to forestall a Syrian attack.

Separate truces were also signed with Syria and Jordan bringing all hostilities to an end by the end of July 1949.

The emergence of the state of Israel was, without a doubt, an event of singularly profound impact on the entire politics of the Middle East. The immediate effects of this were momentous enough: nearly 600,000 Palestinian Arabs became refugees in Jordan, Lebanon, Syria and Egypt. Over the years these refugees spread into Saudi Arabia and the Arab states of the Persian Gulf and gradually emerged as powerful pressure groups in more than a dozen states. In the 1970s the Palestinians created a power structure in Lebanon that amounted to a state within the state. By annexing parts of Palestine, the Hashemite Kingdom of Jordan increased its territory by 7.2 per cent and more than tripled its population. It became a Palestinian state in all but name with a non-Palestinian ruling family. The Zionists, who had been allocated fifty-five per cent of Palestine under the UN partition plan, ended up in control of more than seventy per cent of Palestinian territory. Over 180,000 Arabs found themselves within the frontiers of Israel while a further 150,000 fled to Gaza where the Egyptians tried to set up a Palestinian 'state' with Mufti al-Hussaini at its head.

Demographic changes caused by the creation of Israel were not limited to the 'displacement' of the Palestinians who, in many cases, were persuaded by Zionist terror and Arab propaganda to leave their homes in the hope of soon returning. Between 1948 and 1951 nearly 800,000 Jews from more than thirty different countries arrived to settle in Israel. The vast majority came from western countries. But many long-established Jewish communities in several Arab countries also vanished as immigration to Israel turned from a trickle into a flood. More than a quarter of a million Jews left Morocco, Yemen and Iraq for Israel. Only the Iranian and Turkish Jewish communities did not participate in the mass immigration to the 'promised land' in any significant numbers.

The fact that Israel was predominantly 'European', at least

until the 1980s, emphasized its 'alien' character in the eyes of most Arabs. In subsequent years it was often claimed by left wing Arab intellectuals that the West was hated by Arab masses because it had 'created' Israel. It was, in fact, the other way round: Israel was hated because it represented the West in the eyes of both left wing intellectuals and fundamentalist Muslims. The principal western colonial power of the time, Great Britain, had, in fact, tried to help the Arabs prevent Israel from becoming an independent state. And at least until 1952 it was the Soviet bloc that remained the principal source of weapons for the new Jewish state. It was from the mid-1950s onwards that the theory according to which the western powers had deliberately created Israel in order to perpetuate their dominance of the Middle East was shaped and propagated.

The conservative Arab regimes which had tried to kill Israel at birth were also disturbed by the new state's socialistic structures and the egalitarianism it preached and practised for its own community. Israel's democratic system in which parliamentary rule, press freedom and the presence of numerous political parties made for a lively political life contrasted sharply with both the royal dictatorships of Iraq and Jordan and the sham democracies of Egypt, Lebanon and Syria where oligarchies dominated every facet of national life.

Israel was Jewish, democratic, largely western, socialistic and independent – reasons for which it could not but be disliked and feared by almost all the elites in its neighbouring countries. More importantly, Israel humiliated the Arabs by its very existence. It stood out as a symbol of Arab divisions and weakness, a living testimony to the fact that all Arab nations had fallen by the roadside in the forward march of history. A rational reaction would have been to devote all energies to removing the causes of which the emergence of Israel in the midst of the Arab world was, at least in part, nothing but an effect. But the Arab reaction was emotional. Israel was seen as the cause of all the ills that afflicted the

Arabs. Arab propaganda of both right and left developed the idea that the destruction of Israel would, as if by magic, solve all of the problems faced by Arab societies. Since it is apparently more human to unite against something rather than for something, Israel gradually became the major, if not the only, unifying factor in Arab politics.

While Israel was the principal victor in the 1948–49 war, with Jordan also ending up with more territory, the other parties to the war – Egypt, Iraq and Syria – could not be described as veritable losers. Their principal loss was one of prestige. Their armies failed to make an impression despite their superior weaponry and the fact that they possessed military aircraft which the Zionists lacked. Their casualties, however, were not large and did not have a major impact on public opinion. None of them lost any territory of its own while they could claim to have performed their pan-Arab duties. Nevertheless, the defeat suffered at the hands of the Zionists had a deep impact on the officer corps in Egypt, Syria and Iraq and in due course became the ferment of revolts that led to radical changes in the regimes of all three countries. Paradoxically, the defeat established the Arab armed forces as the principal arbiters of political life. This was a new development with consequences that have continued to the present.

The main loser in the 1948–49 war was, of course, the Palestinian nation. Since the late 1940s the Israelis have tried their best to prove that no Palestinian nation ever existed and that the very concept of such an entity is a figment of radical Arab imagination and designed to provide a premise upon which a denial of Israel's right to exist could be constructed. The fact is, however, that the Palestinians did exist as a distinct people with their own Arab identity. They might not have been aware of their identity as a nation before they lost most of their land. But this could in no way undermine their right of self-determination.

In December 1948 the United Nations approved a resolution demanding that the Palestinian refugees be allowed to return to their homes or compensated for losses suffered as a result of the war. Israel, however, refused to pay any attention to the resolution and other subsequent demands made by the UN on behalf of the refugees. Within a year or so after the cease-fire the villages and towns abandoned by the Arabs had been taken over by new Jewish settlers who could not be evicted except by force. The Israeli leaders could not have used force against the very new immigrants they so desperately sought in Europe and elsewhere as part of their plan to give the new country a credible demographic base.

By 1950 the UN had recognized the problem of the refugees as a long-term feature of the political scene in the Middle East. A new organization, the United Nations Relief and Work Agency (UNRWA), was created to cater to the needs of the refugees pending an increasingly elusive solution of the Palestinian problem.

The Palestinians were not the only people to become refugees in the aftermath of the Second World War. But they proved to be the only people to refuse absorption in other societies. Even those who adopted other nationalities or even emigrated to the United States continued to describe themselves as Palestinians and dreamed of one day returning home. This unusual reaction was, in part, due to the policy of various Arab states which wished to maintain the refugees as a permanent means of pressure against Israel with which they remained in a state of war. Only Jordan, which had gladly, though tacitly, welcomed the partition of Palestine between Israel and itself was prepared to offer Palestinians full citizenship. But the main reason for the Palestinians' refusal to merge with other Arab societies was their own feeling of resentment at having been subjected to an injustice they had not provoked and certainly did not deserve. Thus generation after generation of Palestinians grew up in squalid refugee camps or on the margins of various Arab societies; they became natural recruits for violent political movements committed to revenge.

Israel's treatment of the Palestinians who had stayed

behind did not prove a model of magnanimity either. The new state retained the Ottoman tradition of dividing the community into 'millets' or religious groups and treating them separately. The Arabs were, therefore, divided into sunni and shi'ite Muslims, Druze and Christian groups and subjected to separate legislation in some key domains. The Arabs were barred from serving in the army or working in fields even remotely connected with defence. Intercommunal marriage was made impossible by a decision not to recognize civil marriages. The Arabs were given the right to vote and to seek election to the Israeli parliament, the Knesset, but constituencies where Palestinian voters predominated were often so divided as to make it virtually impossible for Arabs to secure a strong representation. Hopes that the new state might wish to amend its policies in favour of its Arab population were seriously shaken in 1950 when a new law enabled the government to seize the property of the refugees and even expropriate many of those who had stayed behind. Those who had left their homes during the 1948 war, even though for a brief moment, were the first to be expropriated. But the process of depriving the Arabs of land did not stop there. Between 1950 and 1970 the Arabs living within the frontiers of Israel itself lost more than half of the land they owned. Not all of this was due to direct expropriation; the rising price of land also did its work as some Arabs, defying guidelines set by the Palestinian leadership in exile, sold their land in the hope of investing in commerce and small industries.

Despite the political and legal discriminations to which they became subjected, the Arabs who stayed behind in Israel saw their economic standard of living substantially improved over the years. Even in 1988 the income per head per annum recorded for the Arab citizens of Israel was higher than that of any other Arab country with the exception of oil-rich Saudi Arabia, Kuwait and the smaller emirates of the Persian Gulf. The average Israeli Arab enjoyed higher standards of housing, education and medical care than many of his brothers in the Middle East. He was even better off as far as political liberties were concerned. But all this did not prevent Arab Israelis from feeling that they were an oppressed community. The Israeli leaders failed to recognize the collective hopes and aspirations of the Arabs and their sense of belonging to a distinct Palestinian nation which must, one day, find its own 'natural' expression in an independent state. Even if Israel recognized full and equal rights for its Arab citizens, many of them would still feel that their collective rights – chiefly the right to organize a state of their own – remain neglected within the framework of a Jewish nation state.

Shortly after independence, Israel enacted the famous law of return under which the 'promised land' belongs to all Jews wherever they may be – Jews who could exercise their right to return to Palestine and settle there as full citizens of the Jewish state. This does not mean that Israel wishes to house the entire Jewish population of the globe, an impossible task given the size of the territory available, rather it is aimed at offering to those who might face persecution and worse a safe haven – one that they singularly lacked in Nazi-dominated Europe.

6

SOURCES OF CONFLICT

The Middle East, as it emerged from the Second World War, has at times been described as an arc of instability. In this context the term 'the Middle East Crisis' is often taken to be synonymous with the Arab-Israeli conflict which has produced numerous world headlines since 1947. The confrontation between the Arabs and Israel, however, is only one manifestation of the many different conflicts that have contributed to political instability and regional tension during the past four decades.

The sources of these conflicts are varied and complex. A few of the more important ones, however, could be identified and studied. The first of these is the conflict between the extra-regional big powers. Nowhere else in the modern world has rivalry between colonial empires been so acute and so destabilizing as in the Middle East. While it would be wrong to blame all of the region's instability on big power rivalries, a strong case could be made for the contention that colonial conflicts have played a role in virtually every crisis in the Middle East for the past 150 years. Rivalry among the 'classical' colonial powers, such as Great Britain, Portugal, Holland, France and Tsarist Russia over trade and political influence has been a constant factor in Middle Eastern politics ever since the heartland of Islam was virtually encircled with the discovery of new sea-routes between Europe and Asia. From the late 1940s onwards, with the Cold War setting the stage for world politics, the United States and the Soviet Union have fought out a new version of the old colonial war, while China, Britain and France have had to be content with only secondary roles in the Middle East.

The Middle East's immense natural wealth, especially oil and gas, as well as its strategic location make it a prime piece of real estate, a coveted prize for powers seeking world domination. From the 1970s onwards the region was increasingly recognized as a major market for export goods from the leading industrial powers. Military hardware represented an important part of goods imported by the Middle Eastern states. Arms purchases rose from an annual average of $5,000 million in the 1970s to more than $20,000 million a year in the 1980s. While more than twenty different countries participated in this lucrative export market, the lion's share in arms sales to the Middle East went to the USSR, the United States, France and Great Britain in that order.

Most Middle Eastern states have tried to pursue a non-aligned policy whenever given the chance. In reality, however, the non-alignment of most Middle Eastern countries has been more a matter of rhetoric rather than of political substance. In 1988 all of the region's countries, with the exception of Israel and Turkey, were full members of the non-aligned movement. Turkey was a member of the North Atlantic Treaty Organization (NATO) while Israel was a party to a 'strategic alliance' with the United States. A number of other countries maintained close military co-operation with the West. Saudi Arabia and Egypt played crucial roles in the United States' overall defence strategy in the region while Oman, the United Arab Emirates, Qatar, Bahrain and Jordan retained close military links with Britain. Kuwait, although posting a high-profile non-aligned policy, also tilted towards the West. In 1987 the United States assumed the task of protecting the emirate's oil exports through the Persian Gulf.

Iran and Iraq, involved in a prolonged war against each other, pursued ambiguous foreign policies. Nevertheless,

Iraq did not cancel its treaty of friendship and co-operation with the USSR, while Iran, despite its political duel with the United States, remained closer to western positions on almost all crucial international issues. Syria, an established ally of the USSR, was often capable of courting the western powers also, especially as a means of enhancing its own position in the region. The Soviet Union enjoyed its strongest position in the region in South Yemen where the Soviet navy made use of facilities at the port of Aden and on the island of Soccotra. A war-torn Lebanon, meanwhile, was denied the chance to develop and pursue a clear foreign policy.

The second source of conflict in the region consists of the clash between local nationalisms and the policies of the big powers. The movement inspired by Colonel Arabi Pasha in Egypt, the Young Turks' movement in the Ottoman Empire, the 1906 constitutional revolution in Iran and the anti-colonial revolts that later shook Egypt, the Levant and southern Arabia were only some of the manifestations of this type of conflict. Both Atatürk in Turkey and Reza Shah Pahlavi in Iran had recognized the existence of conflicts between their respective nationalistic aspirations and the policies of the major European powers. Both thought they would have a better chance of surviving the duel with the West by making their own societies more western. Decades later the conflict between the Middle Eastern nationalisms and the big powers assumed an additional Islamic aspect as a result of a rising mood of fundamentalism.

The rise of nationalist movements in the Middle East could be described as the most dramatic sign of westernization in the region. The very word 'nationalism' did not have equivalents in any of the region's different languages until the 1920s, which marked the start of the long but fairly rapid progress towards the concept of nationhood among the various peoples of the Middle East. As nationalism thrives best when it is against rather than for, it was not long before the new nationalistic movements of the region assumed strong xenophobic tones. The emerging nations defined their existence in terms of conflict with oppressive foreign powers that had long denied them the right to self-determination and full sovereignty.

The third source of conflict in the Middle East concerns the antagonistic relations that have developed among the region's various nationalisms at different times. The confrontation between Arab nationalism and Zionism is the most dramatic example of this type of conflict. Consistent American support for Israel has often given the so-called Palestinian issue the appearance of a duel between the Arabs and US 'Imperialism', a fact exploited by Soviet propaganda for its own purposes. Some Arabs have also persuaded themselves that Washington has virtually unlimited influence in Israel – a view that sharply contrasts with another Arab myth according to which Israel and the American Jewish lobby determine US policy in the Middle East, if not in the world as a whole.

The Arab-Israeli conflict, however, is essentially one between two rival nationalisms which would have quarrelled with or without any outside encouragement and support. In a sense almost all other causes of conflict in the Middle East could also be found in the Arab-Israeli issue. But the clash of the two nationalisms remains the supreme cause of tension between the two sides.

Conflict between local nationalisms is not limited to Arabism and Zionism. Arabism has clashed with Iranian nationalism on many occasions including during the course of the Iran-Iraq war which began in 1980. Arab and Turkish nationalisms were in conflict during the First World War which led to the dismemberment of the Ottoman Empire. Armenian and Turkish nationalisms in the same period fought a deadly battle that claimed nearly two million lives on both sides. The presence of a strong dose of religious bigotry in the Turco-Armenian duel does not change the fact that rival nationalistic claims were at the root of the savage and bloody events in eastern Anatolia.

Kurdish nationalism has been in conflict with Iranian, Arab

and Turkish nationalisms since the 1920s. At times the struggle of the Kurds for nationhood has led to full-scale wars lasting several years. The Kurdish war in Iraq began in the mid-1950s and continued intermittently until 1975 when it was temporarily halted as a result of an agreement between Baghdad and Tehran. By 1980, however, the Iraqi Kurds were again in revolt.

While there are no open disputes between Iranian and Turkish nationalisms as Iran and Turkey have maintained fairly close ties for more than sixty-five years, much tension seethes beneath the surface in relations between the two. The Turks suspect Iran of encouraging Kurdish secessionism and shi'ite and Naqshabandi Muslim agitation in Anatolia. In return, Iran regards Turkey's keen interest in Turkic-speaking groups in Azerbaijan, especially since 1980, as a sign of less than friendly intentions.

Iranian and Turkish nationalism are, in their own different ways, suspicious of long-term Zionist intentions in the region. Turkey maintains full diplomatic ties with Israel, and Iran has had an ambiguous relationship with the Jewish state since the early 1950s. But both Turkey and Iran resent Israel's 'special relationship' with the United States and suspect it of wanting to dominate the region with help from the West. Both Iran and Turkey have played the Israeli card in their own respective quarrels with various Arab countries and might want to do so in the future. But Israel is perceived as a rival, if not as an enemy, by the more outspoken representatives of Iranian as well as Turkish nationalisms.

Irredentist claims provide yet another source of tension and conflict among the Middle Eastern nations. Almost all of the region's frontiers were drawn by colonial powers between 1920 and 1968. In some cases these frontiers have not been formally recognized and demarcated according to international law. With the exception of its frontier with Egypt, duly recognized and demarcated thanks to the Camp David accords of 1980, Israel lives within cease-fire lines separating if from Syria, Lebanon and Jordan. Israel's announcement in

1982 that it had annexed the Golan Heights was seen by most Arabs as just one example of the Jewish state's expansionist policies. Syria continues to assert its own sovereignty on the Golan and has so far succeeded in preventing Israel from securing any international recognition for the annexation move. Israel's annexation of East Jerusalem, quickly incorporated into a unified capital for the Jewish state, has also failed to gain international recognition. Leaving aside the overall issue of Israel's right to exist as an independent country with secure borders, the Jewish state is involved in a number of territorial disputes with its neighbours. Some of these disputes are related to the sharing of the waters of the Jordan and Litani rivers. But Israel also claims the right to maintain a 'security zone' in southern Lebanon.

Syria, while maintaining its claim on the Golan Heights, pursues an irredentist policy towards Turkey as well. The Syrians refuse to recognize the attachment of Alexandrette to Turkey under an accord signed by France in 1936. Official Syrian maps show that Turkish province as part of the 'Arab Motherland'. The claim, often dormant, has on occasions led to border tension between the two neighbours and is considered by the Turks as an impediment to closer ties between Turkey and the Arab nations. Syria's irredentism does not spare the Arabs either. For Syria has consistently refused to recognize Lebanon as an independent and sovereign country and claims a right of supervision, if not of outright domination of the Lebanese government. Syria has also been in the vanguard of the Arab campaign to change the name of the Persian Gulf into the Arabian Gulf since the early 1960s. Syria's close ties with Iran from 1979 onwards, which included huge Iranian subsidies, did not persuade the Syrian leaders to abandon their campaign in favour of the 'Arabization' of the Persian Gulf.

Arab irredentist claims against Iran are not limited to the Gulf issue. Many Arab governments support an Iraqi claim that Iran's southwestern province of Khuzestan should be turned into a separate Arab state. The province, renamed

'Arabistan' in Iraqi and Syrian propaganda, had a population of 4.2 million in 1987, of which less than seventeen per cent spoke Arabic as their mother tongue. Iraq has three other specific claims of its own against Iran. It has tried to annex the Iranian port city of Khorramshahr (which the Arabs call Muhamarrah) and even occupied it for over a year during the Gulf War. Next, Iraq claims full sovereignty over the Shatt al-Arab border waterway under treaties signed between Iran and the Ottoman Empire and, later, Britain. Finally, Iraq claims as part of its own territory the entire region of Zaynal-Kosh which it has renamed 'Zain al-Kaus' to the north of Khuzestan. A treaty signed between Iran and Iraq in 1975 in Algiers formally ended all these claims and provided the framework for a full demarcation of the frontier between the two states. The accord also settled the dispute over the Shatt al-Arab on the basis of the Thalweg principle and envisaged the joint administration of the waterway by the two neighbours. The agreements were fully respected and put into practice by both sides until the Islamic Revolution of 1979 in Iran. The Iraqi government declared the 1975 accord null and void in September 1980 a few days before ordering an invasion of Iran.

Iran is not the only country to have problems with Iraqi irredentist and expansionist policies. Iraq claimed full sovereignty over the emirate of Kuwait immediately after it achieved full independence from Britain in 1960. Military moves by both Britain and Egypt, as well as some threatening gestures from Iran, dissuaded Iraq from proceeding with its plan to annex Kuwait by force. But the claim on Kuwait has never been formally and irrevocably dropped, although it has been pushed into the background of Iraqi politics since 1965. Various Iraqi regimes have pressed more limited claims against Kuwait. In 1981, for example, they applied strong pressure on Kuwait to cede the islands of Warbah and Bubiyan to Iraq on ninety-nine-year leases. The emirate refused to meet that demand.

Iraq's frontiers with Jordan and Saudi Arabia, as well as the neutral zone which it shares with the Saudis, were fully settled and demarcated only in the 1980s after having been the object of irredentist manoeuvres for more than five decades.

In Iraq's Kurdish north the cities of Mosul and Kirkuk and the oil-rich regions around them have been the subject of Turkish irredentist claims since the 1920s. The Turkish government does not pursue these claims but does not formally abandon them either. Turkish media, on the other hand, keep the claims alive and openly talk of Turkey's 'special rights' in parts of Iraqi Kurdistan. In 1985 the Iraqi government recognized Turkey's right to pursue Kurdish insurgents into Iraqi territory. The Turks lost no time in exercising that right and their armed forces intervened in Iraqi Kurdistan on six different occasions. A number of mountain strongholds captured by the Turkish forces in 1985 had not been returned to the Iraqi authorities by August 1988. Another sign that Turkey considered itself to have special rights in northern Iraq came in the winter of 1988 when Ankara warned Tehran against attacks on the oil pipeline connecting Iraqi fields with Anatolia.

The latent irredentism of Iraq's regional policies has prevented it from concluding the necessary accords on the continental shelf in the northern Gulf with Kuwait and Iran. Such accords are needed to determine the limits of off-shore oil reserves belonging to each of the three countries. Iran has concluded continental shelf accords with Saudi Arabia, Bahrain, Qatar, the UAE and Oman and has initialled a draft agreement with Kuwait also. But the draft could not be developed into full treaty form unless each of the two signatories also reached separate accords with Iraq which shares the waters of the northern Gulf with Iran and Kuwait.

Until 1970 Iran maintained a claim for full sovereignty over the Bahrain archipelago. The claim was officially dropped after a United Nations' mission ruled that a majority of the Bahrainis would prefer independence to annexation by Iran. The UN's decision was formally approved by the Iranian parliament in 1971 and the two countries exchanged am-

Points of Conflict in The Middle East

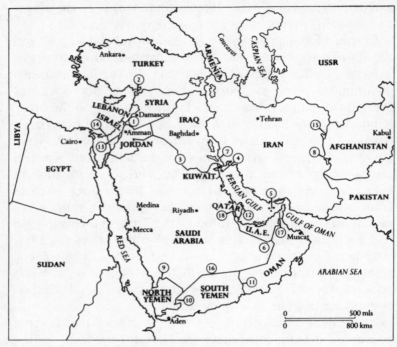

1 The Golan Heights belonging to Syria but occupied by Israel.
2 Iskanderun, belonging to Turkey but claimed by Syria.
3 Long-standing border dispute between Iraq and Saudi Arabia
4 The islands of Bubiyan and Warbah, owned by Kuwait but claimed by Iraq.
5 The islands of Abu Musa, Greater Tunb and Lesser Tunb, owned by Iran but claimed by Sharjah and Ras al-Khaimah (two members of the United Arab Emirates).
6 The Buraimi Oasis, controlled by Oman but claimed by both Saudi Arabia and the United Arab Emirates.
7 The Shat al-Arab border waterway between Iran and Iraq upon which the Iraqis claim exclusive sovereignty.
8 The Hirmand River, Iran and Afghanistan disagree on sharing its waters.
9 The Athir border region: owned by Saudi Arabia but claimed by North Yemen.
10 Dispute over border demarcation between North Yemen and South Yemen.
11 Dispute over border demarcation between South Yemen and Oman.
12 Zibarah Arabs living in the Qatar Peninsula but claimed as "subjects" by Bahrain.
13 West Bank and East Jerusalem, occupied by Israel but inhabited by Palestinian Arabs who want a state of their own.
14 The Gaza Strip, occupied by Israel but inhabited by Palestinian Arabs who want a state of their own.
15 The Parivan River, dispute between Iran and Afghanistan concerning the sharing of its waters.
16 Nomadic tribes on the border between Saudi Arabia and South Yemen. Both sides claim them as subject and disagree on controlling territory used by the tribes.
17 The Khassab and Dibbah enclaves, owned by the United Arab Emirates but claimed by the Sultane of Oman.
18 Khor al-Udaid coastal area in the Gulf. Controlled by Qatar but claimed by Saudi Arabia.

bassadors. But in 1979, shortly after the Islamic Revolution in Iran, the traditional claim on Bahrain, where shi'ite Muslims are in a majority, was revived. An Islamic 'voluntary force', headed by Ayatollah Sadeq Ruhani, even prepared to invade Bahrain in the autumn of 1979. In 1981 a pro-Iranian group tried to stage a *coup d'état* in Manamah, the Bahraini capital, with the specific aim of turning the archipelago into a province of Iran.

Further down the Gulf Iran captured two tiny islands controlled by Saudi Arabia until 1968. The islands were attractive prizes because of their rich offshore oil reserves. In 1969 the United States persuaded Iran to return one of the two islands to Saudi Arabia and keep one for itself.

Four other islands in the Gulf and the Strait of Hormuz remain objects of territorial disputes between Iran and its Arab neighbours. The emirate of Ras al-Khaimah, one of seven forming the UAE, maintains a claim on the islands of Greater Tunb and Lesser Tunb both of which are situated within Iran's territorial waters. Another UAE member, the emirate of Sharjah, has a claim on the island of Abu Mussa which Iran seized on the day British forces left the Gulf in 1971. Iran, for its part, has adopted an on-again off-again claim on the island of Beit al-Ghanam which is controlled by the sultanate of Oman.

The Mussandam Peninsula that dominates the strategic Strait of Hormuz includes isolated pockets of territory over which Oman and several of the UAE members have been in dispute since the nineteenth century. The territory of Oman proper is cut off from Omani possessions at Ras-Mussandam by the enclaves of Khor Fakkan, Khassab and Dibbah which are controlled by the shaikhdoms of Sharjah and Ras al- Khaimah. All these enclaves were originally controlled by the sultans of Oman but were recognized by the British in the 1850s as possessions of the al- Qassemi clan of Ras al- Khaimah.

Another territorial dispute between Oman and the UAE concerned the much-coveted Buraimi oasis, parts of which were claimed by Saudi Arabia and the shaikhdom of Abu

Dhabi. Saudi Arabia and Oman even fought a number of border skirmishes with each other over Buraimi in the 1950s. These armed clashes were, in fact, organized by the Arabian American Oil Company (ARAMCO) which controlled the Saudi oil industry at the time and fought against forces gathered by British oil companies operating in Oman.

Saudi Arabia's borders with its other south Arabian neighbour, the People's Democratic Republic of South Yemen, also provide a potential source of tension. In the 1970s the two countries were involved in a series of border clashes often provoked by tribal raids into villages on both sides of the frontier. Long-standing territorial claims and counter-claims also exist between Saudi Arabia and the Yemeni Arab Republic. A Saudi force captured the oasis of Assir after a brief war against Yemen in 1936. Successive governments in Sanaa, the capital of Yemen, have refused to recognize the annexation of the oasis, while keeping alive a claim on Ta'ef which was also incorporated into the Saudi kingdom in the 1930s.

Officially, the two Yemens aim at forming a single unitary state in the future. Meanwhile, however, they press a number of territorial claims and counter-claims against each other. Irredentist pressures applied by both sides have led to a series of border clashes and tribal wars backed by regular armed forces using fighter aircraft. North Yemen (Sanaa) has also tried to seize control of the island of Perim and the Kamaran archipelago which dominate the strategic Bab al- Mandab, the narrow strait that links the Red Sea to the Gulf of Aden and the Indian Ocean. The importance of Bab al- Mandab (Gate of Tears) increased dramatically in the 1980s as the Red Sea became the main route for exporting crude oil from Iraq, Kuwait and Saudi Arabia to the rest of the world.

The emirate of Qatar has its own territorial quarrels with both Saudi Arabia and Bahrain. The dispute with Saudi Arabia concerns the Khor al-Udaid channel and its offshore oil resources. A number of accords regarding the settlement of the dispute and the joint exploitation of its underwater resources were negotiated in the 1980s. At one point a project for constructing a port was also discussed. But by 1988 there had been no formal announcement that all the claims and counter-claims have been definitely settled.

The Qatar-Bahrain dispute, which provoked naval clashes between the two emirates in 1987, concerns the status of Zibarah tribes. These tribes, probably numbering under 20,000, live in the northwest of the Qatari peninsula but consider themselves as lieges of the al-Khalifah ruling clan in Bahrain.

The quest for territorial aggrandisement has rarely attracted broad mass support in any of the countries of the region. Nevertheless, it has continued to appeal to sufficiently large minorities among the politically active elites to remain a factor in shaping popular consciousness in most countries. A majority of Israelis would probably laugh at those who dream of a Jewish empire between the Euphrates and the Nile. But the 'Great Israel' lobby should not easily be dismissed as a confederacy of cranks. Pan-Arabism, which advocates the creation of a single Arab state from the Atlantic Ocean to the Persian Gulf after the destruction of the Jewish state and the annexation of some territories from both Turkey and Iran, probably reached its peak in the early 1960s. But it would be a mistake to bury Pan-Arabism prematurely as it continues to hold a certain appeal in some Arab nationalist circles.

The Pan-Iranist movement which came into being in the aftermath of Iran's occupation by the Allies during the Second World War never attracted a mass following. But for some three decades it offered an attractive alternative to leftist ideologies which captured the imagination of many Iranian intellectuals. Pan-Iranists want most of the Caucasus to be 'reunited' with Iran, and dream of a vast 'Iranic' federation which will include Afghanistan, Soviet Tadzhikistan, parts of Pakistan, the Bahrain archipelago and the Kurdish regions of Turkey, Syria and Iraq. The Pan-Iranists gave strong support to Ayatollah Ruhollah Khomeini's movement because they believed he would achieve their goal of territorial aggrandisement for Iran in the name of shi'ite Islam in the 1980s.

Pan-Turkism, which was an important ingredient of the nationalist movement in Turkey, was gradually reduced to an eccentricity pursued by small militant minorities. But vague pan-Turkist sentiments could be found in the discourse of almost all Turkish political movements, with the possible exception of Muslim fundamentalists who preach the revival of the caliphate in one form or another. The pan-Turk gospel was gradually monopolized by outright fascist groups such as Colonel Turkes's 'Grey Wolves' who became engaged in terrorist activities in the 1970s.

The failure of the 'pan' movements to attract durable mass following in Iran, Turkey and the Arab countries could be attributed in part to the fact that they are perceived as un-Islamic if not outright anti-Islamic. The Israeli expansionists, on the other hand, have remained outside the mainstream of national politics largely because they are seen as enemies of the country's democratic system of government.

All the 'pan' movements feed upon popular resentment of frontiers drawn by foreign colonial powers. While all Middle Eastern countries have come to consider their own 'colonial' borders as sacred most of them, at least indirectly, perpetuate the myth of unjust frontiers imposed by 'Imperialist' powers of the past. Even the late shah of Iran, a close friend of the West, described his seizure of three islands in the Gulf and his campaign for joint sovereignty over the Shatt al-Arab as an 'anti-Imperialist crusade'.

The sources of conflict discussed so far have to do with relations among the various nations of the region and between the region and the outside world. The importance of international relations in shaping developments in each of the Middle Eastern countries cannot be over-emphasized. A theatre of confrontation between rival power blocs for nearly two centuries, the Middle East is strongly affected by currents in international politics. Handling foreign relations is a major concern of every government in the region, at times at the expense of adequate attention to domestic issues. The general belief that virtually nothing could happen in the Middle East without foreign inspiration and involvement is sustained by the conspiracy theory which sees international affairs as a sum of Byzantine intrigues carried out by unscrupulous powers. This fixation with foreign intrigues at times makes the rulers oblivious to the internal sources of conflict with which they have to contend. And yet it is precisely these domestic sources of conflict that have provoked much of the region's instability in the 1980s.

The most important of these is the conflict between the haves and have-nots. The oil boom of the 1970s and early 1980s created the illusion that all of the region's problem of poverty could be cured thanks to petrodollars. On the eve of the 1990s, however, the gap between the mass of the poor and the privileged classes appears as wide as ever. This gap does not only separate such pauperized nations as the two Yemens from super-rich states such as Qatar and the UAE but is also a potential source of explosions inside some of the larger countries.

A comparison between the annual income of the top five per cent of the population with that of the bottom twenty per cent indicated the immense gap that exists between the very rich and the very poor in almost all of the Middle Eastern countries. The average annes appears as wide as ever. This gap does not only separate such pauperized nations as the two Yemens from super-rich states such as Qatar and the UAE but is also a potential source of explosions inside some of the larger countries.

A comparisonran eight times. Even in such oil-rich countries as Iran, Iraq and Saudi Arabia nearly half the population live in a state of poverty as defined by their own standards.

Some Middle Eastern writers have compared the region's oil income to Spanish gold from the Americas. In both cases huge riches controlled by states that represented the interests of privileged classes left behind no durable improvement in the overall living standards of the population as a whole. This is not to say that living standards have not risen in the oil-rich countries in recent times. But two points must be emphasized. First, the improvements achieved are in line with progress made throughout the world as a result of better health care and the extension of modern communications. Even then the record of Iran and Saudi Arabia, to cite the example of two oil-rich states, is not any better than that of, say, Thailand or Chile in such domains as infant mortality and life expectancy.

The second point is that the gap between the highest and the lowest income groups has widened as a result of the oil boom. In Saudi Arabia, Kuwait and the UAE the lowest income groups consist mostly of immigrant workers. In Iran and Iraq, however, the rural masses and the pauperized populations of the shanty towns compare slight improvements in their own living standards with the unprecedented wealth enjoyed by small urban classes.

In Turkey and Egypt, the region's two most populous states, part of the pressure on the national economy is relieved thanks to emigration. In 1988 no fewer than 3.2 million Turks and some 2.8 million Egyptians worked abroad. Remittances by these workers were estimated at $4,000 million and $3.500 million per annum respectively. In other words manpower represented the single most important source of foreign revenue for both countries. The economic crisis in the oil-rich economies of the region and persistently high unemployment in Western Europe slowed down the emigration of Turkish and Egyptian workers in the 1980s. Nevertheless, both states based their future economic plans on the assumption that they would be able to continue sending substantial numbers of workers abroad. In 1984 Egypt negotiated an accord with Iraq under which a total of five million Egyptians would be settled in the underpopulated areas of Mesopotamia as part of a population transfer plan to be implemented over two decades.

While Turkey, Egypt and, to a lesser extent, North Yemen

remained exporters of manpower, a number of other Middle Eastern countries depended on imported labour in virtually all sectors of their economies. In Saudi Arabia more than forty per cent of the total labour force was non-native, mostly Yemenis. Foreign workers represented sixty-eight per cent of the total force in Kuwait and seventy-five per cent in the United Arab Emirates. Qatar, where non-native workers accounted for eighty-five per cent of the work force, headed the list of regional states depending on imported labour. Iraq, with a population of over fifteen million, hosted more than 1.8 million foreign workers, mostly from Egypt and the Sudan. Even in Iran, with a population of fifty million in 1988, nearly two million foreign workers, mostly Afghan and Iraqi refugees, helped keep the nation's economy afloat.

Some of the foreign workers, notably Palestinians and Lebanese, did quite well in their Middle Eastern host countries. But the vast majority quickly came to represent a poor underclass employed in jobs shunned by the natives.

Between 1985 and 1988 a number of oil-rich countries, notably Saudi Arabia and the UAE, carried out a policy of mass expulsion of foreign workers whose presence was no longer desirable because of reductions in development plans dictated by lower revenues from oil exports. These measures strengthened the feeling among foreign workers of being an underprivileged and exploited substratum of lopsided societies. In 1986 and 1987 a series of illegal strikes hit various industries, including oil, in Saudi Arabia, Kuwait, Bahrain, the UAE and Oman. Non-native workers played key roles in all these rare instances of labour unrest.

Finally, any list of the sources of conflict in the region would be incomplete without the mention of one that has been a major cause of instability in many countries of the Middle East. The established order in almost all countries of the region is challenged by forces advocating radical structural changes in society. The challenge posed by 'overthrow' forces to the established order has inspired numerous *coups d'état* and successful or attempted revolutions in every country of the region with the sole exception of Israel and Qatar. The forces of 'overthrow' are found to the right as well as the left of the regimes in power. Between the 1940s and the 1960s the main challenge to the established order came from leftist and nationalist movements. In the 1970s and 1980s the main challenge came from the right especially in the shape of Islamic fundamentalism.

Substantial forces within each of the Middle Eastern societies find it difficult to reconcile themselves to a status quo which is partly a legacy of the colonial powers. In most countries attempts at social and economic reforms have failed to defuse the situation largely because the state has refused to offer significant concessions in the form of greater popular participation in the process of government. A strong desire for change is often matched by an equally strong fear of reforms that might lead society onto an uncharted path. Conservative and revolutionary coalitions of many different colours exist side by side in most countries of the region. Alliances are made and unmade often on the basis of pure expediency. Until the 1970s the middle classes, the armed forces and the intelligentsia could be counted among the forces of progress in the region while peasants, landlords, tribal groups and the ulema represented the forces of inertia. In the 1980s however, important sections of the middle classes, the intelligentsia and the armed forces rallied to the fundamentalist cause in Iran, Turkey, Egypt and, to a lesser extent, Syria and Iraq in an attempt at cancelling some of the social and economic changes implemented during more than three generations of modernization.

The conflict between the established order and the 'overthrow' forces in the Middle East could not be reduced to a simple expression of class struggle or the duel between a privileged minority and a dispossessed majority. Ethnic, sectarian, religious, cultural, ideological and linguistic factors all play important roles in deciding the make-up of conservative and revolutionary forces in each society at any given time.

One or more of the various sources of conflict described here can be found at the root of the successive and multiform crises that the Middle East has experienced in the past four decades. It is likely that most of these conflicts will continue to affect the political life of the region for many more years to come. The effect of some of these, notably the rivalry among the big powers, is likely to become more limited as the balance of economic and military power continues to shift in favour of new industrial states as well as some of the states in the Middle East itself. Technological changes in weapons systems and new developments in methods of global warfare have reduced the importance of the Middle East as an ideal site for strategic military bases. The region's importance as a source of energy and a major market for manufactured goods and services from the industrial countries, however, will almost certainly continue well into the next century.

Between the late 1940s and the 1980s those factors of conflict that related to the role of outside powers in the region played the key role in shaping the region's political development. The anti-colonial movement, the struggle against foreign control of vital natural resources, chiefly oil, and the need to solve numerous problems left behind by the departing imperial powers provided the central themes of political discourse and action in almost all Middle Eastern countries during that period. This meant that the other causes of conflict, far more important in the long run, were often pushed into the background, creating the illusion that all of the region's many woes were a result of foreign domination and manipulation of regional politics.

7

LIVING WITH THE GIANTS

Between the eighteenth century and the end of the Second World War the rivalry among the big powers interested in the Middle East never took the form of a confrontation between two military and ideological blocs. Almost all western powers, ranging from Portugal and Italy to France, Great Britain and Holland played active roles in the colonial history of the region. Tsarist Russia was also a major actor while Germany tried to secure a role for itself on a number of occasions.

By 1945, however, the Cold War had already started and the Middle East had become one of the first theatres of confrontation between East and West. Within a few years the United States replaced Britain as the major western power interested in the region. The rivalry between Washington and London for influence in various countries in the Middle East continued for some time. But even as early as 1945 it had become clear that only the United States, which at the time enjoyed a monopoly over nuclear weapons, would have the power to counter Soviet ambitions in the region.

The outbreak of war in 1939 was seen by the Soviet leader, Joseph Stalin, as an opportunity for extending Soviet influence and domination in both Eastern Europe and parts of the Middle East. Stalin's negotiations with Hitler in 1940 were not limited to the subject of dividing up Poland between themselves. The Soviet leader also secured Hitler's tacit support for a new Soviet sphere of influence in the direction of the Indian Ocean as well as in Asia Minor. Stalin was especially interested in a revision of the Montreux convention so that the USSR could gain control of the Bosphorus and the Dardanelles, the keys to a Soviet naval presence in the Mediterranean. Stalin was also interested in annexing parts of northeastern Turkey on behalf of the Georgian and Armenian Soviet republics.

As for Iran, Stalin does not appear to have envisaged any direct annexation of the country. He might have been sympathetic to demands by the leaders of the Soviet Azerbaijan's Communist Party for the 'reunification' of the Iranian province of Azerbaijan with their republic. But what the Field Marshal was probably more interested in was a sphere of influence covering the whole of northern Iran. Soviet troops occupied northern Iran and entered Tehran itself in 1941. In 1943 Stalin met the US President Franklin Roosevelt and the British Prime Minister Sir Winston Churchill in Tehran. The three agreed to recognize Iran's independence and territorial integrity and undertook to withdraw their occupation forces from Iranian territory at the end of the Second World War.

On 19 May 1945 Iran officially demanded that occupation forces leave its territory. Two months later the question came up during the Potsdam summit in which the new US President, Harry S. Truman, met Churchill and Stalin. The British premier insisted that all allied troops evacuate Iran at the same time. Stalin, however, demanded a six-months delay in withdrawal of his forces. American forces left Iran on 31 December 1945 and the British followed on 2 March 1946. The Soviets, however, refused to move and thus provoked the first major East-West confrontation in the context of what became known as the Cold War.

During some six years of military presence in northern Iran the Soviets had all but eliminated the influence of Tehran over the political and economic life of several key provinces. The Tudeh (Masses) Party which had come into being with

Soviet financial and organizational support was established as a major political force on the national scene as early as 1942. It drew strength from traditional anti-British sentiments and the militant egalitarianism it preached. In Azerbaijan, however, it was not the Tudeh but a more openly Soviet-controlled political machine that dominated the situation. The so-called Democrat Sect (Dimuqrat Firqasi), led by Jaafar Pishevari, constituted itself into a parallel government structure for the province as early as the summer of 1946. In November of the same year the Sect formally took over the administration of the province and appointed a council of ministers. In December, Soviet-style general elections, with single candidates in each constituency, were organized and 'won' by the Sect. This gave Pishevari the legal basis he wanted for proclaiming the autonomy of the province. Tehran immediately announced its rejection of the results of the elections and ordered a column of the regular army to march on Tabriz, the capital of Azerbaijan. The Iranian force, however, was prevented from entering Azerbaijan by Soviet troops guarding the 'frontiers' of the province.

A similar scenario was played out in the neighbouring province of Kurdistan. The Kurdish Democratic Party, founded and led by Qazi Muhammad, proclaimed the creation of a 'republic' in Mahabad, a small provincial town with a population of 12,000, on 22 January 1946. A certain Mulla, Mostafa Barzani, became minister of war. Three months later the Kurdish and Azerbaijani secessionist authorities signed a treaty of friendship and co-operation with each other. The USSR acted as guarantor.

Meanwhile the Iranian government had called on the Security Council of the newly-created United Nations to intervene and put an end to Soviet military presence in Iran. The UN, however, proved ineffective in spite of American and British support for the Iranian position.

Stalin's strategy in Azerbaijan and Kurdistan contained a number of basic flaws that eventually contributed to its failure. The Soviet leader was not prepared to allow the Soviet and Iranian Azerbaijanis to come together to form an independent state. As a result, Iranian Azerbaijanis saw the Soviet move as little more than an attempt at annexing their province to the Soviet empire. And this was unacceptable to the vast majority of Azerbaijanis who considered the USSR as an atheistic power and an enemy of Islam. Furthermore, Azerbaijani merchant classes and intellectual elites had always played a leading role in Iranian politics and did not wish to become small fish in a Soviet ocean. The manifest unpopularity of the Pishevari regime, especially among the poor who were supposed to provide its base of support, meant that a permanent Soviet military presence would be required in the province.

The situation in Kurdistan was even more difficult for the Soviets. Qazi Muhammad and his entourage were not communists and remained deeply suspicious of long-term Soviet designs. They also lacked a coherent strategy likely to mobilize mass support for their enterprise. The vast majority of Kurds remained hostile or indifferent towards the Mahabad republic.

The Irano-Soviet duel over Azerbaijan and Kurdistan provided the first post-war example of conflicts between a superpower and a Middle Eastern state upholding its national rights. It also provoked the first direct diplomatic confrontation between the United States and the USSR. The fact that the US enjoyed overwhelming military superiority at the time, mainly thanks to its nuclear monopoly, was a factor in eventually persuading Stalin to avoid a full showdown with Washington. But the key factor in the collapse of the Soviet strategy was the clever and prudent political game played by Ahmad Qavam, Iran's elder statesman, who took over as prime minister to deal with the crisis.

Qavam visited Moscow and had extensive talks with Stalin. He promised the Soviet leader oil concessions in northern Iran plus increased political influence for Moscow. On his return to Tehran, Qavam conceded most of the demands of the Pishevari government and appointed a member of the Democrat Sect's Politburo to the post of Governor-General of the province. The premier also reshuffled his cabinet to bring in three Tudeh Party members as ministers, while a noted Russophile served as Deputy Premier and chief government spokesman. The Tudeh was allowed greatly to expand its activities, even in the oilfields of Khuzestan which had been traditionally recognized as part of the British sphere of influence. The impression Qavam gave was that he was the ideal candidate for playing the role of an Iranian Kerensky. Stalin must have pondered the advantages of dominating the whole of Iran rather than ending up with influence in only two provinces.

By December 1946 Iranian troops had seized control of both Tabriz and Mahabad and the two 'republics' were brought to an end. The Soviets did not react beyond vague verbal support for their former allies. Pishevari was helped to escape to Soviet Azerbaijan but Qazi Muhammad was captured and hanged together with eight of his closest aides. In the general election that followed a majority of seats in the Majlis (parliament) was won by Qavam's supporters. The Tudeh secured only two seats. Qavam now opened his hand and called on the United States to help Iran stand up against the Soviet threats. In June 1947 a military accord was signed between Iran and the United States for the first time. American arms donated to Iran were quickly followed by American advisers who began helping the Iranian armed forces rebuild their strength. The United States achieved great popularity as a disinterested power prepared to help weaker nations defend their rights against their more powerful enemies. In other words it was Stalin's adventurist policies that drove Iran into the arms of the United States. Had it not been for pressure from Moscow Iran might have adopted a policy on non-alignment on the same lines as India and, later, Egypt, two countries that did not feel directly threatened by the USSR.

Stalin's experience with Turkey proved equally disastrous

and forced the Turkish leaders to seek alliance with the United States as a means of counter-balancing the Soviet presence on their frontiers.

Stalin had brought up the issue of revising the Montreux convention during his talks with Roosevelt and Churchill in 1943. The allies had at that time hoped to persuade Turkey to enter the war on their side but had failed. In 1945 Stalin, supported by Churchill, secured allied support for a revision of the Montreux convention during the summit conference at Yalta. The USSR was invited to present detailed proposals for such a revision within a few months. Stalin lost little time and two weeks after Yalta announced the unilateral annulment of the Soviet-Turkish treaty of 1925 under which the USSR was committed to full respect for Turkey's independence and territorial integrity. The fact that Turkey had joined the allies towards the end of the war seemed to have had no effect on Stalin's tough posture towards the Turks. The Soviet leader, using a vocabulary that recalled the worst days of the Tsarist empire, spoke of 'new conditions' that dictated a number of territorial and political changes to the detriment of Turkey. The cities of Kars and Ardahan were to be 'restored' to the USSR while the Dardanelles were to be put under joint Soviet-Turkish control. Furthermore, the USSR sought permission to set up a military base on Turkish territory to ensure the security of the straits.

The subject of Soviet demands was brought up at the Potsdam summit despite Turkish protests that their territorial integrity could not be discussed in their absence. Both Truman and Churchill appeared sympathetic to Stalin's openly expansionist claims against Turkey, backed by a military build-up in Armenia, Georgia and Bulgaria. A war between Turkey and the USSR appeared inevitable. In August 1945 the government in Ankara announced that it would agree to a revision of the Montreux convention in principle. Stalin, however, raised the stakes by demanding that the Turkish government, headed by Seracoglu, resign to make way for more accommodating politicians. It became clear that Stalin's long-term plan was direct intervention in Turkey's internal politics.

Unlike Iran, which had lacked the military wherewithal with which to resist Soviet pressure, Turkey possessed a strong army and was fully capable of defending its own territory long enough for international support to be organized in its favour. Thus from the middle of 1946 onwards the Turkish leaders decided to prepare for the worst. Turkish military positions were strengthened in areas vulnerable to Soviet attack and negotiations were opened with Washington with a view to attracting American support. Britain, lacking the economic strength needed for financing its traditional role in the Eastern Mediterranean, encouraged Turkish efforts aimed at involving the United States.

On 12 March 1947 President Truman, in an address to Congress in Washington, announced his policy of helping free people everywhere to resist foreign aggression. He also called for US military aid to be extended to Turkey and Greece. Quickly dubbed 'the Truman Doctrine', the president's address to Congress spelled out some of the basic rules by which the Cold War would be fought in the Middle East. Like Iran before it, Turkey was forced into ending its traditional non-alignment and seeking a place in the Western bloc led by the United States. Stalin had tried to modify the status quo in Turkey and Iran to his own advantage but had ended up by pushing both countries into a militant anti-Soviet foreign policy. In 1952 Turkey formalized its alliance with the West by joining the North Atlantic Treaty Organization (NATO) as a full member. Iran, however, failed to secure a direct alliance with the United States but joined the British-sponsored Baghdad Pact in 1955. Stalin's death in May 1953 eased the tension between the USSR and its neighbours and a formal note from Moscow in September virtually buried all Soviet claims against Turkey. A number of steps were also taken to improve relations with Iran. These included the return of some eleven tonnes of Iranian gold which Soviet troops had taken with them on their way home in 1946.

The consequences of Stalin's expansionist policies towards

Turkey and Iran were many and far-reaching. Of these the most important, from a long-term point of view, was the replacement of Great Britain by the United States as the principal foreign power with influence in the two countries. American global interests and the peculiarities of the US political system, which made the formulation and application of traditional big power policies a hazardous enterprise, were, over the years, to have disastrous consequences especially for Iran.

The duel with Stalin also encouraged the militarization of both Turkey and Iran. In both countries the armed forces had played a central role since the 1920s. They now claimed an even bigger role, which also meant a larger share of the national budget, in their capacity as defenders of the motherland against the Russian threat. The classical dilemma of 'guns or butter' became a vital issue in Iranian and Turkish politics. The victory of the guns lobby meant that fewer resources were available for badly needed development projects.

Russia's policy towards Iran and Turkey prior to the October Revolution had not contained a specific ideological ingredient. Under Stalin, however, Russia was identified with communism and disliked because it was both atheistic and preached revolution. The fact that a number of left wing political parties and trade unions had come into being in Iran and Turkey with financial and political support from the USSR created the impression that the left in particular, and dissident movements in general, were somehow unpatriotic and, as such, enemies of the nation as a whole rather than mere contestants for political power. Fear of the left meant that right wing movements of many different colourings were actively encouraged by the armed forces and the ruling oligarchies. Islamic groups preaching militant anti-communism were given free rein and fascist parties pressing irredentist claims against the USSR made their appearance. The government became increasingly authoritarian as the state was turned into an instrument for encouraging lopsided capitalistic development in the name of free enterprise.

Poor, if not always tense, relations between Moscow on the one hand and Tehran and Ankara on the other meant that the vast land mass of the USSR, the Middle East's natural hinterland, remained closed to normal trade and cultural relations involving the states of the region at least until the late 1950s. The reverse side of the coin was no less significant: the Soviet Union was systematically kept out of the picture in a region of vital importance to its own security and overall development.

With Iran and Turkey firmly allied to the West, the Soviet Union began looking for other potential friends and allies in the region. In the late 1940s and early 1950s Israel appeared a likely partner. The Jewish state suspected Britain of supporting the Arabs and was, as yet, unable to attract effective American sponsorship. France, which also tried to benefit from Israel's dislike of the British, played an important role in helping and arming the Jewish state well into the 1950s, but the Soviet bloc, represented by an uncharacteristically active Czechoslovakia, continued to claim a place of its own. Western, especially British, efforts to draw the Arab states into military alliances aimed against the USSR did not produce the desired results. Unlike Turkey and Iran, most Arab countries did not feel threatened by Soviet power and at times even looked to Moscow as a counterbalancing factor against too much western domination.

In the end, Iraq became the only Arab country to participate in a western-sponsored military pact. But the Baghdad Pact enjoyed virtually no support inside Iraq itself and was deeply resented by the Iraqi armed forces as a device for perpetuating British control over the country's defence and foreign policy options. One of the first decisions made by Brigadier-General Abdul-Karim Qassem after he came to power in July 1958 through a *coup d'état* was to take Iraq out of the Baghdad Pact.

The various Arab countries had their own reasons for maintaining cool, if not openly hostile, relations with both Turkey and Iran. The close alliance these two countries concluded with the West further distanced them from their Arab neighbours who, over the years, identified Israel as a protégé of the West and began drawing closer to the USSR. The fact that Turkey granted Israel full diplomatic relations, while Iran allowed the Jewish state to open a consular office in Tehran, was seen by most Arab states as a direct consequence of western pressure on Ankara and Tehran.

Both Iran and Turkey seized the opportunity provided by their respective confrontations with the USSR for implementing another of their long cherished objectives: the gradual reduction of Britain's influence on their affairs. The replacement of British influence by that of the United States in Turkey, where Britain did not possess major economic and strategic interests of its own, encountered few obstacles. In Iran, however, Anglo-American rivalry, never brought into the open but pursued with some intensity nevertheless, became a factor in the oil crisis that developed from the 1950s onwards.

Ever since the 1920s Iran had pressed for a better deal from the British-owned company that had found and exploited the oil reserves of Khuzestan. Reza Shah had succeeded in securing a new agreement with the Anglo-Iranian Company without achieving any real say in the management of the industry. In 1951 Iran finally decided to take the plunge: the Majlis passed a law nationalizing all of the country's oil resources. The man who had masterminded the move, Dr Muhammad Mossadeq, was appointed prime minister by the shah. This amounted to a declaration of war on the Anglo-Iranian Company in which the British government held a majority of the shares. Mossadeq's move was almost certainly inspired mainly by his own nationalistic sentiments. He argued that there could be no true political independence without an independent economy. And in Iran the national economy was dominated by oil revenues which provided some eighty per cent of badly needed foreign revenues. Nevertheless, Mossadeq must have been encouraged by what he interpreted as gestures of understanding from the United States. The fact that ARAMCO, a wholly US-owned company, had concluded a fifty-fifty agreement with Saudi Arabia in December 1950 could not have escaped Mossadeq's attention. The fact that Mossadeq could not have sought Soviet support without antagonizing the shah as well as the military leaders and the mullahs meant that he had to look to the United States to counter British pressure exercised on his government almost right from the start. He became involved in a complicated game which he could not control. His basic assumption that Britain would not be able to withstand the economic cost of an Iranian oil shut-off proved groundless and his inability to compromise, even on very advantageous terms for Iran, alienated the very Americans on whose friendship he had counted with a mixture of *naïveté* and Machiavellian calculation.

Once it became clear that the United States would not jeopardize its special relationship with Great Britain over Mossadeq's quarrel with the Anglo-Iranian Company the beleaguered nationalist leader began making friendly gestures towards the USSR. But it was virtually impossible to reverse Iran's foreign policy options in a hurry and in the middle of a crisis. Mossadeq was not the man the Soviets could trust and work with; his long record as a strong nationalist opposed to all foreign influence in Iran deprived him of the credentials necessary. More importantly, the USSR itself was still smarting from its double defeats in Turkey and Iran and had not yet developed an alternative policy for dealing with its two neighbours. The death of Stalin made any active Soviet role in the Iranian crisis still more problematic.

Meanwhile Mossadeq's unnecessary quarrel with the shah over the control of the armed forces further isolated his government. The break with Grand Ayatollah Abol-Qassem Kashani early in 1953 also meant that Mossadeq could no longer count on support from the mullahs and the powerful bazaaris who obeyed them. Seen from Washington Mossadeq appeared as a hostage to the Tudeh Party which boasted 50,000 members and organized huge mass rallies dominated by portraits of Stalin and anti-American slogans especially with reference to the US military role in the Korean War.

On 16 August 1953 the shah issued two decrees dismissing Mossadeq as prime minister and ordering General Fazl-Allah Zahedi to form a new government. Mossadeq refused to accept the royal command and ordered the arrest of Zahedi who went into hiding. Mossadeq made the major mistake of revealing the entire episode in some detail over the radio and through the Tudeh-dominated press. This meant that the whole country came to know that the shah, who had left the country precipitously, had indeed exercised his constitutional powers by appointing a new prime minister in the absence of the Majlis which Mossadeq had disbanded a few weeks earlier. The mullahs declared Mossadeq's government illegal and invited the people to revolt. On 19 August massive pro-shah demonstrations took place in Tehran and many other major cities as the armed forces sided with the royalist uprising. Mossadeq was arrested and Zahedi sworn in as premier.

The American Central Intelligence Agency (CIA) played a role in organizing the mass demonstrations in Tehran by providing finance. This role was subsequently blown up out of all proportion by both the opponents of the shah and retired CIA spies in search of self-glorification. British intelligence services and their Iranian agents also played a crucial, though far more discreet, role in bringing Mossadeq's premiership to an end.

With Mossadeq confined to house arrest near Tehran, the shah moved quickly to assert his own personal authority. A new oil agreement was worked out with the West under which Britain lost its exclusive control of the Iranian petroleum industry. The principle of nationalization was preserved with the Anglo-Iranian Company, renamed British Petroleum, receiving no more than forty per cent in Iranian oil. Another forty per cent went to the American oil major while Shell received fourteen per cent. The remaining six per cent was allocated to the Compagnie Française des Petroles (CFP). The United States was established as the principal foreign power with political influence in Iran.

The strengthened US presence in Iran did not prevent the shah from seeking better ties with the USSR. In 1956 he visited Moscow and managed to persuade the new Soviet leadership headed by Nikita S. Khrushchev that Iran would never be turned into a base of aggression against its northern neighbour. During the visit a number of frontier and financial disputes between the two sides were settled in an amicable atmosphere. But the shah remained convinced that only close ties with the United States could protect Iran against long-term Soviet expansionism. In 1959 Khrushchev offered Iran a non-aggression treaty which the shah instantly refused. Instead, the monarch took Iran into the Central Treaty Organization (CENTO) alongside Turkey, Pakistan and Great Britain. At the same time the shah persuaded the US President, Dwight D. Eisenhower, to sign a bilateral military accord with Iran. This took the form of an executive order and fell far short of the shah's demand for a full treaty on the same lines as that signed by the United States with Turkey. Washington also refused full CENTO membership and the US remained an associate member until the treaty ceased to exist when Iran denounced it in 1979.

Another example of confrontation between local national-ism and the big powers was furnished by Egypt where a group of young army officers, describing themselves as 'Free Officers' (Zubat al-Ahrar) overthrew the monarchy in a *coup d'état* in 1952. The titular head of the new revolutionary regime, General Muhammad Neguib, was soon eclipsed by a young lieutenant-colonel, Gamal Abdul-Nasser, who had been the real strategist of the *coup d'état*. Nasser, a charis-matic leader, developed an original discourse of his own in which the concept of Arabism (al-uruba) played a crucial role. He promised Egyptians a better life and freedom from foreign domination. That meant an end to Britain's smother-ing presence in Egypt. Nasser's anti-British posture led both

Moscow and Washington to believe that they could enhance their respective influences in the new Egypt that began to emerge. At first, Nasser turned to the United States, and it was with diplomatic support from Washington that he negotiated a new agreement with Britain regarding the presence of British forces in the Suez Canal zone in the summer of 1954.

Very soon, however, Nasser realized that Washington's real objective was to drag Egypt into an alliance with Iraq and Jordan, and possibly even Saudi Arabia, in the name of combating communism. The Americans did not realize that Egypt, having had no direct experience of Soviet expansionism, did not feel threatened by Moscow and had absolutely no direct interest in entering the Cold War on the side of the western powers. Nasser was cultivating his image as the champion of Arab struggle against western colonialism and had already begun providing military aid for the National Liberation Front (FLN) which fought against French rule in Algeria. A 'hero of the Arab liberation struggle', as he was described by Egyptian propagandists, Nasser could not join a military pact dominated by the very colonial powers he campaigned against. Furthermore, Egypt was now a republic and did not wish to be associated with Arab monarchies which it considered to be reactionary and anti-nationalist. A policy of non-alignment suited Egypt's particular interests best. Accordingly, Nasser began scouting for closer ties with the Eastern Bloc. In 1955 he signed a trade agreement under which Egyptian cotton would be bartered against arms from Czechoslovakia. The Soviets applauded Egypt's new show of independence and encouraged Nasser in his efforts to undermine the Baghdad Pact. Moscow also began to describe itself as a supporter of Arab nationalism and expressed sympathy and understanding for the Palestinian cause.

The immediate result of Nasser's overture towards the east was a series of fresh efforts by the United States and its allies to win favour in Cairo. An attractive package of aid that included financial and technical support for a high dam on the

Nile, Nasser's dream project, was offered to Egypt by the United States with British and French backing in 1955. This was Nasser's day of glory: he had shown how an Arab leader could keep all his options open and still benefit from both camps. The Egyptian leader began to overestimate his own assets and sharpened his anti-western vocabulary. At the same time Egyptian forces on the cease-fire line with Israel in the Sinai began a campaign of harassment against Israeli outposts and thus provoked fresh tension in the area. Egypt also increased its material and propaganda support for the Algerian freedom fighters.

In the spring of 1956 France began supplying arms to Israel, a move that was belatedly approved by Washington. Nasser reacted by extending diplomatic relations to the People's Republic of China, a move that was at the time considered as the supreme snub to the US administration. Washington countered Nasser's purely symbolic move by withdrawing all American support for Egyptian economic development projects, including the Aswan Dam.

Nasser's safest option at the time might have been to sit back and allow tempers to cool for a while. But that might have damaged his image as an intrepid Arab hero. He had to react with vigour and from a position of strength. In July 1956 he announced the nationalization of the Suez Canal Company which was owned by British and French interests. This sent a wave of panic through financial and political circles in Paris and London. The British prime minister, Sir Anthony Eden, had for long seen Nasser as an Arab Mussolini destined to co-operate with the Russian versions of Hitler in a new war aimed at destroying western civilization. Pro-Israeli lobbies in both Europe and the United States played on these fears and warned that any attempt at appeasing Nasser might lead to a repetition of the Munich disaster for Europe. Few people stopped to ask how Egypt, a poor and underdeveloped state unable to feed its own people, might dream of world conquest.

Nasser himself felt flattered by the attacks made on him;

these made him the unquestioned symbol of Arab aspirations for freedom and grandeur. Jordan seized the opportunity for ending British domination over its armed forces and announced that it would fight on the side of Egypt. Syria was even more sanguine in its support of Nasser. Even in Iraq, where the government considered Nasser to be a mad man in search of personal glory, the masses poured into the streets to express their solidarity with Egypt. As always nationalism reached its peaks in a campaign against real or imaginary enemies. The euphoria created throughout the Arab world guided Nasser onto a dangerous path he had no reason to take at that time.

Nasser had to choose between Egypt's narrow interests, which dictated a quick settlement with the western powers which were, after all, the principal users of the Suez Canal, and the irresistible appeal of going for broke in the name of Arab honour and prestige. Nasser chose the latter and was soon overtaken by events he no longer controlled. Arab political rhetoric is a sweet poison that often kills those who distil it. And Nasser's rhetoric was, without a doubt, the most dramatic that Arabs had experienced for generations. The Eygptian leader had posted a broad smile when announcing the nationalization of the canal. This had been the first time in living memory that the Arabs had seen one of their leaders smiling at them at a moment of victory. That smile was subsequently compared with the smile of joy that lights the face of a young man who witnesses the birth of his first son.

In the summer of 1956 Britain, France and Israel concluded a secret accord under which they would take joint military action against Egypt. The United States was not informed of the conspiracy as Eden believed that Washington was incapable of understanding the real world and that it was up to Great Britain to defend the best interests of the West. The fact that Khrushchev was at the time busy dealing with popular revolts in Poland and Hungary meant that the Soviets would not be able to take any significant military action in support of Egypt. The scenario was for Israel to attack Egypt so that

British and French troops could be sent in supposedly to restore order and prevent the war from spreading. Israel opened the war on 29 October by attacking Egyptian positions in the Sinai. The following day French and British aircraft intervened to destroy major Egyptian military targets. Five days later British and French paratroopers intervened to secure control of the canal. They failed to do so despite additional support from an amphibious force brought in on 6 November. All they could achieve was to damage key canal installations and sink a number of ships inside the waterway which, as a result, remained closed for several years.

The Americans wasted no time in asserting their leadership of the West. They could not tolerate two of their European allies and Israel, a country which depended on US subsidies, taking matters into their own hands in so sensitive a region. The US Secretary of State, John Foster Dulles, was convinced that the tripartite attack on Egypt would play into the hands of the Russians and also strengthen the more extremist strands of Arabism. Accordingly, the US went to the UN Security Council and obtained a resolution calling for a cease-fire and the withdrawal of foreign forces from Egyptian territory.

The Suez crisis marked the end of an effective European military presence in the Middle East. It established the United States and the USSR as the only two powers capable of applying military pressure in support of political objectives in the region. But the contest had no long-term winners. The British and the French were prime losers because they were exposed as only medium-size powers compelled to toe the line set by Washington. Israel also lost, despite its military *tour de force* on the battlefield, because it gave itself a new image: that of a local agent for western colonial powers. The Soviets, who had offered only verbal support to Egypt in its hour of need, were no real winners either. They were shown to be unable or unwilling to defend a friendly country against aggression. The United States might have been expected to be a winner among so many losers. But Washington, partly because of its strategic commitment to Israel, also proved unable to secure any lasting gains. Very soon Nasser moved closer to the USSR while becoming more active within the non-aligned movement. Egypt had played a limited role in the Bandung conference of 1955 which had launched the non-aligned movement with China, India and Indonesia in the lead. But from 1957 onwards Nasser, together with the Indian premier Jawaharlal Nehru and the Yugoslav leader Josip Broz Tito, emerged as the most authoritative spokesman for non-alignment. Egypt also increased its support for national liberation struggles, especially in Algeria where France was involved in an unwinnable war.

Nevertheless, even Egypt could not be described as a winner in the Suez crisis. The brief war did not expose the true state of Egyptian defences and created a false sense of security. It also burdened Egypt with Arab nationalist responsibilities it could not bear without damaging its own specific interests. Further, Nasser was forced to draw still closer to the USSR in search of arms. Military dependence on the USSR soon led to other links and it was the Soviet Union that, in the end, helped Egypt construct the Aswan Dam.

In March 1957 the US Congress approved the so-called 'Eisenhower Doctrine' which gave the president leave to use military force to help any Middle Eastern country that faced communist aggression. The new 'doctrine' was put into practice a few weeks later when the US Sixth Fleet entered the eastern Mediterranean in a show of support for King Hussein of Jordan in his struggle against Nasserist forces. There was no communist threat involved in the conflict but few people in Washington bothered to dwell on the exact implications of the 'doctrine'. A year later, the 'doctrine' was invoked again, this time to help the Lebanese president, the Maronite Camille Chamoun, subdue his Muslim opponents. The US marines landed at Beirut in what was the first direct American military intervention in the internal political affairs of a Middle Eastern country. A grateful Chamoun survived but the seeds of a much longer and bloodier civil war were sown in Lebanon.

Meanwhile an Anglo-American plot to overthrow the Syrian government, with financial help provided by Iraq, failed. In February 1958 Syria formally joined Egypt in what became known as the United Arab Republic. The Syrian move was, in part, a desperate attempt by the country's leaders, especially Shukri Quwwattli, to find a solution to the nation's chronic instability. A series of military *coups d'état*, successively led by Hosni Zaim, Sami Hinnawi and Adib Shishakli, had earned Syria the reputation of an Arab version of the Latin American banana republics. Quwwattli, supported by the Syrian Communist Party under Khaled Bakdash, hoped that union with Egypt would prevent future coups in Damascus and associate Syria with a great Arab enterprise it could not attempt alone because of its small population and limited resources. Very soon, however, most Syrians began to feel that their country had been turned into an Egyptian colony in the name of Arabism. The United Arab Republic ended in all but name when Syria withdrew from it in 1961.

In July 1958 it was Iraq's turn to move out of the western orbit. Brigadier-General Abdul-Karim Qassem led a *coup d'état* which led to the overthrow of the pro-British monarchy in Baghdad. The young King Faisal and his old prime minister Nuri Sa'id, the most senior of Anglophile leaders in the region, were murdered along with scores of others including members of the royal family. The mutilated bodies of the king and his premier were dragged into the streets of Baghdad and provoked scenes of unbridled jubilation. The *coup d'état* was strongly supported by the clandestine Iraqi Communist Party and most of the Kurdish leaders in the north. Britain reacted by dispatching paratroopers to Jordan and Washington contemplated action by the marines based in Lebanon. The idea of invoking the 'Eisenhower Doctrine' was brought up by the US but no action was taken because there were no pro-western forces capable of mounting a challenge to the new regime in Baghdad.

The overthrow of the British-sponsored monarchy in Baghdad created a void that the USSR was quick to fill. Moscow used its new Iraqi connection for two purposes: to further limit western influence in the region and to counterbalance the weight of Egypt within the Arab world. Qassem refused to join the Egyptian-dominated United Arab Republic and tried to build up his own image as a champion of Arabism. Using Iraq's oil revenues, an asset not available to Nasser, Qassem launched a major build up of the country's armed forces. The Soviets soon established themselves as the principal suppliers of arms to the region as a whole and to Iraq in particular. Iran, always wary of Iraqi intentions, was forced to speed up its own arms build-up and Israel turned to the United States for the weapons it claimed were needed to counterbalance the Soviet-backed expansion of Syrian, Egyptian and Iraqi arsenals. A full arms race was on with both superpowers becoming more and more involved in Middle Eastern conflicts. The Soviet Union always led the way and became the first power to introduce jet fighter-bombers in the region.

In 1962 the Nasserist cause found a new convert in the shape of the poor and backward Yemen. A military *coup d'état* led by Colonel Abdallah Sallal overthrew the old-established imamate and drove the Imam, Badr Ibn Ahmad, out of the capital Sanaa. Badr managed to rally support among the shi'ite tribes of Sa'adah in the north and declared 'jihad' (holy war) on the Sanaa republic. The civil war that followed soon led to a direct military intervention by Egypt which was to last for years and proved an unbearable burden on the weakling Egyptian economy. Saudi Arabia, on the other hand, sided with the Imam who also enjoyed Iranian support. To make matters more complicated, the United States, which was the closest ally of both Iran and Saudi Arabia, recognized the pro-Egyptian regime in Sanaa while Britain tilted towards support for the Imam. Egyptian air attacks on targets inside Saudi Arabia provoked some angry reaction from Washington. But the US policy of trying to drive a wedge between Egypt and the USSR continued.

In 1963 the Qassem regime, which had in the meantime provoked an economic crisis and a civil war with the Kurds, was overthrown in a new *coup d'état*. Qassem's attempts at annexing Kuwait, which had become independent in 1960, and the tension that his policies caused in Iraq's relations with both Iran and Syria, had isolated his regime and thus made it more vulnerable to plots from within the armed forces. The new regime, which began by murdering Qassem in front of television cameras, was headed by the fallen dictator's closest aide, Major-General Abdul Salaam Aref. A number of other army officers and politicians linked with the clandestine Ba'ath (Renaissance) Party were intimately involved in the *coup d'état*, a fact that gave rise to suspicions of British participation in the plot. At any rate, the new regime scaled down Iraq's relations with the USSR and tried to restore working relations with the West. Moscow reacted by stepping up support for the Iraqi Kurdish rebels and by moving even closer to Egypt.

The 1960s emerged as a decade of wars as well as *coups d'état*. The intervention of the armed forces in politics, however, was not confined to newly independent Arab states. In 1960 the Turkish army staged a *coup d'état* of its own, thus establishing a precedent for similar moves in the following decades. The Turkish coup was led by General Gemal Gursel, the army chief of staff, and presented as a 'corrective' measure rather than a full change of regime. But it was no less violent. The prime minister, Adnan Menderes, was hanged and his Democrat Party declared illegal. The president of the republic, Celal Bayar, an old associate of Atatürk, was sentenced to death but spared on Gursel's orders. He spent the two decades that followed under house arrest on a remote island.

8

THE WATER WAR

By the mid-1960s the Soviet Union was fully established as a major player in the politics of the Middle East. Egypt was a strong ally and Syria was moving ever closer to the socialist camp. Further away, an independent Algeria had emerged as another influential Arab state desirous of joining forces with the USSR in a global campaign against western 'Imperialism'. A united bloc of Arab states, from the Atlantic to the Persian Gulf (in the words of a popular Egyptian song), might tip the balance of power in favour of the USSR in a region of growing strategic and economic importance. Arab unity, however, remained as elusive as ever and the continuation of rivalries involving Egypt, Iraq and Saudi Arabia meant that no pan-Arab strategy could be developed. The civil war in Yemen, in which Egypt was directly involved while the Saudis participated by providing money and arms for the Imam, was yet another illustration of the Arabs' tendency to quarrel among themselves. It was essential that a focus for Arab unity be found.

Various fundamentalist movements had for long argued that only Islam could restore the unity of the Arabs. The argument had found some echoes in both London and Washington. In 1958 , for example, Eisenhower tried to portray the United States as a protector of Islam against Soviet atheism, and the idea of creating an Islamic pact was raised in both Tehran and Riyadh as well as Ankara. The idea did not get off the ground because Turkey wished to remain a secular state while the Saudis would not be associated with shi'ite Iran in an Islamic context. Nationalist and leftist forces in the Middle East in the 1960s considered Islam as an ally of reactionary ruling elites and their western supporters. In ordering the destruction of the Muslim Brotherhood in Egypt, a move that included many executions and mass arrests, President Nasser had branded the fundamentalist organization as a tool of colonialism.

The Russians soon found out that one issue more than any other was likely to unite the Arabs and mobilize their energies against the West. That issue was, of course, the very existence of a Jewish state in the heart of the region that the Arabs considered their own by right. A massive Soviet propaganda and diplomatic campaign aimed at focusing all Arab attention on confrontation with Israel was launched from 1965 onwards. Israel was portrayed as a bridgehead for western 'Imperialism' whose aim remained the colonial domination of the Arab world. The issue of dealing with Israel was pushed to the top of the agenda of virtually all Arab states in the Middle East. This does not mean that the Arabs began to think of Israel as an enemy as a result of Soviet propaganda. What the Soviets achieved was to synthesize the many different sentiments that various Arab political movements already had towards the Jewish state. More importantly, Moscow, which had originally supported Israel as a 'progressive' state in a region dominated by reactionary feudalistic regimes, now told the Arab left that Zionism was only the vanguard of US 'Imperialism'.

In 1966 King Faisal of Saudi Arabia, who had replaced his brother King Saud and sent him into exile, summarized the Arab strategy towards the Jewish state in two words: 'Zaval Israel' (the elimination of Israel). This meant that even Saudi Arabia, the oldest and closest ally of the United States in the region, would be prepared to join forces with radical Arab regimes to challenge the very right of Israel to exist. And because the US could not abandon Israel it was only a matter of time before the Arabs were propelled into an anti-American position. Any crisis in Arab-Israeli relations could, therefore, provide the USSR with a fresh opportunity for scoring gains in its global rivalry with the United States.

One such opportunity arose in 1964–5 when Israel and Syria became involved in a dispute regarding the waters of Jordan. Water is a powerful symbol in the Middle East where the desert predominates and rainfall is often inadequate. In fact, the region loses nearly one per cent of its cultivated area each year because of desertification and salinity. Although in part due to hasty land reform projects, badly designed hydroelectric schemes and the unusual thinness of the humus in most parts of the region, this loss of cultivated land is essentially caused by the absence of adequate and reliable water resources. It was no surprise that an Arab summit was quickly organized to prepare for war in defence of the right to use the waters of Jordan the way Amman and Damascus saw fit. Moscow fanned the flames of the conflict by stepping up its arms deliveries to both Egypt and Syria and sharpening its propaganda campaign against the 'Zionist enemy of the Arab people'. This encouraged Syria to try to divert the waters of Jordan in a way that would turn parts of Israel into virtual desert. The Israelis countered the Syrian moves by using force and the two neighbours became involved in an escalating round of border clashes. Soviet propaganda concentrated on the theme of an alleged Israeli plot to invade Syria and even capture Damascus.

In November 1966 Syria and Egypt, strongly encouraged by Moscow, signed a mutual defence agreement without, however, expecting a major war with Israel. By April 1967 the crisis seemed to have subsided somewhat. Israel had ordered no mobilization and Egypt was far from ready for an early war. On 13 May, however, Moscow speeded up the movement towards armed conflict by presenting Nasser with a top secret intelligence report that speculated about the possibility of an imminent Israeli attack on Syria. Less than twenty-four hours later Nasser issued a strong warning to

Israel and also sent his troops into the Sinai. The Israelis reacted by adopting a low profile in the hope either of avoiding war altogether or, if that became inevitable, of attracting worldwide sympathy as victims of aggression. The Israeli attitude was interpreted by both Nasser and the Soviets as a sign of weakness. Accordingly, Nasser ordered the United Nations' military observation teams, that had been installed in the Sinai to monitor cease-fire violations in 1956, out of Egyptian territory. Israeli and Egyptian armies now faced each other for the first time in nearly twelve years.

On May 22 Nasser announced the closure of the Strait of Tiran, thus shutting Israel out of the Gulf of Aqaba, the Red Sea and the Indian Ocean. The Israeli Prime Minister Levi Eshkol resisted pressures at the Knesset to respond by force and instead asked the US for support. Washington counselled extreme caution and offered to organize a multinational force that would keep the Strait of Tiran and the Gulf of Aqaba open to all shipping. Nasser was at the pinnacle of his prestige as the champion of Arabism and seemed determined to inflict even greater humiliation on the Jewish state.

The crisis was deepened a week later when the Soviets announced that they would counter any move by the USA if and when a war broke out between Egypt and Israel. This was a strange move. The Soviets were, perhaps, convinced that there would be no war in the immediate future and merely wanted to score a propaganda point against the United States. The Arabs and Israel, however, saw the Soviet move as an invitation to war. Once again Nasser made the initial moves. The day after the Soviet guarantee was issued, Nasser declared that what was really at issue was the entire Palestinian question. The Israelis interpreted this to mean that Egypt was trying to provoke a general war with the aim of destroying their state. Ahmad Shukairi, the veteran Palestinian leader, was put under the limelight in Egypt and promoted as the leader of a future Arab state in Palestine. Within a few days Syria, Jordan and Iraq announced that they had put their forces under Egyptian command. Saudi Arabia and Algeria also put their armies on limited alert while even tiny Kuwait did its part by dispatching a token force to Egypt. Arab unity seemed complete and war had become inevitable. It was now impossible for Nasser to defuse the situation without risking major political losses at home and throughout the Arab world. The Israelis, on the other hand, were convinced that their very existence was threatened by an Arab coalition supported by the USSR. Most Israelis believed that the United States would not leave them alone if and when Arab armies entered the territory of the Jewish state. But all Israelis knew that any decisive support from the United States might simply arrive too late. Israel's lack of territorial depth and limited population reserves meant that it would not be able to face the prospect of a prolonged war with its neighbours.

Determined to keep the war within the territory of its enemies, Israel opened the hostilities by attacking Egypt on 5 June 1967. Within hours Israel had succeeded in destroying the Egyptian air force, mostly on the ground. In the afternoon of the same day Israel struck against both Jordan and Syria. A substantial Iraqi force, dispatched to help Jordan, was quickly isolated and virtually held hostage until the end of the war. Deprived of air cover, the Egyptian ground forces were decimated by Israeli air attacks and offensives. In only six days the war was all but lost by the Arabs and Israel's army took positions on the Suez Canal. The Israelis also captured the Syrian Golan Heights, the eastern half of Jerusalem, the West Bank of Jordan, the Gaza Strip and the whole of the Sinai Peninsula. Even a few attols belonging to Saudi Arabia in the Gulf of Aqaba were seized by Israeli forces.

Once the extent of the disaster had become clear, Nasser called on Moscow to seek a cease-fire. The Russians demanded a special session of the United Nations' Security Council and issued vague threats about using rockets against British and French targets. The Security Council quickly passed a cease-fire resolution which was as promptly accepted by the belligerents. Israel was anxious to consolidate its victories while the Arabs wished to limit their losses. The outcome of the war gave Israel a bargaining chip it was not prepared to part with. The concept of exchanging the occupied territories for recognition by the Arabs began to take shape in Israel. The United States supported the concept and refused to pressurize Israel to give up its military gains as it had done in 1956.

The Six Day War, as the conflict came to be known, had been unleashed by a quarrel over water but had ended by creating a much bigger problem in the shape of occupied Arab lands. The war had profound effects on the world view of both the Israelis and the Arabs. To many Israelis the speedy victory achieved by General Moshe Dayan's forces had a much deeper and divine significance. Israeli thinkers began to speak of the God of Auschwitz, who had remained indifferent to the Holocaust, and the God of the Six Day War, who had given the Jews victory as part of his broader promise of redemption for the Chosen People. The war swept aside the bitter internecine quarrels that had marked Israel's politics right from the start and helped create a feeling of nationhood in which differences between the sabras (natives) and the new arrivals, and theological disputes among various sects, suddenly appeared of no more than marginal interest. Israeli vulnerability to internal fractures had been illustrated as early as 1948 when armed right wing groups had clashed with the forces of the left wing government then in power. The 1967 war ended all that for more than a generation. In fact, there are Jews who believe that Jewish history has two beginnings: one marked by the exodus from Egypt led by Moses and another represented by Israel's victory in the Six Day War.

On the Arab side a different picture obtained. Here feelings of humiliation and anger mixed with a sentiment of despair. It was despair that drove Field Marshal Abdul-Hakim Amer, the Arab Supreme Commander, to commit suicide. This was a serious personal blow to Nasser who had loved Amer as a brother and friend. Amer's suicide also raised the issue of Nasser's own future. Would the rais (chief) also commit suicide? Nasser decided to go only half of the way and, after having accepted full responsibility for the defeat, announced that he was ready to stand down as president. The move provoked scenes of delirium in support of the rais throughout the Arab world. Nasser was reassured and promised to stay on and continue the struggle. But his charisma had already disappeared and the stain of defeat could not be cleansed with the passage of time. The June war had killed Nasserism although this fact did not become apparent until several years later.

Nasser now changed his policy of trying to defeat Israel in a single major war and began to prepare for a prolonged conflict in which attrition and guerrilla warfare would eventually produce an Arab victory. The Soviets, having suffered another major blow to their standing in the Middle East, tried to limit their political losses by pouring in fresh arms into both Egypt and Syria. Later they even agreed to Nasser's demand for Soviet pilots and engineers to serve in the Egyptian air force as part of advanced units on the Suez Canal. Moscow also remained active on the diplomatic scene. In November 1967 the UN Security Council adopted Resolution 242 which called for a return of all occupied territories in exchange for Arab recognition of Israel. This was the best deal the Russians could secure at the time. But the Arabs rejected it because it made no mention of a state for the Palestinians.

By the summer of 1969 Nasser's attrition strategy had led to fresh disasters for Egypt. In July the Israelis launched a new, but more limited, operation that resulted in the destruction of most of the new warplanes that Egypt had acquired from Russia. It was now Israel's turn to firmly reject Resolution 242 and begin demanding new and secure borders for itself.

It was in some desperation that Nasser paid a secret visit to Moscow in January 1970 with a new threat of resignation. The Soviet leader, Leonid Brezhnev, reassured the visitor by offering to dispatch thousands of military experts to help reorganize the Egyptian war machine. By spring 1970 some 10,000 Soviet officers were seconded to the Egyptian armed forces, especially the air force which had to be rebuilt from scratch. Very soon, however, it became apparent that the presence of so many Soviets in Egypt was in itself a limiting factor for Nasser in his choice of options. Moscow made it plain that it would not support a new military adventure against Israel and that the Arab military build-up ought to be combined with a diplomatic quest for peace. This new Soviet attitude accorded well with the policy of the Nixon administration, which had come into power in January 1969. The combined pressure of Moscow and Washington led to a new cease-fire agreement in August 1970.

Meanwhile a number of developments beyond Egypt itself had helped create a new post-war atmosphere in the Middle East. The war in Yemen had come to an end as a result of a Saudi-Egyptian compromise. In Iraq the regime of General Abdul-Rahman Aref was overthrown in July 1968 in a *coup d'état*. The new regime, headed by the Ba'athist General Ahmad Hassan al-Bakr, accused its predecessor of treason during the 1967 war with Israel, and declared the 'elimination' of the Jewish state to be its number one objective. Egypt's defeat gave Saudi Arabia an opportunity to build itself up as a major player on the Arab scene. The kingdom's rising oil income, and the prestige that King Faisal had secured as a result of his piety and determination, gave Riyadh important assets in the Arab power game.

King Faisal had all along argued that the Palestinian issue should not remain an exclusively Arab concern and that the energies and resources of non-Arab Muslims should also be mobilized for the purpose of 'wiping out' the Jewish state. Accordingly, he focused attention on Jerusalem, Islam's third holiest city and the base from which Prophet Muhammad made nocturnal visits to the heavens. The king rejected the view held by Nasser and many other Arab leaders that the conflict with Israel was a secular and purely political one. In 1968 an eccentric Australian tourist started a fire in the al-

Aqsa Mosque, one of Islam's holiest shrines in the heart of Arab Jerusalem. The move was instantly presented as a plot by Israel to destroy Muslim edifices in the occupied city in order to rebuild the ancient Jewish temple.

The fire at al-Aqsa, almost certainly the result of an isolated act by a deranged man, created an unprecedented stir throughout the Muslim world. Faisal immediately proposed the holding of an Islamic summit, the first ever. The Shah of Iran, no friend of the Arabs, endorsed Faisal's invitation and the summit was convened in Rabat, the Moroccan capital. More than thirty countries, including secular Turkey, sent their kings, presidents or ministers to the meeting which offered a rare spectacle of Islamic unanimity, though not genuine unity. Nasser himself, however, stayed away from the summit so as not to harm his image as a progressive leader. He did not wish to be seen rubbing shoulders with the 'reactionary, feudalistic rulers' he had condemned for years in vitriolic terms. The Egyptian delegation was led by Nasser's colourful but powerless Vice-President, Muhammad Anwar Sadat, who made a very favourable impression on both the Shah and King Faisal. The Rabat summit produced no immediate results as far as the conflict with Israel was concerned. But it marked the transformation of the Arab-Israeli conflict into a wider confrontation between all Muslims and the Jewish state. A decade later, this very theme was to be seized upon by Ayatollah Khomeini and other fundamentalist leaders in several Muslim countries with far-reaching results for the whole region.

Soon after the June 1967 defeat Nasser had pushed the traditional Palestinian leadership, maintained in the Gaza Strip as a fictitious 'provisional' authority, into oblivion in favour of a new generation of younger and more militant leaders. The Palestine Liberation Organization (PLO) came into being as a coalition of guerrilla groups around al-Fatah (Conquest), whose leader Yasser Arafat, known by his *nom de guerre* Abu-Ammar, was built up into something of an Arab hero within a few months.

The PLO, at first dismissed by some observers as little more than a creature of the Arab secret services (mukhaberat), soon developed an identity and policy of its own. It began preaching a long guerrilla struggle against Israel, a strategy that put the Palestinians themselves in the vanguard of the war, with the Arab states expected to play only a supporting role. Thus the issue of Palestine as a pan-Arab cause was questioned from two opposite positions. Faisal saw it as a pan-Islamic concern while Arafat made it a primarily Palestinian concern. Both positions were to facilitate the task of Egypt in seeking a separate peace of its own with Israel in the late 1970s.

The PLO's analysis of the situation contained another important element. Arafat and his comrades argued that the Palestinian liberation struggle needed a territorial base from which to wage war on Israel. That meant that at least some of the 'reactionary' regimes in the region had to be overthrown as a prelude to the destruction of the Zionist state. The most obvious candidate for overthrow was King Hussein's regime in Jordan. This was a royalist regime created by Britain and still closely linked with the western powers which supported Israel. More importantly, some sixty per cent of the population of the kingdom, now truncated after its loss of the West Bank, were Palestinians. Jordan's long cease-fire line with Israel also provided numerous opportunities for PLO infiltration into the occupied territories. King Hussein, true to the tradition created by his grandfather, believed that seeking peace with Israel would be the best guarantee against future defeats by the Arabs. Also like King Abdallah, he had been involved in secret talks with the Israeli leaders on a number of occasions.

In September 1970 the Popular Front for the Liberation of Palestine (PFLP), a radical component part of the PLO, hijacked four jetliners owned by western air companies at the start of what became a perennial threat to civilian air services in the region. One of the hijacked planes was taken to Cairo and blown up after all passengers had been released. The three others were flown to Amman Airport where PLO elements staged a show of force. The hijacked aircraft were blown up after the release of their passengers. King Hussein's authority seemed more fragile than ever. After consulting with the US as well as Saudi Arabia and Iran, the king declared martial law and ordered all PLO units to surrender their arms to the regular Jordanian army. The PLO responded by opening fire on army positions. Within days a full-scale war had broken out between royalist troops and PLO fighters. On 16 September the PLO called on Syria and Iraq to help. The Iraqis moved some units to their frontier with Jordan but did not go beyond propaganda attacks on King Hussein. Iraq was deeply involved in a war against its own Kurds and also had to face direct military pressure from Iran. Syria, on the other hand, wanted to seize the opportunity and help destroy the Amman regime which it considered as an Israeli 'fifth column' at the time. Syrian troops entered Jordanian territory on 19 September and King Hussein called on Israel to send its air force in to help repel the aggression. On 21 September President Richard Nixon announced that the US would send in troops to help Jordan if either Egypt or the USSR intervened in favour of Syria. Meanwhile, Moscow was also cautioning Damascus against a lengthy war with Jordan. As for Egypt, the question of starting a war against Jordan in support of the PLO and Syria never even arose. All that Nasser was prepared to offer was his mediation which neither side seemed to want. By 22 September, and before either the USA or Israel had completed their contingency plans to come to Jordan's support, the Syrian invasion force, defeated by King Hussein's more experienced army, was in full retreat. The massacre of PLO supporters could continue unhindered. Within a month that was subsequently dubbed 'Black September' by the PLO more than 10,000 Palestinians were killed by the king's bedouin soldiers. The bulk of the PLO's forces, however, managed to escape to Syria which, after a brief interval, pushed them into Lebanon. One direct result of 'Black September' was that the PLO became almost entirely dependent on Syria and its Soviet allies.

On 28 September Nasser died of a heart attack in Cairo, provoking the largest popular demonstrations ever seen in the region. More than six million people gathered in Cairo to march behind the cortege of the rais. All of Nasser's mistakes were forgiven. And soon many of his policies were forgotten. The Soviet premier, Alexei Kosygin, flew to Cairo for Nasser's funeral and appeared as Egypt's effective ruler for a few confused days. From his base at the Soviet Embassy compound he urged the more pro-Moscow factions within the Egyptian leadership to accept Sadat as temporary head of state in accordance with the constitution. Soviet influence in the Middle East appeared at its peak.

Meanwhile, Moscow had found a new ally in the region in the shape of the People's Democratic Republic of South Yemen which gained its independence from Britain in 1968. The new state, the first and only one among the Arab states to describe itself as Marxist–Leninist, was the result of a fusion between the British crown colony of Aden and a number of British-protected sultanates and shaikhdoms in southern Arabia. A liberation movement had been launched in Aden from North Yemen in the early 1960s with the well-organized trade unions in the port city as its main base of support. The movement assumed the name of Front for the Liberation of Occupied South Yemen (FLOSY) and depended on Egyptian financial and ideological support. Its principal leaders, Abdallah al-Asnag and Abdul-Qawee al-Makawee, were not particularly anti-British. The British government, however, continued to believe that Nasser was a long-term threat and that anyone who co-operated with him had to be treated as an enemy.

British refusal to treat with the relatively moderate FLOSY encouraged the emergence of another and far more militant liberation movement, the NLF (National Liberation Front), which began by forging a Chinese connection before ending up as an ally of the USSR. The terror campaign, especially against British troops and installations in Aden, intensified and led to mounting casualties that the government in London could not easily explain away. An early settlement with FLOSY might have enabled Britain to withdraw from Aden and southern Arabia earlier and at a lower cost. But London preferred to deal with the NLF which, in the end, took over as government after having killed or chased away many of FLOSY's leaders and activists.

The pro-Soviet factions within the NLF eventually seized full control after a palace coup that ended with the murder of President Qahtan al-Sha'abi. Within a few months the USSR had established a military presence in the port of Aden as well as the strategic island of Soccotra. From 1970 onwards South Yemen also became a base for guerrilla activities against the Omani province of Dhofar. Moscow seemed determined to enter the Persian Gulf from the back door as it were. Soviet military presence in Somalia in the Horn of Africa also meant that Moscow exercised a certain military pressure on that strategic part of the Indian Ocean.

The US reaction took the form of the so-called 'Nixon Doctrine', which committed the United States to arming its regional allies so that they could defend themselves against any Soviet or Soviet-sponsored aggression. The Vietnam syndrome meant that Washington would think twice before promising direct military support to its friends in the Third World. This was also an era of *détente* and the Nixon administration did not seem overly disturbed by the expansion of Soviet influence in the Middle East and Africa. Even when Cuban troops were dispatched to Hadhramaut, in South Yemen, to boost that country's defences against possible attacks by Iranian and Omani forces from Dhofar, the USA remained unusually reserved.

The rebellion in Dhofar, led by the Front for the Liberation of the Occupied Arab Gulf (FLOAG), was seen by both Britain and Iran as a direct threat to the Strait of Hormuz through which some seventy per cent of the West's oil imports passed at the time. By 1971 Britain had completed its military withdrawal from the Persian Gulf, enabling Bahrain, Qatar and the United Arab Emirates to become independent. Meanwhile, the obscurantist Sultan Sa'id ben Teymur of Oman had also been overthrown by a *coup d'état* organized by Britain in the name of the sultan's son, Qabas, who was quickly declared king. Oman's ability to fight a rebellion had been badly impaired by years of misrule as well as a civil war in the Jabal Akhdar region. That civil war had been brought to an end after the rebel leader Ghalib Ben Ali, who claimed the right to rule the country in his capacity as the Imam of the Ibadhi Muslim sect, fled to Saudi Arabia.

With Qabus duly installed as sultan, the British began reorganizing the Omani army and also called on Iran to help. The shah dispatched a task force of 6,000 men complete with an impressive arsenal of American-made weapons. The Dhofar rebellion was finally crushed in 1976 and the shah, for a while, toyed with the idea of an Irano-Omani campaign against South Yemen itself. But this came to nothing after Britain opposed it.

Iran became involved in another campaign to roll back Soviet influence in the region. From 1970 onwards, Iran began to train, finance and arm Iraqi Kurdish insurgents led by Mullah Mostafa Barzani. Both Israel and the United States also participated in the scheme whose principal aim was to destabilize and then overthrow the Ba'athist regime in Baghdad. Iran exerted a more direct pressure on Iraq by cancelling the 1936 treaty that defined their respective rights in the Shatt al-Arab border waterway. The Iranian navy began escorting ships in the Shatt and Iran's ground forces captured a number of strategic hills previously allocated to Iraq by British forces in 1941. A little publicized but no less deadly border war continued between the two neighbours until 1975. The pressure exerted by Iran pushed the Ba'ath regime closer to Moscow. In 1971 Iraq offered naval facilities to the USSR and Soviet ships became frequent visitors to the Iraqi port of Um al-Qasr at the head of the Gulf. A year later Iraq and the Soviet Union signed a treaty of friendship and co-operation which was rumoured to have secret clauses providing for direct Soviet military aid in case Iraqi territory was invaded, presumably by Iran.

The complex power game played by more than a dozen regional and outside powers in the Middle East found its most complete and one of its deadliest manifestations in Lebanon. The smallest of all the Middle Eastern states in terms of territory, Lebanon is a veritable mosaic of peoples, religions and secular ideologies. No census has been taken in the country since the 1930s but estimates showed that nearly forty per cent of a total population of around three million in 1975 were Christians, with the Maronites accounting for more than two-thirds of that number. The Muslim community was divided between shi'ites (forty per cent of the total population) and sunnis (fifteen per cent). The Druzes, an esoteric sect with a mixed faith in which elements from Islamic doctrine are mixed with Zoroastrian beliefs and Hindu traditions, accounted for the remaining five per cent of the population.

Lebanon's already tangled ethnic and sectarian set-up was further complicated by the presence of numerous political parties, armed groups and publishing companies financed by various powers ranging from Egypt and Israel to Syria, Iran and Iraq. Both superpowers were also present, either through their regional allies or the Lebanese politico-military groups. By the early 1970s the line-up of forces was more or less clear. The Druzes, although a feudal community ruled over by hereditary chiefs, had somehow established themselves as the vanguard of socialism in Lebanon and supported the interests of Syria and the USSR which financed and armed them. The Maronites had forged a discreet but wide-ranging relationship with Israel, largely through the influential Gemayel family, and with Iran through the Chamoun clan. In a broader sense they also maintained close ties with France and the United States. The shi'ites were largely financed and controlled by Iran and, to a lesser extent, by Israel. Sunni Muslims looked to Egypt for leadership but accepted financial support from a wide variety of other sources including Saudi Arabia, Iraq, Kuwait and Libya. The only non-sectarian political grouping in the country was the Lebanese Communist Party, a small but active pro-Soviet outfit.

The Lebanese state had weathered the storm of the 1958 civil war surprisingly well, largely thanks to the wisdom of President Fuad Chehab. But it was still in no position to exercise full control over the various sects or to defend the country against a major external attack. It devoted its energies to protecting the delicate balance of all the many different internal and external interests that made Lebanese politics a veritable minefield. That balance was shattered by the sudden eruption of the PLO which, chased out of Jordan, moved into Lebanon from Syria with a view to creating a state within the Lebanese state. A population base of some 150,000 Palestinian refugees, concentrated in camps where living conditions were poor to say the least, already awaited the PLO near Beirut and in parts of southern Lebanon. The PLO's move into Lebanon was at first strongly supported by Syria which hoped to use Arafat's organization as a Trojan horse. Under General Hafez al-Assad, who had come to power in a *coup d'état* in 1970, Syria became more determined in the pursuit of its long-cherished aim of annexing Lebanon.

The PLO, however, had no intention of playing Syria's game. Attracting financial aid from Saudi Arabia and other oil-rich states it also established its own direct line to Moscow, by-passing Damascus. By 1975 southern Lebanon, where shi'ites were in a majority, was under PLO control and generally referred to as 'Fatahland'. With more than 30,000 well-trained and heavily-armed troops, the PLO represented the strongest military force in Lebanon. It also enjoyed support from a variety of smaller armed groups recruited mostly among the sunnis and the Druzes. PLO camps around Beirut and in southern Lebanon became major centres for the training of Iranian, Turkish, Armenian and Lebanese shi'ite guerrillas and terrorists. The number of those trained by the

PLO in the 1970s was estimated to be more than 20,000.

The PLO used its positions in southern Lebanon for attacking Israel's northern districts. The Israelis retaliated both directly by attacking southern Lebanon and through client forces they set up with help from shi'ite and Maronite groups. In 1975 factional fighting that involved the PLO and other armed groups, notably the Maronite Kata'eb (Phalangist) party led by Pierre Gemayel and his son Bechir, degenerated into a series of full-scale battles accompanied by the massacre of civilian populations. In the summer of 1976 Syria, officially acting on behalf of the Arab League, dispatched troops to Lebanon to help restore order and discourage an Israeli intervention. The Lebanese civil war, however, was not halted and continued into the 1980s. Syria changed sides a number of times, alternating between its role as the protector of Lebanese Christendom and its declared responsibilities towards the PLO. Syrian troops were directly involved in the massacre of both Palestinians and Christians at different stages of the conflict in Lebanon.

While almost all other sects were drawn into the civil war in one way or another, the Lebanese shi'ites managed to stay out of the conflict. This was due to a decision by their new charismatic leader, Hojat al-Islam Muhammad Mussa Sadr, an Iranian mullah sent to Lebanon by the shah in the early 1960s to mobilize support for Tehran's policies. Sadr practised the shi'ite tactic of 'taqiah' (dissimulation) and spent the shah's money for his own purposes. In the late 1960s he took the title of Imam (Guide) and created the Movement of the Dispossessed which, in turn, developed into the Amal (Hope) Organization. Originally conceived as a charity outfit, Amal soon began recruiting and training an armed militia. By 1975 Sadr's break with Iranian security services had become final and he began receiving financial aid from Libya where an ebullient Colonel Muammar Gaddafy saw himself as true heir to Nasser's dream of pan-Arab unity.

The rise of the shi'ite power in southern Lebanon was strongly encouraged by Israel in the hope that Sadr's forces would not tolerate the PLO presence in their midst. Sadr's tactic of 'taqiah' encouraged the Israelis in their belief that the shi'ites would remain objective allies of the Jewish state. Nevertheless, Israel provided itself with a second insurance policy by creating the South Lebanon Army, a force of Christian and shi'ite mercenaries charged with the task of protecting a strand of territory that Israeli military commanders described as a 'security zone' along their northern border.

For its part, Syria consolidated its hold on northern Lebanon and the Bekaa Valley and also ensured the election of its own friends to almost all the key posts in a Lebanese state structure that gradually lost much of its authority. Under the successive presidencies of Suleiman Frangieh and Elias Sarkis the ghost that was left of the Lebanese state came to be considered as just another expression of Syrian domination. This encouraged the various ethnic and sectarian groups to strengthen their own structures of authority. The path was open for the *de facto* division of Lebanon into miniature states exercising authority in the name of this or that religion or political ideology. Lebanon, which had once boasted about its ability to offer a model of religious and ethnic harmony and won the title of 'the Switzerland of the Middle East', had by 1976 relapsed into the fragmented state that characterized it in medieval times.

The Lebanese civil war claimed more than 200,000 lives between 1975 and 1988. It also forced a further 800,000 people into exile, at times as far as Latin America. This meant that nearly a third of the country's population either died or emigrated as a direct result of political upheavals. Material damage done to the country was variously estimated at between $5,000 and $12,000 million as many parts of Beirut, once one of the most prosperous cities in the eastern Mediterranean, were destroyed in years of fighting. The war did not spare the countryside either and many Christian and Muslim villages were turned into rubble and their inhabitants massacred or expelled from their homes. An estimated

300,000 Lebanese, some ten per cent of the population, became refugees in their own country. Many of them shi'ites from the south, settled in the shanty towns near Beirut. It was in these shanty towns that the Hezb-Allah (Party of God) was born in 1980 with revolutionary mullahs sent from Tehran acting as midwives.

Between 1975 and 1988 Lebanon experienced the presence of Palestinian, Syrian, Israeli, Libyan and Iranian army units on its soil. American, French, British and Italian troops were also dispatched to Lebanon on peace-keeping missions in the mid-1980s but had to be withdrawn after their own safety could no longer be assured. Lebanon became both a prime target for terrorist attacks and the main centre for the training of terrorists in the Middle East.

9

THE JOURNEY TO JERUSALEM

In September 1970 when Muhammad Anwar Sadat was sworn in as President of Egypt few people expected him to remain in power for more than a few months. In his position as a largely ceremonial Vice President Sadat, who lacked a power base of his own, had been kept out of major decisions by the regime for a number of years. More importantly, he had no political contacts in Moscow at a time when Soviet influence played a crucial role in Egyptian politics. Also, Sadat gave the impression that he was not interested in supreme power.

Within a few months, however, Sadat had intervened with unexpected decisiveness in a power struggle from which he had been all but excluded by the military chiefs and the leaders of the Arab Socialist Union, the government party created by Nasser. Having already established discreet contacts with the United States, through Saudi Arabia and Iran, Sadat struck against the pro-Soviet faction in May 1971. All of Moscow's closest friends, notably Ali Sabri and Sha'arawi Gumm'ah, were arrested and accused of treason.

The Soviets reacted by pressuring Sadat to sign a treaty of friendship as a sign of his goodwill towards the Socialist bloc. Sadat, a pragmatist to a fault, signed the fifteen-year treaty and began to act as Moscow's most loyal ally within Egypt. This enabled him to purge the army and the civil service of pro-Soviet elements while broadening his own contacts with the United States.

Sadat knew that nothing but a war with Israel could consolidate his authority within Egypt and give him the popular base of support he needed for imposing major changes in his country's foreign and internal policies. From the end of 1971, and despite a reduction in Soviet arms supplies, he began to prepare for war. The two superpowers, however, appeared to be in a rare agreement over the need to avoid a new flare-up in the Middle East. During the Nixon-Brezhnev summit in Moscow in June 1972 the USA and the USSR even concluded an accord aimed at helping prevent an Arab-Israeli war. To Brezhnev *détente* was a more effective means of expanding Soviet influence in the region than would be a new military adventure by Egypt.

Less than a month later Sadat responded to the Nixon-Brezhnev accord by ordering the expulsion of nearly all of the 10,000 Soviet military advisers who had come to Egypt at the invitation of Nasser. Sadat also cancelled Russia's right to use military facilities on Egyptian soil. Sadat followed up his dramatic move by inviting the United States to help impose a negotiated settlement under which Israel would evacuate the Arab territories it occupied. The Israelis, however, saw Egypt's break with Moscow as a setback for Arab capability to wage war and became even more intransigent. Washington, for its part, felt that it had achieved the goal of eliminating Soviet influence in Egypt without the need for offering any concessions to Sadat.

The Egyptian leader became more than ever convinced that only a war could break the log jam by forcing the United States to pressure Israel into meaningful negotiations. Sadat's own political survival depended on his ability to bring in some movement on the Arab-Israeli issue. He had received the sobriquet of 'the man who could do nothing' from many Egyptians and his authority was under heavy strain by the end of 1972. The war option, however, seemed suicidal. Egypt no longer had access to Soviet arms and material and Israel appeared militarily stronger than ever.

Nevertheless, by the summer of 1973 Sadat had put his

armed forces on a war footing. He did not aim at a decisive victory against Israel and was even prepared to accept a partial defeat. What mattered was for him to be able to show to his people that he had tried both diplomacy and war. The Egyptian forces attacked on 6 October 1973, in the midst of the Muslim fasting month of Ramadan and on the day the Jews were marking the Yom Kippur. Exactly at the same time, Syrian forces launched a series of attacks against Israeli positions in the Golan. As Egyptian forces crossed the Suez Canal and broke into Israel's famed Bar-Lev defensive line in the Sinai the myth of Israeli invincibility was badly shaken. The Israelis did better on the Golan front and destroyed large quantities of Syrian military hardware. This forced the Soviets to ferry fresh supplies to Damascus by air, using Iranian and Iraqi air spaces. Moscow also put three of its airborne divisions on full alert to discourage possible US intervention in support of Israel. The Soviets seemed anxious to associate themselves with what looked like the first ever Arab military success against Israel. At the same time, however, Brezhnev advised Sadat to accept a quick cease-fire lest the tide of war turn in favour of the Israelis. Sadat, now buoyed by the enthusiastic support his action had received from almost all Arab countries, decided to press on.

Six days after the start of hostilities, the Israeli prime minister Golda Meir telephoned Nixon to tell him that Israel felt its very existence threatened and would, therefore, feel free to use whatever means it deemed necessary to repulse the Arabs. This was interpreted by analysts in Washington as a threat to use nuclear weapons. Israel was known to have developed a nuclear capacity at Dimonah in the Negev desert with initial help received from France in the 1950s. The Americans counselled restraint and speeded up their weapons shipments to Israel. By October 15 the tide of the war had turned against Egypt. In a flanking operation led by General Ariel Sharon, the Israelis crossed to the west bank of the Suez Canal and began isolating the Egyptian forces in the Sinai. The Israelis gained control of part of the north-south highway at a distance of less than sixty miles from Cairo. On the Syrian front, Damascus itself was now within reach of Israel's advance artillery. Sadat felt that he had no choice but to accept a new cease-fire.

On 22 October the UN Security Council adopted resolutions 338 which called for an end to hostilities. Sadat accepted the resolution immediately but Israel, now dreaming of total victory, rejected both resolutions 338 and 339 which had been passed two days later. Sharon's forces poised themselves for action aimed at destroying Egypt's Third Army Corps in the Sinai. Sadat appealed to both Washington and Moscow to restrain Israel and impose a cease-fire. Moscow responded by putting all its airborne divisions, as well as some naval units, on full alert. The United States reacted with a global alert of its own forces. But both Moscow and Washington knew that neither wanted a global confrontation. The idea was to reassure both Egypt and Israel so that hostilities could be ended.

On 25 October Moscow and Washington agreed on the formation of a United Nations peace-keeping force to separate the belligerents and monitor a cease-fire. The Israelis were, in effect, forced to withdraw from the west bank of the Suez Canal and accept territorial losses to Egypt. With both banks of Suez now controlled by Egyptian forces Sadat was able to order the reopening of the canal for the first time since 1967. An armistice was signed between Egypt and Israel on 11 November 1973. Syria, however, refused to sign a truce and continued to fight, without much success, for several more weeks. Although Syria suffered very high losses, its intransigent attitude enhanced its image as the champion of Arab resistance against Israel.

The Yom Kippur, or Ramadan, War was accompanied by an unprecedented show of Arab unity most dramatically illustrated by the oil embargo imposed by seven oil-exporting Arab countries against the United States and Japan as well as a number of European states accused of supporting Israel. Non-Arab Iran, although a key member of the Organization of Oil Exporting Countries (OPEC), did not join the embargo but helped the Arab war effort by supplying Egypt with oil and non-military goods. Iran also loaned some of its transport aircraft to ferry men and arms from Saudi Arabia to Syria.

The oil weapon, used by the Arabs with dramatic effect, established OPEC as a power to reckon with. The embargo pushed oil prices through the roof and forced the West to look for alternative sources of energy. The shock of 1973 led to a steady decline in western dependence on Middle Eastern oil as new oilfields in north and south America and the North Sea became economically attractive. The mobilization of western financial and technological resources to make sure that there would be no repeat of the 1973 shock reduced the share of OPEC in the global oil trade by more than sixty per cent within the next twelve years.

The increase in the power of OPEC in 1973 meant that Saudi Arabia and Iran emerged as key players in the Middle East. That, in turn, meant a greater role for the United States which maintained special relations with both the shah and the Saudi ruling family. Seizing the opportunity provided by a combination of circumstances the US Secretary of State Henry Kissinger began to promote himself as the ideal mediator between Cairo and Jerusalem. Conscious that the Soviets could not be totally excluded from a peace process at that time, Kissinger agreed that the USA and the USSR should jointly chair an international conference in Geneva. The conference was convened in December. Egypt, Israel, Jordan, the United States and the Soviet Union were represented. Syria refused an invitation to attend and most Arab countries also adopted a hostile attitude.

The Geneva Conference, adjourned to allow for Israeli general elections to be completed, was never reconvened. Kissinger's appetite for influence in the region had sharply increased and he saw no reason why Moscow should be given any part of the credit for an eventual settlement in the Middle East. The Israelis were also anxious to work their way out of

Geneva where they felt surrounded by too many enemies. Early in 1974 Israel suggested that Kissinger act as sole mediator between itself and Egypt. The American secretary of state was more than elated. Egypt also agreed and thus became a party to what was, at least in part, an anti-Soviet move. Sadat was now committed to a peace process. The Israel–Egypt disengagement agreement was signed on 18 January and seen as a triumph for American diplomacy. Kissinger then offered his 'shuttle' diplomacy to Syria also and succeeded in negotiating a disengagement accord between the Syrians and the Israelis four months later. Attempts at working out a similar accord between Israel and Jordan failed because more and more Israelis began to call for an outright annexation of the occupied West Bank which they called 'Judea' and 'Samaria'.

Once again the Arab world was divided. Radical Arab regimes such as Syria, Iraq, Libya, Algeria and South Yemen formed various groupings under different names such as 'the rejection front' and 'the resistance bloc'. They preached a new war aimed at liberating Arab lands occupied by Israel. But their rhetoric was not matched by action. In the autumn of 1974 an Arab summit at Rabat designated the PLO as the sole legitimate representative of the Palestinian people. This was a major victory for Arafat and a setback for King Hussein. Arafat seized the occasion for reminding the world that the PLO remained dedicated to the destruction of Israel and its replacement by a Palestinian state in which Jews would be able to live as citizens with full rights.

Egypt continued to foster closer ties with Washington throughout 1975. Kissinger convinced Sadat that Washington would be a more profitable ally for Egypt than Moscow had ever been. He persuaded the Israelis to agree to the creation of a new no-man's-land east of the Suez Canal and to give up the strategic Mitla and Gidi passes in the Sinai. The rich oilfields at Abu-Rudais were also handed back to Egypt. In exchange, Kissinger assured the Israelis that they would not be attacked again by Egypt and that the United States would also counter any Soviet military moves against Israel. Egypt's full entry into the American camp came in the spring of 1976 when Sadat formally abrogated the Soviet-Egyptian treaty of 1971. Washington welcomed Sadat's move by announcing it would resume selling arms to Egypt again after a lapse of some twenty-five years. American economic and technical assistance to Egypt was also resumed.

The US presidential election in 1976 resulted in victory for the Democratic party candidate Jimmy Carter. This meant that Kissinger would no longer be able to pursue his step-by-step plan for creating a formal peace agreement between Egypt and Israel. The new American administration did not believe in patient and secret diplomacy and favoured a broader framework for talks that would also include the Palestinians. The net effect of Carter's policy was that the whole peace process came to a halt. Israel had moved sharply to the right and was more reluctant than ever to talk to the Palestinians or get involved in Geneva-style negotiations. The disarray caused in Washington's policy in the Middle East was exploited by hardline Arab states which began to pressure Sadat to join the so-called 'rejection front'.

Sadat, however, was determined to seek peace with Israel in the best interests of Egypt even if that meant sacrificing Palestinian and pan-Arab goals in the region. Sadat, who described himself as Egyptian, Muslim and Arab in that order, had changed his country's official name from the United Arab Republic back to Egypt and all but abandoned Nasser's pan-Arab dreams. In September and October of 1977 Sadat, using the services of discreet emissaries, asked the Israelis whether they would be prepared for direct talks with Egypt. The answer was positive and in November Sadat told an astonished world that he planned to travel to Jerusalem to address the Israeli parliament and negotiate peace with government leaders there. The fact that the Israeli government was at the time headed by Menachem Begin, a former leader of the Zionist terror groups in

Palestine and considered by many Arabs as 'enemy number one', did not seem to deter Sadat.

Begin looked like the last person likely to become a peacemaker. His entire political career had been built on his preaching of war against the Arab 'enemies' who would understand nothing better than the language of force. Begin also sympathized with the partisans of the 'Greater Israel' who dreamed of a Jewish state extending from the Euphrates to the Nile. But more than anything else Begin was a shrewd and realistic politician. He knew that his wafer-thin majority in the Knesset would not allow him the freedom to pursue a warlike policy towards the Arabs. He was also anxious to bury the Geneva talks for ever. Making a separate peace with Egypt would also make it impossible for other Arab countries to launch a new war against Israel. Sadat visited Jerusalem at the invitation of Begin and the two men quickly established a personal relationship that helped the peace momentum.

Sadat's dramatic move left the Carter administration with little choice but to abandon its own unrealistic plans and offer to act as mediator in direct Egyptian-Israeli peace talks. In September 1978 Sadat and Begin joined Carter at his presidential weekend home at Camp David and agreed to a series of accords leading to Israeli withdrawal from the Sinai in exchange for full diplomatic recognition by Egypt and the signing of a general peace treaty between the two countries. Israel also received the right to use the Suez Canal and the Strait of Tiran. The Palestinian issue which had for years been at the centre of Egyptian-Israeli conflict was treated as secondary in the Camp David accords. The two sides agreed to continue the peace process with the aim of providing limited self-rule for Palestinians in the West Bank and the Gaza Strip. But all along it was clear that Begin had no intention of relinquishing control over the occupied Arab territories outside the Sinai.

One direct result of Sadat's decision to seek a separate peace with Begin was the intensification of PLO attacks on Israel through Lebanon. One such particularly bloody attack on the Israeli settlement of Kriyat Shemonah gave Begin the excuse he needed for invading southern Lebanon in the spring of 1978. This was the first time that Israeli and PLO forces faced each other on the battlefields of regular warfare. The Israelis emerged victorious and left Lebanon in June. But the PLO had in the meantime established its credentials as a determined fighting force. Guerrilla operations by the PLO and diplomatic pressures by the 'rejection front' countries, however, did not prevent the signing of the Egypt–Israel peace treaty on 26 March 1979 by Sadat and Begin in the presence of Carter. The American president smiled upon what many saw as his only major foreign policy success.

Begin interpreted the Camp David accords to mean that Israel had the right to dictate the terms of a series of separate peace treaties to its other Arab neighbours. In 1981 he announced the formal annexation of the Golan Heights, giving it the same status as East Jerusalem which had also been incorporated into the Jewish state and described as 'non-negotiable'. The move made it virtually impossible for any Syrian regime to contemplate a peace settlement with Israel. Begin also encouraged the multiplication of Jewish settlements in the West Bank in an attempt at altering the demographic situation there.

Sadat, who had won the admiration of his people in war, became an object of intense hatred in Egypt as a result of his separate peace with Israel. Numerous Muslim fundamentalist and radical Arab leaders openly called for Sadat's assassination as an 'enemy of Islam and of Arabism'. Their wish was fulfilled in October 1981 when fundamentalist commandos led by Lieutenant Khaled Ahmad Showqi al-Islambouli opened fire on the rais as he sat watching a military parade. The funeral ceremony organized for the murdered president became a purely official event in contrast with Nasser's funeral a decade earlier. Then the Egyptian people had poured into the street to a man to mourn their rais. Now they mostly stayed home and greeted Sadat's brutal murder either with indifference or with ill-disguised joy. Nasser had been the architect of the most disastrous military defeat in Egyptian history. Sadat, on the other hand, had given the Arabs their first and only military triumph in more than 500 years. Nasser's funeral had been attended by all Arab leaders and most of the Muslim heads of state. At Sadat's funeral, however, Menachem Begin occupied the stage front. Not a single Arab head of state was present and many Muslim countries did not even send representatives.

Israel's decision to formally annex East Jerusalem in 1980 seemed to endorse the view of those who believed that the Zionists were enemies of Islam as a whole and that the struggle against them should be recognized as a pan-Islamic cause. That view had lost one of its principal advocates in the person of King Faisal Ibn Abdul-Aziz of Saudi Arabia who was assassinated by one of his own cousins in 1975. But by 1980 even secular Turkey was prepared to support the idea of a pan-Islamic 'Jerusalem Committee' charged with the task of ensuring an end to the Israeli occupation of the holy city. Morocco's King Hassan II became head of the committee which remained largely inactive. The king's close but secret relations with various Israeli leaders, notably Shimon Peres, made it virtually impossible for Morocco to adopt a radical policy on the issue. Nevertheless, the annexation of Jerusalem gave the Arab-Israeli conflict a new and sharpened religious edge and helped Muslim fundamentalists single out the Jewish state as the principal enemy of all Islam in the region.

Sadat's murder gave the radical Arabs a fleeting moment of hope that the new Egyptian leader, Muhammad Hosni Mubarak, might seek to modify at least part of the Camp David accords and bring Egypt back into the Arab fold. Syrian president Hafez al-Assad even went out of his way to describe Mubarak as 'my heroic brother'. But Mubarak continued to apply Sadat's foreign policy without any significant change. Peace with Israel and increasingly closer ties with the United States remained the two pillars of Egyptian foreign policy.

With peace with Egypt assured Israel turned its attention to Lebanon where the PLO was growing as a long-term military threat. In 1981 the Israelis bombarded the PLO's headquarters in Beirut in the hope of killing Yasser Arafat. This was Israel's second attempt at eliminating Arafat in Beirut. In 1973 an Israeli commando unit had been dispatched to the Lebanese capital with orders to murder as many PLO leaders as possible. The attackers killed several Palestinian leaders, including three of Arafat's most senior associates. But the PLO Chairman, absent from his headquarters at the time of the attack, was not hurt.

In 1982 the Israelis decided to engage the PLO in a decisive battle in Lebanon. A large Israeli task force entered southern Lebanon and began moving towards Beirut. The PLO and its local allies were outgunned and outnumbered and forced to retreat. The Israelis also took on the Syrians positioned in the Bekaa Valley and used the opportunity for destroying the network of anti-aircraft missiles that Syria had installed against possible Israeli air raids on Damascus. Syria also lost nearly two-thirds of the new fighter-bombers it had acquired from the Soviet Union.

The Israeli forces had at first been greeted as liberators by some shi'ite elements in southern Lebanon. The PLO had become unpopular among the shi'ites who resented the arrogance of Arafat's men and their leftist ideologies. But the atrocities committed by the invading forces and their mercenary Christian allies under one Major Sa'ad Haddad, quickly altered Israel's image in southern Lebanon. The Israelis were in close contact with Bechir Gemayel's Phalangist militia and seemed to want to help the Maronite minority reassert its political domination in Lebanon.

Despite pressure by the United States which was concerned about the dangers of a wider conflagration, the Israelis finally entered Beirut and forced the PLO to withdraw from Lebanon. But before that process was completed the invading army of General Ariel Sharon allowed a group of Maronite gunmen, led by the leader of the Force Libanaise,

Elie Hobeika, to enter the Sabra and Shattila refugee camps in the suburbs of Beirut. Hobeika's gunmen organized a veritable massacre of the Palestinian women and children who had been left behind in the camps. An estimated 1,300 people were murdered in the most atrocious manner as the Israeli army watched from a safe distance. Reports of the incidents sent shock waves throughout Israel and dealt a serious blow to Begin's stature as a national leader. A commission of enquiry was created and soon provided a full and factual report on the tragedy.

As Lebanon tottered on the brink, a multi-national force of American, French, Italian and British soldiers was invited by what was left of the Lebanese government to help restore peace and ensure a full Israeli withdrawal. The force was seen by militant Muslim groups in Lebanon as an objective ally of the Christian minority. The election of Bechir Gemayel as president of Lebanon under questionable circumstances convinced the Muslims that Israel, supported by the western powers, wished to turn the country into an Israeli protector-ate under Phalangist domination. The haste with which Gemayel signed a 'peace treaty' with Israel confirmed Muslim suspicions. Syria, which had succeeded in maintaining troops in northern Lebanon, emerged as a powerful ally of the Muslims. Revolutionary Iran also began helping radical Muslim groups by sending money and arms and training shi'ite fighters in special camps both inside Iran itself and in Lebanon.

By 1983 the Hezb-Allah, using a variety of labels such as 'Islamic Jihad', 'Revolutionary Justice Organization' and 'The Mobilization of the Downtrodden', had established itself as a new force on the Lebanese scene. Using the shi'ite tactic of 'leading from behind', the partisans of Allah hid behind the outwardly moderate Amal Organization led by the pro-Syrian lawyer Nabih Berri. Slowly, Amal was turned into an empty shell which served as a cover for the activities of Hezb-Allah.

For a while Syria found Hezb-Allah's activities to its own

advantage. And it was joint action by Hezb-Allah suicide units and Syrian secret services that led to a number of spectacular terrorist attacks on American, French and British positions in Beirut. Israeli positions and military convoys in southern Lebanon were also attacked by suicide squads that at times included teenage girls. In two dramatic attacks on buildings used as dormitories by French and American troops near Beirut, shi'ite terror squads killed more than 300 marines and paratroops on 23 October 1983.

The American and French soldiers became targets in part because of deteriorating relations between Tehran on the one hand and Washington and Paris on the other. But local politics also played a role. The shi'ites believed that the western powers would use their military presence to help the Phalangists come out on top in a civil war that had continued for more than eight years. The murder of Bechir Gemayel, no doubt organized by Syrian secret services with help from some of the Phalangist leaders' Christian enemies, had not halted the Maronites' attempts at expanding their zone of influence. Amin Gemayel, Bechir's elder brother, had been quickly installed as the new President of Lebanon while Phalangists established offices and arms caches in Muslim-dominated West Beirut.

By the summer of 1983 the Lebanese civil war had begun a new and far more violent phase which the western powers neither understood nor could come to grips with. The fighting involved the Lebanese regular army, the Phalangists, Amal, Hezb-Allah, the Druze and a variety of other, mostly sunni or Christian, armed bands. Shi'ite forces succeeded in gaining control of southern Beirut and the areas adjacent to the international airport. This put them in a strategic position which they later used for establishing their domination of West Beirut as well. The eastern districts of the city, mainly inhabited by Christians, remained under the control of Maronite forces. The western soldiers present in Beirut were gradually sucked into the conflict and sustained several casualties.

In September 1983 the Israelis withdrew from the Shouf mountains near Beirut, thus signalling new clashes between Druze and Christian forces. The Druze, backed by Syria, scored a series of victories against the Maronites and began to threaten the predominantly Christian town of Souk al-Gharb. It was then that the US mediator Robert MacFarlane persuaded Washington that American naval and ground fire should be used in support of the Christian-led Lebanese Army. The United States became a party to the Lebanese civil war and American marines came to be considered legitimate targets for Muslim and Druze attacks. The Soviet Union, for its part, increased its financial and material support for the Druzes and some of the Muslim militias through Syria. The rivalry between the two superpowers assumed the form of sectarian killings in Lebanese villages and the slums of Beirut.

The Israeli withdrawal from Lebanon was completed by 1985. This was partly prompted by high casualties inflicted on the Israelis by shi'ite suicide squads in southern Lebanon, an unexpected development that undermined the position of the war party inside Israel itself. The Israelis retained control of parts of southern Lebanon through their mercenary forces but failed to stop attacks on border settlements. The shi'ites took over from the PLO forces in southern Lebanon and continued the harassment of Israeli settlements across the border. From 1987 onwards the PLO succeeded in restoring part of its presence in what had once been the 'Fatahland', forcing the Israelis to intervene frequently in southern Lebanon to save the South Lebanon Army from annihilation by combined Palestinian and Hezb-Allah forces.

Israel's Lebanese adventure proved the costliest of all its military conflicts with the Arabs. Yet it produced no lasting results. The issue of an eventual state for the Palestinians remained unsolved and Israel's allies inside Lebanon could not protect the gains made on their behalf by the Tsahal (the Israeli army). Even the so-called 'peace accord' never became more than a piece of paper. Amin Gemayel was forced to formally abrogate it as a condition for his own continued presence in the isolated presidential palace at Babdah.

Sadat's dramatic visit to Jerusalem, the Camp David accords and the war in Lebanon all dealt serious blows to the idea of Arab unity. The 1980s developed into a decade of brutal realism for Arab leaders, with each trying to protect his own country's narrow interests to the detriment of the broader goals of Arabism that had once captured the imagination of the masses as well as the intelligentsia.

In some cases, this pursuit of national interests assumed an unusually brutal form. Syria, determined to establish itself as the paramount Arab power in the Levant, had no difficulty in changing allies when and if necessary. This Syrian attitude assumed horrific proportions in Lebanon where a group treated as friendly one day might well face massacre the next. Syria was above all anxious to dominate Lebanon and achieve hegemony over the Palestinian liberation movement. This latter objective made a confrontation with the PLO inevitable. Mobilizing support from some of its old clients within the PLO Syria began to campaign for the dismissal of Arafat as Chairman. The Syrian party was led by a former Arafat aide, Colonel Abu Mussa.

Arafat and the bulk of the PLO leadership were expelled from Damascus under particularly humiliating conditions. For a while Arafat, with his men scattered between North Yemen and Tunisia, looked like a spent force. But the PLO had vast financial resources at its disposal and continued to enjoy support from conservative Arab states. Arafat, establishing new headquarters in Tunis, survived and gradually moved closer to Egypt in a bid to counter-balance Syria. More importantly, he succeeded in remaining on good terms with the USSR which continued as Syria's principal supporter throughout the 1980s. Syria failed to monopolize the Palestinian card and in 1988 President Assad played host to Arafat in Damascus. The two men posted an appearance of unity but remained enemies. Sporadic fighting between pro-

Arafat and pro-Assad Palestinians continued in Lebanon and claimed far more casualties than were caused by Israeli operations against the PLO.

Syria also maintained a close alliance with revolutionary Iran which became involved in a war with Iraq from 1980 onwards. The Syrians argued that it was unwise for the Arabs to break totally with one of the two principal non-Arab but Muslim countries of the region and condemned Iraq for having started the war. In exchange, Syria received more than $4,000 million from Iran in the form of cash gifts and cut-price crude oil between 1980 and 1988.

Egypt developed its economic and military relations with the United States throughout the 1980s and came to represent a major American asset in the global East-West rivalry. In 1988 all Arab countries, with the exception of Libya and Syria, restored full diplomatic ties with Egypt. The country's boycott by Arabs was at an end and Egypt also regained its full membership of the Islamic Conference. The Arab change of heart towards Egypt was partly dictated by the fear of Iran; only Egypt was powerful enough to counter-balance the pressure exerted by the Iranian revolution on the Persian Gulf and beyond. Egypt, nevertheless, played a very cautious hand and maintained a low profile both on the subject of the confrontation with Iran and the Palestinian issue.

Egypt's low profile, Syria's involvement in Lebanon and alliance with Iran, Libya's lack of population resources and Iraq's entanglement in a seemingly endless war meant that all the usual candidates for pan-Arab leadership were kept out of the race. That left the field wide open for Saudi Arabia. But the traditional Saudi fear of being found under the limelight prevented the kingdom from exploiting the new situation to its own advantage. To be sure Riyadh played an active role in the creation of the Gulf Co-operation Council (GCC) which grouped together all the Arab states of the Persian Gulf with the exception of Iraq. But the GCC did not become a political alliance and its various members pursued their own, at times contradictory, policies vis-à-vis Iran and Iraq. The GCC achieved a measure of economic and technical success, however, indicating that it was in those domains, rather than the risk-ridden field of politics, that the best chances for Arab co-operation might be sought.

10

THE CHALLENGE OF ISLAM

Throughout the 1970s Iran and Turkey faced a serious threat from urban and rural guerrilla organizations determined to overthrow the established order by force. Most of these organizations described themselves as Marxist-Leninist and based their strategies for the conquest of power on the theories of the Chinese Communist leader Mao Zedoung. They recruited their first members among Iranian students and Turkish workers in Western Europe during the 1960s. China, North Korea, Cuba and, from 1970 onwards, South Yemen and Albania provided training facilities, ideological guidance and money. After 1973 the PLO, based on southern Lebanon, also began training and arming Turkish and Iranian guerrillas.

Solidly allied to the West, both Turkey and Iran believed that the new guerrilla movement launched against them was inspired by the Soviet Union as part of its traditional expansionist policies *vis-à-vis* its neighbours. Neither the Shah of Iran nor the Turkish leaders would consider the possibility of destabilization caused by anything except big power conspiracies. And in the 1970s the big power believed to have an interest in fomenting trouble was none other than the USSR.

Initially, Iran's reaction to the guerrilla challenge was far more energetic, even bordering on paranoia. The shah saw the slightest expression of dissent as a mortal danger for the survival of his regime. Iran had entered the 1970s with a buoyant economy which was soon further boosted by quadrupling of oil prices. The shah's regime, which had beaten off a challenge by the mullahs in 1963–4, enjoyed a certain measure of popularity because of its policy of reforms and economic liberalism which offered opportunities for individual self-enrichment. Nevertheless, this was a politically isolated regime. Its basic domestic and foreign policy options were not shared by the mass of the people – partly because they were never clearly formulated and explained. Even the growing middle class, which owed its existence and prosperity to the regime, did not feel itself politically committed to the shah.

The shah's aggressive foreign policy, meanwhile, meant a gradual cooling of relations with the USSR and its regional allies. Iran was involved in a virtual war against Iraq, one of Moscow's closest allies in the Middle East, between 1970 and 1975. At the same time Iranian forces intervened in Oman to beat back a rebellion sponsored by South Yemen, another of Moscow's allies. Iran's support for Pakistan antagonized India, also an ally of the Soviets, while the shah pursued a high profile policy in many parts of Africa, notably the Horn, where Moscow was seeking to consolidate its own gains. The 1973 *coup d'état* that overthrew the monarchy in Afghanistan was seen by the shah as a Soviet move. Mohammad Daoud Khan, the new ruler of Afghanistan, had cultivated his own image of 'a progressive' leader opposed to a pro-American and 'feudalistic' king.

The shah minimized the importance of Iran's deep-rooted and genuine problems with both Iraq and Afghanistan and exaggerated Soviet influence in Baghdad and Kabul. As a result he began to see himself as the target for a vast Soviet conspiracy in which the urban guerrillas had the task of applying internal pressure in harmony with the pressure applied by Soviet allies from the outside.

The real opposition to the shah's regime, however, came neither from the urban guerrillas nor from the Soviet Union and its allies. This fact was more than established by 1976. Iran ended its war with Iraq and the two countries began acting as the closest of friends. In Kabul, the Daoud regime had been brought under strong Iranian influence as early as 1974. And by 1976 it was beginning to look like a threat to the Soviets. Moscow had always regarded Afghanistan as something of a glacis in its strategic plans. The prospect of Daoud leaning towards the West appeared to be a departure from Afghanistan's traditional neutrality. In 1977 the Soviets reacted by helping overthrow Daoud in a bloody *coup d'état* which brought the Communist People's (Khalq) Party to power under Nur-Muhammad Taraki. But even Taraki and his successors were not in a position to threaten Iran's stability in any way.

The urban guerrilla groups, for their part, were all but crushed by 1976 after having killed some 300 people and lost a further 200 of their own members in clashes with the security forces led by SAVAK, the shah's political police. The guerrillas hit the headlines with a number of spectacular acts including the murder of five American military officers seconded to the Iranian forces. But their main achievement was the hardening of the regime's attitude towards all forms of dissent. In 1975 the shah dissolved all political parties and ordered the creation of Rastakhiz (Resurgence) as the nation's sole legal political movement. SAVAK crackdown against the media, trade unions, student organizations and other possible forums of dissent also intensified. The number of political prisoners jumped from under 400 in 1970 to more than 3,000 in 1976. The main victims of the new repression were the middle class groups who, in ordinary logic, should have been considered as the shah's natural constituency. Only one forum remained available to those who did not wish to endorse the shah's policies one hundred per cent. That forum was the shi'ite mosque which had never fully accepted the legitimacy of the secular power in place.

The mullahs, estimated to number more than 80,000 in 1977, dominated a unique nationwide network of associations, charities, religious schools, interest-free banks, guilds, fraternities and endowments that amounted to a state within the state. Every year, during the mourning month of Muharram when shi'ites mark the martyrdom of their third Imam, Hussein, in the seventh century, the mullahs mobilized millions of believers especially in Tehran and other major cities. Their main base of support was provided by the traditional bazaar shopkeepers, the lumpen elements of the shanty towns, ruined peasants come to town and sections of the urban working class. The new repressive policy imposed by SAVAK from 1970 onwards forced many students and other members of the intelligentsia towards the mosque as a line of defence against absolutism.

The mullahs had their own quarrels with the shah's regime. Basing themselves on a strict interpretation of the shi'ite doctrine, many mullahs believed that only the clergy had a divine right to rule the country. A compromise had been worked out in 1906 under which the monarchist constitution, which envisaged parliamentary rule, recognized the authority of the mosque by providing for the formation of a council of five mullahs with the right to veto all legislation they saw as un-Islamic. The council, however, was never formed and under the shah the parliament itself was reduced to a mainly ceremonial role.

After 1906 the mullahs never succeeded in dominating the Iranian political scene although they remained major actors. In the 1940s and 1950s they organized assassination squads, known as Fedayeen of Islam, mainly to combat communism and exert pressure on the government of the day. In the early 1960s they tried to stop the shah's reform plans which included a land reform, legal equality for women in certain fields and plans to replace all religious schools by secular ones. Led by one Ruhollah Khomeini, then a middle-ranking mullah, the clergy provoked a series of bloody riots but failed to attract genuine popular support.

Khomeini was forced into exile, first to Turkey and then to Iraq in 1965 where he built up his religious authority and achieved the title of grand ayatollah. By 1977 he was recognized as number five on a list of six grand ayatollahs who formed the highest echelon of shi'ite leadership. It was in his capacity as a 'marja'a taqleed' (source of imitation) that Khomeini issued an edict that declared the shah's regime to be 'illegitimate' and the monarch himself an 'enemy of Allah'. The ayatollah also invited all opponents of the shah to unite under the banner of the clergy in order to replace the monarchy with an 'Islamic government'.

Khomeini's courage and resolution was in sharp contrast with the quietism of the other grand ayatollahs who had all tacitly accepted the separation of the mosque and the state as inevitable in modern times. Few mullahs could support the shah. The monarch and his father before him had done much to diminish the influence of the ulema and to secularize the state. The forcible abolition of the veil, the creation of a secular judiciary, the seizure of land owned by mullahs and religious endowments, the banning of polygamy and the recognition of the right of divorce for women were but some measures taken by the two Pahlavi shahs in defiance of strict Islamic rules.

Khomeini knew that fighting the shah on issues that interested the mullahs only could not mobilize the mass support needed for counterbalancing the armed forces which remained loyal to the regime. Accordingly, he abandoned some of his extremist slogans of the 1960s and began to address the people as a political rather than exclusively religious leader. The presence of a number of Americans of Iranian origin among Khomeini's closest aides in exile was interpreted by the shah as a sign that the new administration of President Jimmy Carter in Washington was encouraging opposition elements. Carter's campaign theme of human rights had already persuaded the shah that the Democrat president would not look upon Iran's authoritarian system of rule with the same degree of understanding as had been the case with Presidents Richard Nixon and Gerald Ford.

The shah's various opponents shared that view and

persuaded themselves that Carter would somehow help them get at least a share of power in Tehran. They saw the shah's decision to 'liberalize' certain aspects of his rule in 1977 as a direct result of pressure from Washington. Under his new 'liberalization' policy the shah offered concessions to his opponents and, instead, jailed some of his former ministers after having accused them of corruption and mismanagement. Suffering from cancer and told by his doctors that he would not have long to live, the shah sought to placate his enemies in the hope of preparing the way for a smooth transfer of power to his son, Reza, then aged only seventeen.

Meanwhile, Iran had entered a period of economic crisis provoked by an inflationary spiral which had itself resulted from the sharp increase in oil revenues. By 1977 the gap between the country's achievement in real terms and the expectations aroused among the masses had become so wide that some form of political unrest seemed inevitable. Had the country possessed normal channels for the expression of political and economic grievances the whole situation might have remained under control within the institutions of the regime. In pluralist societies differences of opinion and clashes of interests lead to the emergence of political parties. In societies living under a single, centrally imposed ideology, no matter of what type, dissent is bound to assume a religious aspect and often seeks its expression in sectarian militancy.

The spark that set off the fire of revolution in Iran was provided by a fake letter published by *Ettelaat*, a Tehran daily with close links with the royal court, in January 1978. In that letter the anonymous writer accused Khomeini of being a British agent of Indian origin as well as an alcoholic and a pederast. The form and substance of the letter scandalized almost everyone, including those mullahs who had no love for Khomeini. The publication of the letter led to a demonstration in the holy city of Qom where pro-Khomeini mullahs tried to seize a police station. In the clashes that ensued several people were killed. This became a signal for nation-wide mourning ceremonies marking the seventh day and then the fortieth day of the Qom incident. Each of the new ceremonies led to clashes between the police and the demonstrators which often produced new 'martyrs of Islam'. Thus the circle of mourning ceremonies remained unbroken until the fall of the shah's regime on 11 February 1979.

The regime's inability to mobilize its own supporters combined with the shah's lack of resolve led to a rapid decline in the authority of the state throughout 1978. Khomeini, expelled from Iraq in the autumn of 1978, moved to Paris where he quickly established himself as the supreme guide of the anti-shah movement. The ayatollah missed no opportunity for emphasizing the religious aspect of the revolt in Iran but remained suitably ambiguous on a number of issues that might have alienated the middle classes at home or the western powers interested in Iran. As mass demonstrations and strikes brought the country to a virtual standstill and continued to claim casualties, a desperate shah began to think of nothing but leaving the country. Rejecting the advice of his more hawkish aides he refused to provoke a bloodbath and flew into exile on 16 January 1979. Two weeks later Khomeini flew into Tehran and within ten days was the master of the country. He ordered a series of executions and mass arrests and turned Iran into an Islamic Republic within three months of having seized power.

The Carter administration, always several steps behind the events in Iran, completely misunderstood the nature of the anti-shah revolt and the true intentions of its leadership. Intoxicated with its own propaganda about human rights, the administration assumed that any change of regime in so-called Third World countries would necessarily be for the better. The 'dictators' would give their place to democratic groups who would respect human rights in countries as different one from the other as Iran and Nicaragua. Accordingly, Khomeini was described by some of Carter's advisers as a saintly man who would retire into his prayers once he had chased away the 'tyrant'. The road would then be open for pro-American liberals to form a government in Iran.

Between 1978 and 1979 the Carter administration tried to support a variety of 'liberals' ranging from Shapour Bakhtiar, who served as prime minister in the last five weeks of the shah's regime, to Mehdi Bazargan who was appointed premier by Khomeini and used as a front man to reassure the middle classes.

The mullahs interpreted Carter's constant search for 'liberals' and 'moderates' within a manifestly illiberal and extremist revolutionary movement as a sign of American unwillingness to recognize the emergence of the shi'ite clergy as the new rulers of Iran. They soon began to suspect the USA of plotting to deprive them of the fruits of their victory and to help restore American influence in Iran in a new form. The fact that Bazargan's cabinet included five naturalized Americans of Iranian origin appeared to confirm that view. The more radical mullahs, encouraged by the pro-Soviet Tudeh Party, which resumed legal activity after forty years of clandestinity, began to speak about the need for a 'second revolution' that would aim at rooting out American influence in Iran.

The signal for the 'second revolution' was given by a group of militant youths, who described themselves as 'Muslim Students Following the Imam's Line', when they stormed the American embassy in Tehran and ended up by holding fifty-three US diplomats hostage. The crisis led to a formal rupture of diplomatic relations between Tehran and Washington and a freezing of Iranian assets, estimated at over $14,000 million, in US banks. The Carter administration, still unable to read signals from revolutionary Iran, tried a variety of contradictory policies that included a military rescue mission in April 1980. The mission came to grief because of technical problems caused by a sandstorm in the Iranian desert.

The attack on the embassy, on 4 November 1979, had come in response to Carter's decision to allow the ailing shah to enter a New York hospital for urgent treatment. The shah was forced to leave the United States and, after a brief and unpleasant stay in Panama where the local dictator, General

Omar Torrijos, wanted to hand him over to Iran in exchange for money, ended up in Egypt. The shah died in July 1980 but the hostage crisis continued until January 1981. The hostages were released minutes after the newly-elected President Ronald Reagan had been sworn in at a Washington ceremony. The crisis had in the meantime enabled the mullahs to bring down the government of Mehdi Bazargan and to consolidate their own hold on power.

In 1981 the mullahs had to face a serious challenge from a leftist Islamic urban guerrilla group known as the People's Mujahedin (Strugglers) which carried out a series of terrorist attacks against the top officials of the regime. More than 200 leading mullahs and politicians were killed by the Mujahedin within a few weeks. Abol-Hassan Bani-Sadr, one of Khomeini's economic advisers who had been elected as president of the Islamic Republic, sided with the urban guerrillas and was dismissed from his post on orders from the ayatollah. The Mujahedin failed to provoke a popular revolt against Khomeini and their leaders were forced to go first into hiding and then into exile. Bani-Sadr went with them and the Mujahedin challenge was brutally suppressed in the summer of 1981. More than 3,000 members of the group were shot or hanged without trial and more than 6,000 others sentenced to long prison terms.

By the autumn of 1981 the mullahs were in full control of the country and began eliminating other active or potential opponents of their regime. By 1983 all but one of the many political parties that had become active after the fall of the shah had been banned, with their leaders either shot or imprisoned or forced into exile. The one remaining political party, which had been founded by Khomeini himself, was also dissolved by the ayatollah in 1987. The theory according to which Khomeini was the representative of Divine Will on earth was firmly established as a cornerstone of the republic's political philosophy. In 1984 a group of Pakistani shi'ites living in the United Kingdom suggested at a pan-Islamic conference that the caliphate be revived and that Khomeini be named Caliph and the only legitimate ruler of all Muslims. But the idea of a return to the caliphate, especially under a shi'ite leader, met with a cool reception from the sunnis and was abandoned.

What was not abandoned was Khomeini's dream of creating a universal Islamic republic capable of uniting all Muslims and establishing itself as a world power. Using Iran's unprecedented oil revenues the ayatollah had begun 'exporting' his revolution as early as 1980. By 1982 thousands of Muslim militants from more than sixty countries were being trained for propaganda and urban guerrilla activities abroad, and Iranian mullahs were roaming the world to spread Khomeini's message. More than two dozen Islamic fundamentalist groups were either created or revived in Lebanon, Iraq, Kuwait, Bahrain, Pakistan, Afghanistan and Turkey among other countries.

Two countries had been specially targeted as more receptive to Khomeini's message of revolution: Iraq and Lebanon. Iran began spending large sums of money among militant shi'ite groups in Iraq in the summer of 1979. Members of the clandestine ad-Da'awah (The Call) group began training in propaganda and urban guerrilla techniques in Tehran from July 1979. Within a few months ad-Da'awah was able to orchestrate a campaign of violence against the Ba'athist regime in Baghdad. Several local officials were murdered but an attempt on the life of Tareq Azis, the number two leader of the Ba'ath and the closest adviser of President Saddam Hussein, failed. Hussein seized the opportunity for ordering a crackdown on shi'ites. More than 400 people were executed within a few weeks, among them Ayatollah Muhammad-Baqer Sadr who was universally recognized as the principal theorist of shi'ite fundamentalism. Many of those executed were related to Khomeini or other powerful mullahs in Iran. The government in Tehran retaliated by launching an unusually violent campaign against the Iraqi leaders. President Hussein was declared 'Mahdur ad-damm', a religious term which means 'he whose blood must be shed'.

The radio war between the two neighbours was accompanied by a series of border skirmishes in which the Iranian armed forces performed poorly. Iran appeared to be in no shape to fight a major war. The mullahs had executed hundreds of army and air force officers and purged or imprisoned thousands more. Hundreds of other officers had fled into exile. The revolution had also disrupted the process of conscription and many units existed only on paper. The situation had been further complicated because of the action taken against the armed forces by the Mujahedin, the Tudeh and other left wing groups. Arms stores had been pillaged or destroyed and military documents burned or stolen in many parts of the country. The sophisticated computer system that was used for the management of arms stocks and the organization of logistics was also sabotaged by the Mujahedin and their temporary allies, the People's Fedayeen Guerrillas.

In the summer of 1980, therefore, Iran seemed to be in no position to defend itself. This view was confirmed to the Iraqis by some leaders of the Iranian opposition in exile who travelled to Baghdad and offered to collaborate with Iraq in destroying the ayatollah's regime. The fact that Iran no longer had easy access to its main source of arms, the United States, because of the hostages crisis also persuaded Hussein that he would have little difficulty in winning a quick war. Early in September Hussein cancelled the 1975 treaty with Iran and declared a general mobilization. The Iraqi invasion, code-named Qaddassiyah after a battle in which Muslim armies had defeated a Sassanid force in the seventh century, came on 22 September 1980.

The initial successes scored by Iraq led some Iranian leaders to begin to seek a quick settlement. To Khomeini, however, war was 'a divine blessing'. He declared that the war should continue until President Hussein be brought to justice. The course of the war, however, remained favourable to Iraq until 1982 and Hussein announced that Khorramshahr, Iran's largest port, had been annexed by Iraq 'for ever'. He also called for the creation of an Arab state in

southwestern Iran and the transfer of three Iranian islands in
the Gulf to two Arab emirates. These Iraqi demands led to an
upsurge of nationalistic feelings which were deftly exploited
by Khomeini. Using the shi'ite tactic of deceiving one's
enemies when necessary, the ayatollah began adopting a
nationalistic tone and, for the first time, spoke of Iran's
territorial integrity as 'sacred'. Previously and throughout his
life he had condemned patriotism as another form of
'idolatry'. A good Muslim should love only God, he had
argued.

Iran's most urgent problem was to secure arms and spare
parts for its air force. Here, some of Iran's former Israeli
connections proved useful. Israel itself supplied Iran with
only limited quantities of arms and spare parts after the
revolution. Israeli contacts, however, enabled the mullahs to
secure access to black market arms and find new suppliers in
Brazil, Argentina, Portugal, Spain, Italy, Holland, Switzerland and France. The Israelis had seized the opportunity of
the war for knocking out Iraq's nuclear centre near Baghdad
in 1981. The French-built centre, as yet incomplete, was
suspected by Israel of having the capacity to produce a
nuclear device likely to be used as a weapon of war.

As the war dragged on against all expectations, Iran found
new arms suppliers in China, North and South Korea,
Taiwan and the United Kingdom. More importantly, Iran's
superior morale and fighting spirit turned the tide of the war
against the Iraqis early in 1982. In the two years that followed
Iran recaptured all of its own territory occupied by Iraq and
began to advance in parts of southern Mesopotamia. Iranian
forces attacked and seized the Majnun islands in the southern
Iraqi marshes and thus gained control of one of the richest
oilfields in the world. From 1983 the port-city of Basrah,
Iraq's second largest urban centre, came within range of
Iranian forces. Hussein retaliated by taking the war into the
Persian Gulf. His air force began attacking Iran's oil terminal
on Kharg Island and also raided tankers carrying Iranian
crude oil. Iran retaliated by attacking ships and tankers

engaged in trade with Saudi Arabia, Kuwait and the other Arab emirates of the Gulf. The financial and logistical support given by the Gulf Arab states to Iraq was cited by Iran as the reason for these attacks. The conflict thus assumed a broader dimension.

In 1986 Iraq took yet another initiative and started massive air and missile attacks on civilian targets. Iran retaliated and the 'War of the Cities' assumed awesome proportions. The two adversaries destroyed each other's cities and industries without being able to achieve any meaningful political concessions likely to bring the war to an end. Iraq also expanded its use of chemical weapons, principally mustard gas, which had begun in 1983. This was the first time since the First World War that this type of weapon was used on such a scale. In 1988 the two neighbours seemed to have reached the stage of total war and Tehran and Baghdad suffered missile attacks for weeks. Within one week Tehran alone received more than 200 Iraqi missiles which caused thousands of casualties.

Iranian attacks on Arab shipping forced the emirate of Kuwait to appeal to the superpowers for help. The USSR agreed by chartering three of its own oil tankers to Kuwait. The United States sent in an armada of around forty ships, the largest ever assembled since 1945, to the Gulf to help escort eleven Kuwaiti tankers that had been re-registered and re-flagged as American. Washington and Moscow also worked together and passed resolution 598 at the UN Security Council demanding a cease-fire in the Gulf war and the withdrawal of Iranian and Iraqi forces to pre-war frontiers.

Baghdad instantly agreed to abide by the resolution but Iran rejected it after a series of diplomatic manoeuvres aimed at dividing the Council's five permanent members. Iran tried to test American resolve in the Gulf through the planting of mines and largely symbolic acts of harassment. The USA retaliated by destroying a number of Iranian offshore oil installations and sinking nearly half of Iran's war fleet. Although the UN Security Council failed to agree on an arms embargo against Iran, the western powers succeeded in reducing arms supplies reaching the Islamic Republic to a mere trickle. This, combined with sharply reduced oil revenues, put Iran in a weak position when Iraq began a series of new offensives of its own. Iraq succeeded in liberating the Fao Peninsula, which had been captured by Iran in 1986, and also regained control of the border city of Shalamcheh. In July 1988 the Iraqis scored new victories and regained control of the oil-rich Majnun islands and the Zubaydat Heights. Almost at the same time a United States warship shot and destroyed an Iranian civilian aircraft flying over the Strait of Hormuz on a scheduled flight. All the 296 people aboard were killed. After a series of enquiries the U.S. agreed that the attack had been unprovoked and the result of a serious error by the captain of the American ship, the *Vincennes*.

The incident a mood of gloom in Iran and was used by supporters of an end to the war for the purpose of focusing Iranian public opinion on the country's exposed situation. On 18 July the Islamic Republic announced that it would accept a cease-fire within the framework of resolution 598, which the Security Council had unanimously approved in July 1987. Khomeini appeared on Iranian television to announce the decision which entailed the humiliation of his regime. 'To accept this resolution is worse than swallowing a cup of poison,' he said.

Iran's principal military commanders and most of the high-ranking religious leaders refused to endorse the ayatollah's decision in public. Nevertheless, it was evident that the continuation of the war had become virtually impossible for Iran, at least for some time.

The Iran-Iraq war was certainly the longest, the costliest and the bloodiest war in the history of Islam. Estimates made in the summer of 1988 showed that the war had claimed more than 1.2 million lives, two-thirds on the Iranian side, and a further 2.2 million wounded. A total of 4.2 million men, some thirty-eight per cent of the male adult population of the two countries, had taken part in the war between 1980 and 1988.

Material damage caused by the war was estimated at more than $350,000 million, more than sixty-five per cent of it on the Iranian side. Among Iran's losses were its major port facilities at Khorramshahr, the Abadan oil refinery, which had been the largest in the world, more than a dozen onshore and offshore oilfields and more than 3,000 industrial units of all sizes. A total of 157 Iranian towns with populations of more than 5,000 were partly or wholly destroyed by the war which also wiped some 1,800 border villages off the map.

The savagery of the fighting, the use of chemical weapons, the murder of war prisoners, the use of children to clear minefields and the rage for destruction manifested by both sides made the Iran–Iraq war one of the ugliest in recent history.

The war destabilized the whole of the Persian Gulf region and forced even the relatively more liberal states such as Kuwait and Bahrain to adopt repressive measures aimed at containing dissent. The tension between Iran and its Arab neighbours in the Gulf reached its height in July 1987 when Iranian pilgrims in Mecca organized a political demonstration during the Haj season. The aggressive attitude of some of the demonstrators caused panic among the outnumbered Saudi policemen on duty. Rumours that the Iranians might want to seize control of the ka'aba provoked a violent reaction from the Saudi reinforcements which soon arrived on the scene. In the clashes that ensued some 600 people, including more than 450 Iranian pilgrims, were killed. Relations between Tehran and Riyadh continued to deteriorate until Saudi Arabia severed its diplomatic ties with the Islamic Republic in 1988. Ayatollah Khomeini reacted by declaring the Saudi rulers to be 'enemies of Islam' who should be put to the sword. He also proposed the formation of a pan-Islamic authority to administer the holy shrines in Mecca and Medina.

The Islamic revolution in Iran and the Gulf War that followed it also affected the political situation in Turkey. By the summer of 1979, shortly after Khomeini had seized power in Tehran, a number of Kurdish secessionist groups fighting for the separation of eastern Anatolia from Turkey began to organize forays into Turkish territory from bases inside the Iranian border. It was obvious that the new rulers of Iran were either unable or unwilling to control the situation. Tension in eastern Anatolia reinforced the general feeling of insecurity that reigned throughout Turkey. Leftist guerrillas had even carved up the various districts of Istanbul among themselves and spoke of 'liberated zones'. They also attacked army and police arms depots and isolated outposts in preparation for what they described as a full-scale civil war aimed at establishing a Marxist-Leninist government in Ankara.

In September 1980 the Turkish military commanders, led by Chief of Staff General Kenan Evren, staged a *coup d'état* which brought down the democratically elected government of prime minister Suleiman Demirel. Martial law was imposed throughout the country and a nationwide hunt of the guerrillas organized. Within three years an estimated 700 guerrilla leaders were executed, and a further 1,600 were killed in encounters with the security forces. Thousands of others were arrested and kept in what amounted to concentration camps. In three years of full military rule more than half a million Turks appeared in front of military tribunals on various charges. Many of them spent some time in prison while most, together with a further five million people, had part or whole of their civil rights suspended for varying lengths of time.

The military crackdown was essentially focused on the urban middle classes and, particularly, the Turkish intelligentsia. The military rulers, like the Shah of Iran before them, believed that only the left could foment revolutionary trouble. The Turkish generals began to encourage and finance Islamic fundamentalist groups in the hope that these would, in time, destroy the influence of the left, especially among students and trade unionists. For more than three years the fundamentalists enjoyed the kind of freedom and official support that they had never dreamed of since the abolition of the caliphate by Atatürk. Many kemalist principles were pushed aside or simply forgotten as the Turkish top brass tried to use militant Islam against the 'atheist' left.

In 1983 General Evren, under pressure from the United States, organized a referendum in which a new constitution was approved. Evren himself was elected president at the same time. In the general election that ensued a new group, Anavatani Partisi (Motherland Party), led by the technocrat Turgot Ozal, won a majority. Ozal kept an Islamic profile, starting many of his public meetings with recitations from the Qur'an. The teachings of Atatürk were toned down and Turkey became a full member of the Islamic Conference. The basic contradiction between Turkey's Islamic personality and the desire of its ruling elites to see their country accepted as a full member of the European Economic Community (EEC) was best reflected in the Ozal premiership. Ozal, who won a second general election in 1987, performed a double act. At home he emphasized the Islamic credentials of his government and strengthened his political ties with various 'tariqat' (path) fundamentalist orders, especially the Naqshbandis. In dealing with the western powers, however, Ozal gave prominence to his liberal economic policy and the unshakeable attachment of his government to NATO.

The inherent weakness of such a policy had all but become apparent by 1988. Turkey's modernizing elites resented Ozal's flirtations with Islamic fundamentalists and doubted his sincerity about their country's European destiny. The fundamentalists, on the other hand, did not feel they could trust Ozal precisely because he wished Turkey to become a junior partner in an enterprise created and dominated by 'Christian' powers.

11

ANATHEMA AND WITHDRAWAL

The nature of the relationship between religion and the state has been one of the most crucial issues in Middle Eastern politics since the early years of this century and is likely to remain so for some time yet. Theoretically, the question would be of only academic interest in a truly Islamic society modelled on Medina during the reign of the Prophet Muhammad. In such a society all matters pertaining to the life of the community are religious issues by definition. Because life as a whole is sacred no part of it could be ignored by religious jurisdiction.

Nevertheless, the question of what is a genuinely Islamic state is not answered merely by being posed. With the exception of Israel and Lebanon, all existing Middle Eastern states, including the Marxist-Leninist South Yemen, claim at least some Islamic credentials. In every case, however, that claim is contested by important sections of society, at times through acts of violence.

The western domination of the Middle East, which began from the last years of the eighteenth century, gradually created a *de facto* separation of the mosque and the state in most countries of the region. By the end of the First World War all of the Middle Eastern countries had become either colonies or protectorates of Britain and France or had their basic political options dictated to them from the outside in spite of their apparently independent status. The state apparatus came to be seen by the masses as an instrument in the hands of foreign 'infidels' determined to humiliate Islam and plunder the natural resources of the region. Modernity came to mean defeat for Islam and ascendancy for Christendom, while tradition evoked the golden days of Islamic glory.

The anti-colonial movement that took shape throughout the region from the 1920s onwards was dominated by western-style nationalists and thus was itself a symbol of the success achieved by the European powers in pushing Islam into the background of politics in the Middle East. Nationalism pretended to replace faith and was, therefore, irreconcilable with Islam. It presupposed the existence of free individuals who, together, created a larger reality that transcended the frontiers of faith and tribal divisions.

By the early 1960s the last theoretically Islamic state, the Imamate in Yemen, had disappeared. All the states in the Middle East based themselves as much on nationalism as they did on religion. Even the state created by the Wahhabites under Saudi leadership described itself as an 'Arab kingdom'. Islam became only an ingredient, albeit a very important one, in the different brands of nationalism that found their expression in the different states of the region. Only Israel was the product of a different process. In its case a faith (Judaism) was developed into an ideology (Zionism) which in turn provided the basis for a state.

The first problem that every state faces is that of legitimacy. A state that cannot properly prove and defend its claim to represent authority as a matter of right is bound to be challenged and destabilized sooner or later. In the Middle East today four types of legitimacy can be distinguished regardless of the economic and foreign policies pursued by the different states concerned.

The first of these could be described as dynastic: the state claims to enjoy legitimacy because it is headed by a ruler who has inherited his authority in accordance with certain specific and widely accepted rules. A typical example is Saudi Arabia where King Fahd assumed the title of 'the Guardian of the

Holy Shrines' of Mecca and Medina in 1987. The Middle Eastern dynastic system is seldom purely monarchical as in Europe. King Hussein of Jordan, for example, is a bedouin tribal chief first and a monarch only afterwards. The Sultan of Oman and the emirs of the Gulf are also more leaders of clans than of European-style monarchs. Iran's system of kingship tried to bolster the dynastic principle by presenting the person of the monarch as the expression of the nation's unity and continuity.

The second type of legitimacy is religious. Israel is the most outstanding example. Although a secular Israeli identity has been developed during the past four decades, it is Judaism that still represents the basis for Israel's existence. Israel is a faith translated into a state. In Iran, on the other hand, an already existing state was captured and re-interpreted by a very peculiar version of Islam. Almost all the states of the region base part of their claim to legitimacy on Islam. The 1980s was a decade of 'Islamicization' in Egypt, Kuwait, Bahrain, Oman, the UAE and even Syria and Iraq, where rival wings of the secular pan-Arab Ba'ath Party were in power and a series of laws aimed at giving the state a stronger Islamic content was put into effect. Turkey, the very first officially secular state in the Middle East, was not spared either. Between 1983 and 1988 the parliament amended a number of laws related to family relations, adoption and inheritance in order to dilute their western content with the introduction of elements from Islamic law (shari'ah).

The third type of legitimacy could be described as revolutionary. This almost invariably means that the regime is a product of a military *coup d'état* that pretends to be a popular uprising. Egypt, Syria, Iraq, North Yemen and South Yemen have all experienced one or more *coups d'état*. In all these countries the armed forces act as guarantors of the state's legitimacy. If a particular set of leaders is deemed by the armed forces to be deviating from the 'path of the revolution' a new *coup d'état* is organized and a new set of military leaders assumes power. Sometimes, the new rulers describe their own rise to power as a new revolution and, therefore, a new source of legitimacy for their rule. Often, however, the initial *coup d'état* that ended civilian rule is retained as the original 'revolution' and subsequent *putsches* by the army are described as 'corrective movements'.

In some cases the regime assumes a civilian appearance complete with one or more political parties, parliamentary elections and even, as has been the case in Egypt since Nasser's death, general elections to choose the head of state. But in every case it is the army that represents the reality of power. Turkey could also be included in this category of states dominated by the military. For in spite of the fact that a genuine multi-party parliamentary system has been allowed to function in different periods since the 1920s, the Turkish armed forces have claimed the right to seize and exercise power whenever they feel that the security of the state is threatened.

Paranoia about security represents one of the main characteristics of the Middle Eastern state. Lacking an adequate popular base the Middle Eastern state is conscious of its fragility. It does not feel secure within its borders, often arbitrary lines resulting from colonial accidents, and lives in fear of invasion. Since 1939 every single one of the states of the region has been involved in one or more military clashes with its neighbours. Israel has been involved in four major wars with Egypt, Syria and Jordan in which a number of other Arab states also played a part. A fifth Israeli-Arab war was fought on Lebanese soil between the forces of the Jewish state on the one hand and the PLO and Syrian units on the other.

In the past four decades the Middle Eastern state has dramatically increased its role in society. In Iran, for example, the government employed a total of 32,000 people in 1939 and more than 2.1 million in 1988. In the same period the number of Saudi government employees increased more than seventy times. The state, jealous of all other institutions, gradually dominated or destroyed any institution likely to challenge its authority. Clan and tribal structures, guilds,

professional associations and religious fraternities either fell
under the financial and political control of the government or
lost much of their importance.

The average Middle Eastern state, regardless of its political
colourings at any given time, assumes the responsibilities of a
highly centralized almost Soviet-style structure without
possessing the powers of mobilization, indoctrination and
surveillance that are the hallmark of totalitarian power. In
most cases, even the lowliest of officials are appointed by the
centre which also takes the most routine of local decisions.

One undeclared goal of the Middle Eastern state is to stand
above all classes and be accountable to no one but itself. The
typical state in the region considers the people it administers
as primarily a source of insecurity. It does not need the people
to vote for it because elections, where they are held, often
represent little more than a ritual exercise. The state does not
depend on the people for its income either. Those countries
that export crude oil – that is to say Iran, Iraq, Kuwait, Saudi
Arabia, Qatar and Oman – offer their governments a ready
source of income far greater than any taxes that might be
collected within their boundaries. These are *rentier* states
with access to cash often far beyond their capacity for
absorption. Egypt, which also exports some oil, gets more
from the remittances of Egyptians working abroad than it
does from income tax collected locally. It also depends on
foreign loans and cash and kind gifts from more than twenty
countries. The Turkish state draws much of its income from
the numerous monopolies it controls – ranging from hotel and
resort holdings to mining – and also benefits from money sent
home by Turkish workers abroad. Syria, North Yemen and
South Yemen keep their budgets balanced thanks to foreign
aid, borrowings from abroad and exports of government-
controlled agricultural products. Even Israel, where a more
normal relationship exists between the state and the people,
hugely depends on foreign aid and subsidies as a state.

With the exception of Israel all the other states in the region
have had to compete with Islam for the loyalty of their

subjects. Everywhere the initial tendency was for the state to try and create an identity of its own. Atatürk changed the name of his country and created a republic. The new Turkish republican flag was red, the colour of revolution, with the crescent retained as a symbol not so much of the Muhammadan faith but of Ottoman glories. In Iran Reza Shah revived many of the pre-Islamic traditions and symbols of ancient Persia. The new Iranian flag was a tricolour – green, white and red – with a golden lion and sun as the emblem of the state. The lion represented Ali, the first Imam of shi'ism whose title was 'the lion of Allah'. The sun, however, was the symbol of Mithra (Mehr) and a reminder of Mithraism, one of the many religions of Iran before Islam. The Egyptian republic, created by Nasser, adopted the Roman eagle as its symbol, while other Arab republics chose two or more stars. The Saudi state's emblem is two crossed swords that symbolize tribal valour rather than religious belief. Lebanon's national emblem, the cedar, was chosen because it was supposed to be free of religious and sectarian connotations.

The Middle Eastern state advocated an alternative set of values designed to modify or even partly supplant those defended by Islamic political traditions for centuries. Such concepts as 'Watan' (homeland), 'qowm' (people or ethnic group), 'mellat' (nation), 'mihan' (fatherland) and 'jumhuriyat' (republic) were all alien to Islam but strongly upheld and propagated by the state.

More importantly the state enacted and applied laws of its own which, in many cases, were based on western legal systems and in contradiction to 'shari'ah'. The eclipse of 'shari'ah' had begun long before the emergence of any of the modern Middle Eastern states. In a sense, the decline of 'shari'ah' could be said to have started with the fall of the Abbasid caliphate. The new Mongol, Tatar and Turkic invaders introduced elements of their own legal traditions in the parts of the Middle East that they conquered. This, in turn, permitted many pre-Islamic laws and legal customs to be revived, especially in Iran and Anatolia.

The dream of a return to a fully Islamic way of life, complete with a legal system based on 'shari'ah', however, continued to live on. In the nineteenth century a number of intellectual and practical attempts were made at reforming Islam so that it could cope with the modern world – a world designed and dominated by the western powers. Sayyed Jamaleddin Assad-Abadi, a mullah but also a freemason who took the code name of 'Afghani', preached pan-Islamism in the hope of creating an empire in which western advances in industry, economy and administration would be combined with the traditional Islamic values. The idea that Islam needed its own reformation was later preached by the Syrian Rashid Rada and the Egyptian Muhammad Abdoh.

In the 1920s Egypt witnessed the birth of a fundamentalist movement of a new kind. This was the Ikhwan al-Moslemeen (the Muslim Brotherhood) founded by Shaikh Hassan al-Banna, a primary schoolteacher in Ismailiah in 1924. Banna had initially thought of setting up a European-style political party in the vague hope of contesting parliamentary elections and winning power through the ballot box. Both the royal court and the British who dominated the Suez Canal Company encouraged the shaikh's movement in its early stages as a force capable of countering the rise of communist influence among Egyptian middle class students. Banna's organization, however, soon developed into a secret society more interested in winning its way through bullets. The brotherhood continued to publish magazines and organize schools and maintained a legal appearance. But its strategy was increasingly based on preparation for a violent conquest of power. After a series of assassinations aimed against high officials, including two prime ministers, Banna himself was assassinated, almost certainly by a police agent, in 1949.

Meanwhile, the Brothers had developed into a genuine pan-Islamic movement with many followers throughout the Arab world as well as in Turkey and Iran. The idea of a militant Islam using force to save the community from perdition became firmly implanted in the minds of many young Muslim idealists. The Brothers played an important role in the Arab war effort against Israel in 1948 and later helped Nasser seize power in 1952.

Relations between the Brotherhood and the new regime in Egypt, however, were under strain right from the start. The 'Free Officers' led by Nasser were quickly attracted by socialist ideas which enjoyed a vogue in Third World countries during the 1950s while Banna's heirs, notably the charismatic Sayyed Muhammad Qutb, preached a pure and unalloyed Islam. The break between the government and the Brothers came in 1954 when a member of the Muslim Brotherhood fired on the rais in Alexandria. Some historians of the Muslim Brotherhood later suggested that the incident had been set up by Nasser's secret services, the dreaded Mabahith, as a pretext for a crackdown on the Brotherhood. More than a thousand Brothers were arrested and dispatched to concentration camps in the desert. Seven were sentenced to death by hanging, among them Qutb who quickly became 'the martyr saint' of the movement. A vast purge was also ordered against members of the Brotherhood throughout the administration and affected more than 5,000 people. Many more left the country and went into exile, often in Saudi Arabia and the Gulf states as well as the Sudan, to escape political persecution and economic pressure.

Almost at the same time that Nasser was attacking the Muslim Brotherhood in the name of Arab socialism, the Shah of Iran was engaged in a crackdown on the Fedayeen of Islam, the shi'ite version of the Egyptian fundamentalist movement. The fedayeen had come into being in the 1940s under the leadership of Mujtaba Mir-Lowhi who used the *nom de guerre* of Muhammad Nawwab-Safavi. The fedayeen were responsible for a series of political murders between 1946 and 1952 and could be more aptly regarded as a terrorist organization rather than a mass movement.

By the end of the 1950s Islamic fundamentalism had been largely driven underground where it remained until the Islamic Revolution in Iran in 1978–79. A number of local

revolts against the shah's reforms in the early 1960s gave
Ayatollah Khomeini some prominence in Iran but did not
lead to a mass movement. In Egypt the Muslim Brotherhood
moved towards the centre of the political spectrum and
renounced the use of murder as a legitimate political weapon.
Branches of the Brotherhood in Jordan, Saudi Arabia,
Yemen and Iraq took the Egyptian lead and concentrated
their efforts on education and propaganda rather than terror
and conspiracy against the state. Only in Syria did one branch
of the Muslim Brotherhood continue to have recourse to
violence, including the assassination of government officials.
In Turkey the fundamentalist movement was dominated by
the 'tariqats' or sufi fraternities which also believed in
permeation as the surest means of conquering political
power.

The 1970s, however, ushered in a new phase in the history
of Islamic radicalism. The Muslim Brotherhood was seen by
the more radical activists as little more than a debating society
without any real impact on society. A number of new
clandestine organizations came into being with the aim of
conquering political power by force if necessary. They re-
read Qutb and found in him the prophet they had looked for.
Qutb preached the rejection of the existing corrupt society
through an act of 'hegirah', akin to the movement of the
Prophet from Mecca to Medina. True believers had to stay
away from a society that had forgotten the teachings of the
Qur'an. They also had the duty to anathemize such a society,
to expose and oppose its 'black, heathen depth' and, later, to
fight it on the battleground.

In Iran the new fundamentalists were strongly influenced
by Maoist and Marxist ideas and hoped to raise a guerrilla
army capable of defeating the shah's mighty war machine. By
1973 at least half a dozen guerrilla groups, mostly led by
Muslim radicals, were active in some Iranian cities. In
neighbouring Iraq a new radical Islamic movement was
created by the shi'ite leader Ayatollah Muhammad Baqer
Sadr. The movement, ad'Da'awah (the Call), was not

involved in acts of violence until 1980 when it tried to assassinate a number of Ba'athist leaders, including the regime's second-in-command Tareq Aziz. The government's reaction was exceptionally brutal. Sadr and many other mullahs and shi'ite activists were executed in the holy cities of Karbala and Najaf. Hundreds of activists were imprisoned and thousands were forced to cross the border into Iran.

The assassination of President Sadat in 1981 revealed the existence in many parts of Egypt of an underground network of Muslim militants known under the general code-name of 'takfir wal hegirah' (anathema and withdrawal). But Egypt was by no means the only Arab country where the new Islamic radicalism assumed a different and more violent form. In Syria a series of attacks by armed bands of Muslim Brotherhood supporters on army and police units provoked an extremely brutal reaction from the government in 1981. Syrian army and presidential guard units moved into the city of Hamma where they massacred between 10,000 and 15,000 supporters of the Muslim Brotherhood during two days of house-to-house search for alleged terrorists.

Throughout the 1980s Islamic radical groups kept up their pressure on almost all governments in the Middle East. Even in Iran, where Ayatollah Khomeini ruled in the name of fundamentalist Islam, groups more radical than his government pressed for a more accelerated programme of Islamicization. In Egypt, the Muslim Brotherhood succeeded in becoming a major force in the parliament and was instrumental in forcing the government to cancel a series of laws considered as 'un-Islamic'. The more radical groups, however, stayed outside mainstream politics and kept up their pressure on the state in the form of occasional riots as well as selective assassinations of local officials.

Fearful lest their legitimacy be questioned in the name of Islamic purity, the various Middle Eastern states have adopted different policies *vis-à-vis* radical Muslim groups. Syria, Iraq and South Yemen relied on ruthless repression while Egypt, Jordan, North Yemen and Oman tried to co-opt as many of the radicals as possible. In Turkey, the generals used Muslim radicals to counter the influence of Leftist groups between 1980 and 1983. And from 1983 to 1988 Premier Turgot Ozal relied on Muslim fraternities for part of his nationwide support. In 1988 no fewer than eight members of Ozal's cabinet were members of the Naqshbandiah, a semi-secret sect with supporters in Turkey, Iran, Syria and Iraq and led by a shaikh living in Houston, Texas.

The use of terms such as Muslim radicalism or Muslim fundamentalism might suggest the existence of a monolithic movement throughout the Middle East. In fact there are many different versions of radical Islam with a variety of different strategies aimed at conquering power. The groups inspired by Ayatollah Khomeini, and generally known as Hezb-Allah (Party of God), aim at seizing power through an Islamic revolution based on the 'mustadhafin' (the down-trodden). The idea is that because most Middle Eastern states are either led by the military or dominated by the army, only a force capable of counterbalancing the political weight of the armed forces could bring about a radical change in society. That force, the theorists of Hezb-Allah argue, could only be that of the poor masses who are not afraid of death because they find life so hard and unrewarding. And these masses, the argument continues, could not be mobilized in the name of secular, often imported, ideologies; only Islam can persuade the 'mustadhafin' to pour into the streets to bring down the governments.

The mainstream Muslim Brotherhood, especially in Egypt, seeks power in two ways: by acting as a political party capable of winning a parliamentary majority and by building itself up as the centre of an economic empire. In 1988 the total assets of some 500 Islamic enterprises, ranging from interest-free banks to factories, supermarkets and investment organiz-ations, were estimated at more than $8,000 million. The radical Muslim groups demonstrated their economic power in May 1988 by withdrawing millions of dollars' worth of savings from state-owned banks within a few days. Two Islamic investment organizations, ar-Rayyan and as-Sa'ad, boasted assets of $4,000 and $3,200 million respectively in 1988. Most of these came from small savings especially in rural areas.

The attempt to build up an 'Islamic' economic power base by the fundamentalist groups is only one aspect of their overall strategy of 'withdrawal' from societies which they consider to be 'satanic'. Interest-free banks and Islamic investment houses are already established as important forces within the economies of countries as different as Oman, Turkey and Egypt. But it was in the field of education that the strategy of 'withdrawal' was more dramatically at work. In 1988 no fewer than four million Egyptian children and young people attended Qur'anic schools, either as full-time pupils or to complement the state education they received. Even in secular Turkey more than two million people received Qur'anic education on a full-time or part-time basis. Also in Turkey an estimated 280,000 young men and women received scholarships from the various 'tariqats' while attending secondary school or university either at home or abroad. The idea, as formulated by the Naqshbandiah theorists, was that a fully-educated Islamic elite would better be able to bring society back to the 'right path'.

'Withdrawal' from the 'satanic' society also took the form of refusing to obey the laws of the 'un-Islamic' state wherever and whenever possible. In Turkey and Egypt this took the form of tax evasion and refusal to register marriages and divorces with the governmental authorities. In Iraq and North Yemen the avoidance of national service was a popular form of fundamentalist protest. This, in the case of Iraq which was at war with Iran, meant that thousands of young men had to escape to Turkey, Syria, Kuwait, Jordan and even Iran to avoid conscription.

The signs of 'withdrawal' could be seen throughout the Middle East. The most obvious of these signs was the unprecedented popularity of the 'hejab' (veil) for women. In 1968 hardly a woman could be found wearing the veil on the campuses of Turkish, Iranian and Egyptian universities. By

1988 those wearing the 'hejab' were in a majority. In the case of men it was the popularity of beards that could be seen as a sure sign of fundamentalist progress in the Middle East. The beard, denounced by progressives throughout the Middle East as a relic of the feudal and decadent past, was by 1988 established as a symbol of Islamic protest against the existing state structures. All the manifestos of fundamentalist groups in the region emphasize the crucial importance of the beard in the process of 'withdrawal', whose chief aim is to distinguish between 'true Muslims' and those who have been led astray.

Another sign of 'withdrawal' was the renewed popularity of purely Islamic names as opposed to names inherited from the pre-Islamic past. From the 1920s onwards more and more Turks, Arabs and Iranians, influenced by nationalist move-

Illiteracy in The Middle East

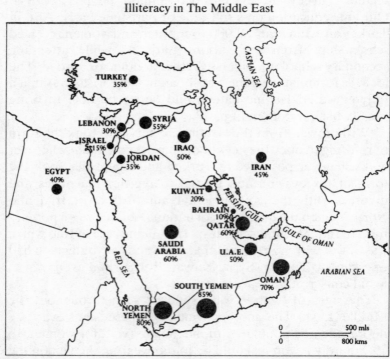

● Percentage of illiterates in the school-age population

ments, chose non-Islamic first names for their offspring. The governments encouraged this trend and by the 1950s many 'pagan' names had gained immense popularity throughout the Middle East. In 1979 the newly-established Islamic Republic of Iran banned the use of non-Islamic names such as Cyrus, Darius and Artaxerxes. There was no similar official move anywhere else in the region but many fundamentalist groups made it a priority to discourage the use of non-Islamic names wherever they could. Purely Islamic names became fashionable even in outwardly secular Iraq and Syria as well as Lebanon, Jordan and the Israeli-occupied territories.

Islamic fundamentalism also showed its strength in the field of publications and propaganda. Between 1980 and 1988 Iran trained an estimated 50,000 preachers from more than 60 countries. A majority came from various parts of the Middle East. The number of mosques and other places of Islamic worship increased dramatically: it rose by fifty per cent in Iran but nearly doubled in Turkey and Egypt. In 1988 more than 150 fundamentalist publishing companies took part in an exhibition in Istanbul. Together they had published more than 3,000 different titles, all dealing with various aspects of the fundamentalist message, between 1983 and 1987. More than forty weekly, monthly or periodical fundamentalist magazines were available in Turkish, Arabic and Persian in 1988. In Iran the fundamentalists controlled all the daily newspapers. In Egypt and Turkey they controlled at least one daily.

The 'anathema' aspect of the fundamentalist movement manifested itself in many different ways. These ranged from the idea of persuasion, setting an example by being a 'good Muslim', as preached by many intellectuals in Cairo or Istanbul, to the concept of 'jihad' or holy war as developed by Khomeini and the shi'ite pamphleteer Ali Shariati. While the Egyptian Omar al-Talmassani, one of the founders of the Muslim Brotherhood, believed that anyone who saw Islam in real life would quickly adopt it as his own, Shariati developed the idea of martyrdom in the service of the faith. Khomeini's celebrated dictum that 'to kill and to be killed is the supreme task of all true Muslims' was based on Shariati's claim that one had either to destroy the enemy or to deny him the fruits of his victory by destroying oneself.

The avowed aim of most intellectual efforts deployed by the many different fundamentalist movements is the development of an Islamic alternative to the leading western systems of legal and political organization of society. The fundamentalists claim that only their version of Islam can solve the problems of Muslim societies today and also save the entire human race from war, racism, inequality and poverty. Because the world is culturally, economically and politically dominated by the western powers and the USSR, which is considered to be part of the West by the fundamentalists, virtually all attempts at creating an Islamic 'alternative' assume an anti-western dimension.

Some fundamentalists do not go beyond simple assertions regarding the need for government based on the experience of Muhammad during his governorship of Mecca. Others try to provide a synthesis of western socialistic ideas and Islamic traditions of care for the poor and militancy against unjust rulers. The results range from interesting and provocative to bland and boring. What is certain is that few of the existing Middle Eastern states could think of their immediate future in purely secular terms. Even Israel is forced to take into account the growing demands of its own fundamentalists.

The fact that almost none of the region's many different states could claim to have solved its basic problem of legitimacy on a long-term basis means that the fundamentalist challenge will remain a crucial element in Middle Eastern politics for the foreseeable future. For it to achieve stable legitimacy the Middle Eastern state would need to accept some form of consensus politics. Under present circumstances that could mean many more concessions to fundamentalists, concessions that few states feel like offering because of the evident risks involved. The general retreat of the left, especially communists, and the decline of secular nationalism in the past two decades, have rendered the process of democratization, needed for a new form of legitimacy to be developed, far more problematic than ever before. Muslim fundamentalists, who regard parliamentary democracy as anathema to the teachings of Muhammad, are in the strongest position for winning power through any genuine electoral system in many countries of the region. In Israel, which is always a case apart, the right wing Likud bloc is itself a manifestation of a fundamentalist approach to politics.

In Egypt the fundamentalists already dominate the legal opposition inside and outside parliament and might well win an outright majority in a free and fair election. In Turkey almost all political parties are aware of the fact that they would not be able to secure a majority without support from the fundamentalist voters. For the first time since the Second World War it is fundamentalism that dominates opposition to regimes as diverse as those of Iraq, Syria, Kuwait, Bahrain and Egypt. It is probably only in the Islamic Republic of Iran that the regime is opposed by western-style movements ranging from nationalist-monarchist to Marxist-Leninist to liberal and democratic. Even in Turkey, where the left remains powerful, especially among the dissident Kurds, the main threat to the existing order comes from fundamentalist groups dedicated to the destruction of the kemalist state and the creation of a society based on the 'shari'ah'.

The crucial role played by fundamentalist parties in Afghanistan's armed resistance against Soviet occupation between 1980 and 1988, and the propaganda campaign waged by khomeinists against the United States throughout the region, persuaded many Muslim intellectuals that only by mobilizing the masses in the name of the faith could one stand up to the challenge of the two superpowers. The idea that Islam drove the Americans out of Iran and the Russians out of Afghanistan might appear simplistic to most outside observers. But it has an undoubted appeal for many Muslims who are genuinely persuaded that most of their social, political and economic problems result from foreign intervention.

Throughout the 1980s the fundamentalists scored major successes in creating their own realities within the broader reality of a state which they considered alien to Islam or at least deviant. Their strategy of anathema and withdrawal proved effective in enough cases to make them credible. Nevertheless, they failed to develop a coherent view of the contemporary world and its problems as a whole. The alternative they sought to western politics and economics continued to elude them.

12

A TRADITION OF VIOLENCE

Political violence in both physical and moral forms has been a major feature of public life in the Middle East during the past four or five decades at least. Employed as an instrument of rule by most governments in the region, political violence has also been recognized as the principal means of defying the authority of the state.

With rare exceptions the Middle Eastern states suffer from a feeling of insecurity that borders on paranoia. They are suspicious of any individual or group that might wish to take an initiative in public affairs and act beyond the narrow limits dictated by the rulers. Even non-political bodies such as cultural associations and sports clubs are seen as potential threats to the authority of the state. Such organizations are put under close surveillance, infiltrated and eventually brought under government control or, if that proves difficult, destroyed.

In some cases even the ruling party itself is regarded by the state as a source of danger. All ruling parties, in one-party states, are infiltrated by members of the secret police and watched by parallel organizations run by the security services. These parties are subjected to periodical purges and changes of name and of ideology in accordance with the wishes of the rulers. In Egypt, for example, the Arab Socialist Union (ASU), created by Nasser to advocate socialist central planning, was re-formed by Sadat into a liberal party that defended free enterprise. The party's name and ideology changed but most of its leaders and almost all of its members remained the same.

The virtual impossibility of changing governments through the ballot box in most Middle Eastern countries has provoked more than 240 successful or abortive attempts at *coups d'état* in Turkey, Iran, Iraq, Syria, Jordan, Egypt, North Yemen, South Yemen, Oman, Bahrain and the emirate of Sharjah since the Second World War.

Even in monarchies where the state theoretically has at its disposal generally accepted traditions aimed at facilitating the succession the establishment of a new king has at times come about in the context of a palace revolution. Faisal Ibn Abdul-Aziz, for example, acceded to the throne of Saudi Arabia after forcing his brother King Saud Ibn Abdul-Aziz to go into exile in Egypt. In Jordan the military commanders and tribal chiefs declared King Talal Ibn Abdallah 'insane' before putting his son Hussein on the throne. And in Oman Crown Prince Qabus became king after overthrowing his father Sultan Sa'id ibn Teymur in a *coup d'état* supported by Britain and Iran in 1970. In 1953 Shah Muhammad Reza Pahlavi of Iran regained his lost throne through a *coup d'état* with British and American help.

The Middle East has also experienced a number of civil wars and armed revolts provoked by the absence of political structures needed for greater popular participation in the process of decision-making and the formation of governments. Iran experienced a full-scale civil war in 1909–1911. Turkey had its own civil war in the aftermath of the First World War. In Arabia the civil war of the 1920s led to the domination of the country by the new Al-Saud dynasty. In the 1950s and early 1960s Oman had to face a civil war provoked by the revolt of the Ibadhi sect in the Jabal Akhdhar region. In the 1960s and 1970s the sultanate went through another civil war, this time in the southern province of Dhofar. Lebanon experienced its first civil war in 1958, a conflict that was ended with the arrival of the US Marines. A second civil war, started in 1975, continued with varying degrees of intensity in Lebanon well into the 1980s. North Yemen fought its own civil war throughout much of the 1960s, while two separate civil wars ravaged South Yemen in 1969 and 1986. Even the Arab-Jewish armed conflict in mandate Palestine in 1947 could be described as a civil war.

Since the First World War the Middle East has experienced more than thirty major armed revolts, often provoked by autonomist or secessionist movements. The authority of the government was re-established in Iran in the 1920s after Reza Khan succeeded in quelling revolts by Kurdish, Turcoman, Baluchi, Luri, Arab and Mamasani tribes. In the 1940s Iran experienced several other tribal uprisings, notably in Kurdistan. The Kurds and the Turcomans raised the standard of revolt once again in 1979–1981 but were crushed by the Islamic government of Ayatollah Khomeini. Iraq experienced Kurdish revolts in the 1930s, 1960s, 1970s and 1980s. Turkey fought its first Kurdish war in the 1920s and faced revolts by the Kurds in 1983, 1984 and 1987. South Yemen experienced tribal revolts in Aulaqi and Hadhramaut in the 1970s.

Border clashes and full-scale wars have also been important features in Middle Eastern politics. Israel and the Arab states have fought four major wars in 1948, 1956, 1967 and 1973. And in 1982 Israel launched a full invasion of Lebanon and also engaged some Syrian forces. But by far the most important of the wars in the region has been the Gulf War between Iran and Iraq, a conflict that began in 1980 and was not yet fully ended in 1988. Iran and Iraq had fought a more limited war in the 1970s over the issue of sharing sovereignty and control over the Shatt al-Arab border estuary.

The Arab states have been involved in a number of wars against one another. In 1936 Saudi Arabia and the imamate of Yemen fought a border war that led to the annexation of some oases by the Saudis. Saudi Arabia was involved in border wars with Oman (in the 1950s), North Yemen (in the 1960s) and South Yemen (in the 1970s). The Syrians invaded Jordan in 1970 and in 1975 intervened in Lebanon. In 1988 the Syrians seized control of almost all of Lebanon with the exception of the south and the eastern boroughs of Beirut. Through much of the 1970s Oman and South Yemen were involved in a series of border clashes in which Iranian forces supported the army of the sultanate.

The region's recent history contains a number of large-scale massacres, largely of civilians, either directly by government forces or with indirect encouragement from the authorities. Between 1915 and 1925 Turkey was the scene of a series of massacres in which more than a million Armenians, Assyrians and Greeks were put to death by Kurdish, Turcoman and other tribesmen with support from the regular armed forces. In exchange, the Assyrians and Armenians, supported by the Tsarist armies until 1917, massacred some 250,000 Muslim Turks and Kurds in eastern Anatolia and parts of Mesopotamia. The Druzes, the Yazidis, the Maronites and other non-Muslim minorities in the region have also been subjected to frequent massacres by their Muslim neighbours and have, in turn, participated in anti-Muslim pogroms on many occasions.

In 1975 Syria allied itself with Christian Phalangists in Lebanon in the massacre of Palestinians. And in 1982 the Israeli army watched as Christian Lebanese gunmen murdered more than 1,200 Palestinian women and children in the camps of Sabra and Shatila. In 1981 Ayatollah Khomeini's Revolutionary Guard invaded the West Azerbaijani village of Naqadah and killed more than 1,000 Kurds, mostly women and children, with help from Azaris from neighbouring villages. The massacre of Muslim Brotherhood supporters in the city of Hama in 1981 was not the only example of an Arab government organizing the massacre of its own people. In 1988 the Iraqi army bombarded the Iraqi Kurdish city of Halabcheh with chemical weapons and killed more than 5,000 people.

The massacre of Palestinians in Jordan in 1970 was not the only example of state violence used as a means of solving a political problem. In 1979 Saudi and Jordanian troops quelled an armed revolt inside the holy shrine of Ka'aba at Mecca and killed more than 1,000 fundamentalist militants. In 1981 Egyptian troops killed more than 700 Muslim extremists during a series of riots in Upper Egypt. In 1986 an estimated 10,000 people were killed in South Yemen during a bloody struggle for power. Some 2,000 Soviet army and navy officers and technicians watched the massacre but did not intervene.

At times government forces crossed international boundaries in search of armed opponents of the state. In 1984 and 1987 Turkish troops crossed into Iraq and killed hundreds of Kurdish guerrillas and captured several thousand Kurdish women and children who had sought sanctuary in Iraqi villages. In 1988 Iranian troops destroyed five Iraqi villages that had sheltered anti-Khomeini Kurdish and communist guerrillas.

Another tactic used by some governments against their opponents consists of mass expulsion. The Iraqis expelled more than 200,000 shi'ites between 1970 and 1974. Jordan solved its problems with the PLO by expelling more than 80,000 Palestinians in 1970. In 1947 and 1948 Israel forced an estimated 400,000 Palestinians to flee their homes. The Jewish state has used the arm of expulsion against the Palestinians ever since. The number of Arabs forced by Israel to leave their homes since 1967 works out at an average of 1,200 a year.

One direct result of political violence in various countries of the region has been the emergence of a long-term social and economic problem in the shape of millions of displaced persons. In 1988 there were 2.2 million Afghan refugees in Iran with a further three million in neighbouring Pakistan. Iran also sheltered an estimated 400,000 Iraqi shi'ites and Kurds. In exchange there were an estimated 1.2 million Iranian refugees in Turkey with a further two million scattered in the rest of the Middle East and in more than thirty other countries. The Palestinians, who numbered an estimated 1.2 million outside Israel and the occupied territories, were officially classed as 'refugees' only in Jordan and Lebanon but were present in all other Arab states of the region. The presence of some two million Yemenis and Omanis in Saudi Arabia and the Gulf emirates could not be directly attributed to political conditions in home countries. Nevertheless, many of the exiles had left their country of origin for political or religious reasons.

State violence comes in still other forms. Between 1948 and 1988 some 120,000 people were executed in various countries of the region. Iran, with an estimated 55,000 executions between 1979 and 1988, headed the list of countries where capital punishment, especially for political reasons, was most frequently applied. Iraq was second with nearly 40,000 executions between 1958 and 1988. There were more than 10,000 executions in South Yemen between 1968 and 1988. North Yemen, with 3,000 executions in the period 1962–1988, also figured prominently on the list. Between 1952 and 1988 just under 2,000 executions were carried out in Egypt. Turkey, with some 1,500 executions between 1945 and 1988, was not far behind. Executions were carried out in all other countries of the region including Israel where capital punishment was reserved only for Nazi criminals. During the period 1979–1988 more than eighty per cent of all executions carried out in the world took place in the Middle East.

Imprisonment is yet another important form of state violence in the region. Between 1945 and 1988 millions of people were imprisoned for varying lengths of time in almost all the states of the region. Between 1979 and 1988 the number of Iranians who passed through the government's political prisons was estimated at more than one million. In Turkey no fewer than half a million people were held in custody for periods of varying length between 1980 and 1988. According to conservative estimates more than eighty per cent of all political prisoners in the world were in the Middle East. The Islamic Republic of Iran with more than 65,000 political prisoners headed the list and Iraq, with 45,000 people in jail, came second. Israel held some 10,000 political prisoners, mostly Palestinians in Gaza and the West Bank. A further 4,000 Palestinians were in prison in Syria together with an estimated 3,500 Syrian fundamentalists. There were political prisoners in all other countries of the region with the exception of Qatar and the United Arab Emirates.

Making political opponents 'disappear' was a well established practice of many Middle Eastern states long before Latin American dictatorships discovered the device. In 1988 thousands of people remained 'disappeared' in Iran, Iraq, Turkey, Syria, Lebanon, South Yemen and North Yemen. In Lebanon the 'disappearance' device was complemented by the seizure of hostages by various terrorist organizations financed and led by different governments in the region. The fact that American and European diplomats, journalists, teachers and businessmen were among the people kidnapped in Lebanon focused international attention on a problem that might otherwise have remained confined to the borders of the Middle East. The tactic of holding hostages as a means of exercising political pressure on real or imagined opponents of the government was, in 1988, widely practised in Iran, Iraq, Syria and South Yemen. In all these countries army officers, key civil servants and managers of major state enterprises were not allowed to travel abroad in the company of their spouses and children for fear that they might choose not to return. At least one member of each family concerned had to stay behind as an unofficial hostage.

The practice of keeping people in prison without charge was widespread in Syria, South Yemen, Iraq, Iran and Turkey. In most cases a promise of an early release was used as a means of psychological pressure on the relatives of the hostages thus held. In Iran seizing hostages was, in 1988, a source of revenue for revolutionary organizations: a hostage could be set free in exchange for a 'voluntary' contribution to a cause supported by the authorities.

Ransom money also played a role in ensuring the release of more than thirty French, American, West German, Soviet, South Korean, Saudi, Kuwaiti and UAE hostages held by the

Party of God in Lebanon between 1983 and 1988. In some cases the ransom paid took the form of arms shipments to Iran. France also paid a total of $1,000 million to the Islamic Republic on two occasions in exchange for the release of its hostages. The payments, although made in settlement of financial claims sustained by Tehran, amounted to political ransom because of the linkage established with the hostages' issue. The Party of God itself received an estimated $180 million over five years as part of deals negotiated by Iran for the release of western hostages.

Political violence practised by various Middle Eastern states also takes the form of murder squads that operate against the opposition both at home and abroad. Between 1968 and 1988 Iraqi murder squads assassinated thirty-two opponents of the regime in twelve different countries including Britain. Among those gunned down were the former prime minister Abdul-Razzaq al-Na'ef, and the former vice-president, Hardan Abdul-Ghaffar al-Takriti. During the same period murder squads dispatched by Iran gunned down forty-five of the regime's opponents in ten countries including Britain, France and the United States. Among those murdered were General Gholam-Ali Oveissi, a former commander of the Iranian ground forces, and Rear-Admiral Sharyar Shafiq, who had once commanded the Iranian navy in the Persian Gulf.

The tactic of murdering one's opponents, however, was not started by Ayatollah Khomeini in Iran, although he made more frequent use of it. Under the *ancien régime* more than two dozen left wing opponents were killed by SAVAK gunmen between 1970 and 1976. In 1970 a SAVAK murder squad landed in Baghdad aboard a jetliner which had supposedly been hijacked. The gunmen masquerading as hijackers described themselves as opponents of the shah and contacted the exiled General Teymur Bakhtiar who quickly took them under his wing. Bakhtiar was killed by his new recruits a few days later and the SAVAK murder squad escaped back into Iran across the border. In 1971 Ahmad

Aramesh, a former deputy prime minister who had joined the shah's opponents, was assassinated by SAVAK gunmen in a park in Tehran.

In Egypt the practice of eliminating opponents was widespread under Nasser. An estimated 100 opponents of the rais were killed by Mabahith gunmen in Egypt and other Arab countries between 1956 and 1967.

Between 1970 and 1988 more than twenty opponents of the Syrian president Hafez al-Assad were murdered in Europe and the Middle East. The most prominent among them was Salah Bitar, a former prime minister and a founding father of the Ba'ath Party. Another distinguished victim of Syrian murder squads was Salim al-Lawzi, publisher of the weekly *al-Hawadith* (Events) and one of Lebanon's leading journalists.

Israel used political murder as a weapon in its war against the Palestine Liberation Organization. In 1973 an Israeli death squad entered Beirut and murdered three of the PLO's highest-ranking leaders. Since then more than thirty PLO leaders or activists have been murdered in more than half a dozen countries. In 1988 an Israeli commando squad landed at the Tunisian coastal village of Sidi Bu-Sa'id and murdered Khalil al-Wazir, alias Abu-Jihad, the PLO's military commander.

While having recourse to violence against their opponents, most Middle Eastern states have had to cope with the challenge posed to their authority as a result of terrorism practised by different political parties of both left and right. The tactic of murdering rulers as a means of imposing changes of governmental policy and behaviour had been perfected in the Middle East by the sect of the Assassins (Hashasheen) in the eleventh century. This tradition was revived in Iran in the early 1900s when Heydar Amoqli, an Azerbaijani social democrat, created a secret society named 'Komiteh Vahshat' (Committee of Terror) with the aim of murdering the leading members of the government. The most prominent victim of the 'Komiteh' was the prime minister Atabak, whose murder shook the Qajar state to its foundations.

Political murder did not remain a prerogative of the left and was adopted by the Muslim Brotherhood as part of its overall strategy for bringing the Middle East back to the 'Right Path'. The most prominent of the Brotherhood's earliest victims was Imam Yahya of Yemen.

Since the end of the Second World War the Middle East has witnessed more than 5,000 political assassinations carried out by more than two dozen different political groups, ranging from the fundamentalist Fedayeen of Islam and the communist Tudeh (Masses) Party in Iran to the fascist Grey Wolves in Turkey and the Anathema and Withdrawal group in Egypt. In the case of military *coups d'état* the task of murdering rulers and high officials has been entrusted to regular army officers.

Among the heads of state murdered in the Middle East since the Second World War are King Abdallah (Jordan), King Faisal (Iraq), King Faisal (Saudi Arabia), President Qahtan Shaabi (South Yemen), President Salim Rubaye-Ali (South Yemen), General Abdul-Karim Qassem (Iraq), President Ibrahim Hamdi (North Yemen), President Muhammad-Ali Raja'i (Iran), President Anwar Sadat (Egypt), President Bechir Gemayel (Lebanon) and Shaikh Khaled (Sharjah).

The list of prime ministers murdered or executed includes the following: Abdul-Hossein Hazhir (Iran), Haj-Ali Razm-Ara (Iran), Hassan-Ali Mansur (Iran), Noqrachi Pasha (Egypt), Maher Pasha (Egypt), Adnan Menders (Turkey), Saad Zaghlul (Egypt), Amir Abbas Hoveyda (Iran), Mohammad-Javad Bahonar (Iran), Rashid Karame (Lebanon) and Nuri-Sa'id Pasha (Iraq).

Much longer lists could be compiled of the names of other ranking politicians, ministers, parliamentarians, party leaders, journalists, university professors, leading doctors, poets, writers, historians, scientists, civil servants and army officers who have been assassinated for political reasons during the past four or five decades. A list of public figures who have been the subject of assassination plots would read like a political *Who's Who* of the Middle East.

In several countries of the region terrorism has been an almost constant feature of public life since the 1940s. Until the 1980s the threat came mainly from leftist or secessionist movements as well as Palestinian groups. In the 1980s, however, it was the Islamic fundamentalist movement in its many different expressions that most frequently used the arm of terror against its enemies.

Two countries have been specially affected by terrorism. Turkey has had to cope with Armenian terrorism, orchestrated by the so-called Armenian Secret Army for the Liberation of Armenia (ASALA), as well as Kurdish terrorist groups led by the Maoist Kurdish Workers' Party (PKK). Throughout the 1970s Iran was the scene of intense activities by the leftist People's Fedayeen Guerrilla, a Marxist-Leninist organization, and the People's Combatants (Mujahedin), a leftist-Islamic urban guerrilla group. After 1979 both the Fedayeen and the Mujahedin soon ran into confrontation with the new Islamic regime and became victims of an unprecedented repression. Nevertheless, they continued to fight the authorities through selective assassinations and acts of sabotage against the armed forces and industrial centres.

The fundamentalist terror groups active in the rest of the region included the Hezb-Allah (Party of God), the Islamic Jihad (Holy War), ad-Da'awah (The Call) and Hezb al-Tahrir al-Islami (Islamic Liberation Party). These groups were responsible for more than ninety per cent of all terrorist acts carried out in Bahrain, Kuwait, Saudi Arabia, Iraq, Lebanon, Jordan and Egypt in the 1980s.

Between 1970 and 1988 more than 3,200 acts of terrorism were recorded throughout the region. These included more than 400 cases of successful or abortive hijackings of civilian aircraft. Explosions caused by booby-trapped cars, setting fire to public buildings, sabotage of bridges and railways and the burning or poisoning of crops were among the tactics used by terror groups. The terrorist attacks claimed thousands of lives and affected every country in the region with the exception of Qatar. In Turkey alone the terrorist campaign claimed nearly 12,000 lives. In one incident in Iran more than 600 people were burned alive when a cinema was set on fire by Muslim fundamentalists in the city of Abadan in 1978.

The Palestinian strugle for self-determination and the creation of an independent state has included the use of terrorist tactics against Israel. While many of the operations carried out by the PLO could be described as bona fide acts of war against the Israeli armed forces, violence has also been used against Israeli civilians. In almost every case Israel has reacted by even more brutal acts of revenge, including the destruction of homes owned by Palestinians. Between 1970 and 1988 alone an estimated 17,000 Palestinian homes were either partially or totally destroyed by the Israelis. Another frequent form of Israeli revenge has been the use of bombing raids carried out against Palestinian refugee camps in Lebanon. In most cases the majority of victims have been women and children.

During the 1980s the PLO gradually moved away from acts of violence as part of its new strategy aimed at bringing about the creation of an independent Palestinian state through international, especially superpower, pressure on Israel. Some groups within the PLO, however, continued to use the terrorism arm as did dissident factions such as those led by Sabri al-Banna (Abu-Nidal) and Ahmad Jibril. These terror groups, together with Georges Habache's People's Front for the Liberation of Palestine (PFLP) were often backed by various Arab states including Syria, Libya and Iraq.

The policy of ruthless retaliation practised by Israel did not achieve its declared aim of ending terrorist attacks. And from 1983 onwards the Israelis faced a new terrorist threat in the shape of the Lebanese Party of God. Israel's invasion of Lebanon in 1982 had been code-named 'Peace in Galilee' and presented as a move aimed at ending all terrorist attacks from across the Lebanese border. A number of dramatic terrorist raids on Israeli targets, however, proved that something more than military operations was needed for peace to be established in Galilee.

Violence in the Middle East at times overspilled into other regions, especially Western Europe which became the scene of many dramatic acts of hijacking and terrorist attacks during the 1970s and 1980s. The massacre of Israeli athletes during the Olympic Games at Munich in 1972 and the killing of thirty-two passengers on a West German jetliner at Rome and Athens airports by five Palestinian terrorists helped focus international attention on the problem of violence in the Middle East. In 1975 another dramatic event hit the world headlines. A Libyan-sponsored commando squad, headed by the Venezuelan terrorist Ilych Ramirez Sanchez, alias Carlos, attacked the OPEC headquarters in Vienna and seized eighty-one hostages including thirteen oil and finance ministers of the member states. Iran and Saudi Arabia paid a ransom of $25 million to secure the release of their ministers.

Between 1970 and 1988 more than 100 western diplomats and businessmen, including two American and one French ambassadors and a Belgian chargé d'affaires, were murdered by Middle Eastern terror groups. None of those responsible for the killings was brought to justice as few Middle Eastern countries wished to take the risk of standing up to terrorist groups that did not directly threaten them. A similar attitude was adopted by most western governments which often went out of their way to appease Middle Eastern terror organizations.

The Middle East in general, and Lebanon and the Islamic Republic of Iran in particular, emerged as important centres for the export of political violence to other regions of the world. Western European, North African and even Japanese terrorist groups enjoyed the protection and support of Palestinian, Lebanese and Iranian revolutionary authorities at different times in exchange for their help in planning or executing terror operations outside the Middle East.

From 1983 onwards the leftist terrorist organizations of Iran, Turkey and Iraq began co-ordinating their efforts within the framework of 'the International of the Downtrodden', a shadowy outfit that also mobilized support for such diverse groups as the Peruvian Sendero Luminoso (the Shining Path) and the New People's Army of the Philippines. The backbone of the 'International' was provided by the Turkish PKK (Kurdish Workers' Party) and the Kurdish-Iranian Komalah Marxist-Lenninist movement. Both groups had their headquarters in Stockholm, Sweden, with active offices in Paris and Hamburg.

Two incidents illustrated the degree of cooperation that existed among the various guerrilla and terrorist groups working for a new 'international'. In June 1988 Turkish police arrested eight Iranians during a police raid on a safe-house in the city of Van. The men seized were members of a group called 'Marxist-Lenninist Storm' and was allegedly involved in gun-running for the PKK.

The second incident came in July when three members of Abu-Nidal's terrorist group were arrested in Lima, Peru, and confessed to links with Sendero Luminoso. The three, all Palestinians with Iraqi passports, also spoke of joint missions involving Peruvian and other Latin American terrorists in Europe and the Middle East.

Between 1970 and 1988 more than 200 acts of terrorism directly traceable to the Middle East have been recorded in Western Europe and the United States. These acts have led to more than 300 deaths, mostly among people in no way involved in any of the Middle East's different conflicts.

13

CENTRES OF CRISIS

The Middle East, situated at the heart of what geostrategists describe as an 'arc of crisis', a vast region extending from Mauritania to Indochina, is likely to remain a source of instability for more decades to come.

The Arab-Israeli conflict, probably the most complex of the crises that the region has had to live with in its recent history, will continue to dominate the world headlines. It is, however, not the only crisis likely to plunge the region into a new war with the possibility of external powers being dragged in.

The term 'Arab-Israeli conflict' is used as a convenient shorthand for a more complex phenomenon. There are, in fact, several different interrelated sets of crises, each with its own dynamics, woven into what is described as 'the conflict'. The first of these is the conflict between Palestinian aspirations to nationhood on the one hand and the refusal by a majority of Israelis, at least until 1988, to recognize the legitimacy of such aspirations. Under the British mandate in Palestine, the Palestinians fought their own battle for self-determination against both the Zionists and Great Britain. After 1947 the Arab league seized control of the Palestine issue and turned it into a dispute between itself and the Jewish state. The Palestinians were somewhat pushed into the background and treated as pawns in an international power struggle.

The creation of the Palestine Liberation Organization

(PLO) in the wake of the 1967 Arab defeat by Israel held the promise of restoring the Palestinian people to the centre stage in a conflict that directly concerned them. But the PLO, despite pronouncements made by its leaders, quickly became involved in inter-Arab rivalries and was at times used as an instrument of pressure by Egypt, Syria, Iraq and even Saudi Arabia. The fact that most of the PLO's leaders were in exile and that the organization depended on contributions by Arab governments – despite a five per cent tax imposed on Palestinians working in the 'diaspora' – meant that the PLO was more involved in regional power politics than a day-to-day struggle against Israel. Nevertheless, the PLO succeeded in focusing attention on the Palestinian core of the conflict. Israel had tried, and to some extent succeeded, in pushing the very words 'Palestine' and 'Palestinians' out of the international vocabulary. Diplomats spoke of the 'Middle East crisis' and 'the Arab-Israeli conflict' as if the Palestinians represented little more than a side issue. The famous Resolution 242 of the United Nations' Security Council, approved in 1968, does not mention Palestine or Palestinians once. Instead it speaks of 'the refugees'.

A number of Arab states, notably Jordan, Syria and Egypt under Nasser, also tried to push the Palestinians into the background by pretending to speak on their behalf. King Abdallah of Jordan did all he could to dissolve the Palestinian issue and worked for a permanent division of Palestine between his own kingdom and Israel. His grandson, King Hussein, pursued a similar policy and maintained secret contacts with Israeli leaders.

In 1982, however, the Arab 'summit' at Fez, Morocco, reasserted the legitimacy of the PLO as the sole representative of the Palestinian people. Nevertheless, the summit also approved the broad outlines of a peace plan under which a Palestinian state would be created in the West Bank and the Gaza strip. The plan also implied Arab recognition for Israel. The Fez Plan, as the ensemble of summit decisions came to be known, represented a major step towards recognizing the right of the Palestinians to choose and apply their own strategies in their struggle for independence. But the Arab leaders were not prepared to go all the way and considered it both a right and a duty to decide the broad outlines of an eventual settlement with Israel. They maintained their basic assumption that Israel could be persuaded to accept the creation of a Palestinian state under international diplomatic pressure especially from the United States and Western Europe.

During the 1960s and part of the 1970s the PLO kept the issue of Palestinian demands for nationhood in the headlines through a series of dramatic guerrilla operations and terrorist acts. But it failed to work out a coherent long-term strategy that could fulfil Palestinian national dreams. In 1976 a majority of Palestinians in the Israeli-occupied territories voted for the PLO in the last of the municipal elections held there. Nevertheless, Israel refused to recognize the PLO as a legitimate partner for any future peace talks. This Israeli attitude helped undermine the PLO's position within the occupied territories. Yasser Arafat's organization was seen as one incapable of producing a diplomatic framework within which Israel would have to recognize the Palestinian right to self-determination. The PLO remained popular, partly because it was so hated by the Israelis. But a growing number of Palestinians in the occupied territories began to think of other means of struggle as early as 1982.

The Camp David process that led to a separate peace between Israel and Egypt in 1980 had included provisions for a negotiated settlement of the Palestinian issue as well. Very soon, however, it became clear that there was almost no chance of realizing any of the major goals of the Palestinians within that process. Camp David marked the limits of what diplomacy could achieve: complex territorial disputes between neighbouring states could be settled through negotiation but the dream of a Palestinian state could not be realized in smoke-filled back rooms of diplomatic endeavour. This did not mean that the only alternative left to the

Palestinians was a whole series of future Arab-Israeli wars as preached by Syria. Israel's military superiority, which included the possible possession of a nuclear capability, combined with Arab disunity meant that there was little chance of the Palestinian issue being settled on the battlefield.

The strategy advocated by Muslim fundamentalists could not be taken seriously either. This was based on the assumption that only a pan-Islamic 'jihad' (holy war) could push the Jews into the sea and create an Islamic Palestine. For one thing it was not certain that any call for 'jihad' would have much echo in the Muslim world. The call to 'jihad' had never been effective since the early decades of Islam. In 1918 the Ottoman Caliph declared 'jihad' but received little response except from some Kurdish tribes in eastern Anatolia. In 1948 and 1968 the al-Azhar University in Cairo, sunni Islam's most important theological centre, declared 'jihad' against Israel without creating much of a stir. In 1980 Ayatollah Khomeini launched his own 'jihad' for the liberation of Jerusalem – which for him had to come after the overthrow of the Ba'ath regime in Baghdad – but attracted little support outside Iran.

The possibility of urban guerrilla groups ever being able to force a solution on Israel was equally remote. Leaders like Georges Habache and Nayef Hawatameh, not to speak of Abu Nidal, remained marginal players at best. Their rhetoric about destroying Israel through terrorist attacks strengthened the hand of Israeli hardliners who opposed the very notion of a Palestinian state in any imaginable form. But a majority of Palestinians knew that it was not by throwing bombs in Jewish market-places or by hijacking school buses in the Negev that the flag of an independent Palestine would one day fly over any part of the occupied territories.

The various scenarios aimed at Israel's defeat or even outright liquidation as a state through the use of force failed to attract support among the Palestinian masses, not only because such schemes had little chance of being realized but also because more and more Palestinians had become genuinely reconciled to the idea of living side by side with a

Jewish state. The Palestinians of the 1940s and 1950s were probably more interested in seeing Israel, which they saw as a symbol of injustice and an affront to Arab honour, destroyed than in seeking the creation of a state of their own. The Palestinians of the 1980s, contrary to claims by the Israeli hardliners, did not dream of destroying Israel; their dream was that of having their own independent state in a world of nation states. Such a dream could not be realized by commando raids and diplomatic efforts alone; it had to take shape on the ground and among the inhabitants of the occupied territories.

Israel's occupation of Gaza and the West Bank created a number of new realities on the ground. With a population just under half that of Israel itself (1.6 million in 1988) the occupied territories developed into the second largest market for Israeli goods after the United States. They also became an important source of cheap labour for Israeli industries and services. In 1988 more than 120,000 Palestinians from the occupied territories worked in Israel itself. Between 1970 and 1980 Israel carried out a policy of de-industrialization in the occupied territories. By dumping goods, including poultry and milk products, Israel prevented the West Bank from maintaining and expanding its own industrial base. The result was a greater interlocking of the economy of the occupied territories with that of Israel itself.

During that period Arab living standards, helped by wages earned in Israel, improved appreciably. But the people of the occupied territories lagged behind their neighbours in Jordan and earned less than a third of what was earned by the average Israeli worker. The economic links created between Israel and the occupied territories were, by 1988, too strong to be ignored by either side.

Another new reality created on the ground was the growing presence of Jewish settlers in new developments in the West Bank as well as the occupied Golan Heights. In the West Bank alone the number of settlers had exceeded 50,000 by 1988. This meant that the West Bank was the scene of a triangular conflict in which the Jewish settlers and the Israeli security forces were not always on the same side. Macropolitical problems concerning Palestinian demands for statehood often mixed with local conflicts provoked by the settlers and added further tension to an already tense situation.

It was against this background that a new form of Palestinian struggle began to develop from the end of 1987 onwards. This consisted of almost daily acts of rebellion aimed at defying the occupation authorities. The rebellion, quickly dubbed 'al intifdat al-hajarieh' (the uprising of the stones) because it featured children and adolescents throwing stones at Israeli army units, began as a largely spontaneous movement in which individual and local initiatives played the main part. The PLO was certainly not involved in either planning or leading the 'intifada', at least in its earlier stages, and was plainly taken by surprise just as were the Israeli leaders.

The leadership of the 'intifada' was provided through youth clubs (shabibah) and social and charitable organizations as well as the network of religious teachers and jurists. The uprising was most severe in Gaza where poverty and political frustration created an explosive mix.

Israel's initial reaction to the 'intifada' was one of panic. The army was sent in to face stone-throwing school-children and old women. Between December 1987 and August 1988 more than 300 Palestinians were killed in almost daily clashes. A further 2,700 were wounded. Thousands of Palestinians were interned, often in what resembled concentration camps, especially in Gaza. But the 'intifada' did not die down. As the world began to count the Palestinian dead, many Israelis began to feel uneasy about playing the role of oppressors of a people that rejected occupation.

Strikes, riots, political demonstrations and mass protest meetings became almost daily occurrences and created a situation that the Tsahal could not control without harming the morale of its troops. By August 1988 some villages and parts of some cities in the occupied territories were described by their inhabitants as 'liberated territories', meaning that the Israeli security forces could not penetrate there and that occupation authorities were not obeyed by the inhabitants. An important element in the 'intifada' was a movement aimed at reasserting the Palestinians' attachment to their soil. During more than twenty years of occupation, the number of Palestinian farmers continued to decline while more and more people, especially in Gaza, became seasonal workers gleaning a meagre life on the margins of Israeli society. The 'intifada' encouraged the cultivation of the land. A number of new co-operative farms were developed and people were encouraged to grow food on any available plot of land, including some city squares.

The central slogan of the 'intifada' was 'ma fi khawf' (there is no fear). In a sense, fear changed sides during the 'intifada': it was now the Israelis who began to feel frightened. They did not fear defeat or annihilation as they had during the earlier wars with the Arab armies. What they were afraid of was being dragged into an endless confrontation in which they would have to continue killing women and children in order to hang on to a land that refused their rule.

Although the PLO remained popular in the occupied territories it did not succeed in gaining full control of the 'intifada' despite contrary allegations by the Israeli authorities. The uprising became an almost integral part of daily life in the occupied territories. Almost everyone participated in it, each according to his abilities. More than anything else since the 1960s the 'intifada' strengthened the Palestinians' sense of belonging to a national community distinct not only from the Israelis but also from other Arabs. The estimated 650,000 Arabs inside Israel itself provided the 'intifada' with a major reservoir of political and moral support while the Palestinian 'diaspora' mobilized financial aid and propaganda.

The 'intifada' showed that the Palestinian issue was not one of an external security threat to Israel's existence. There was

no Arab army that the Tsahal could destroy in a surprise
attack and no 'terrorist camp' across the border that could be
razed to the ground. The soldiers of the 'intifada' were
everywhere and their strength lay in the fact that they were
unarmed.

As a form of political protest the 'intifada' was an
undoubted success. But its limits soon became apparent. It
failed to produce clear goals set within a realistic strategy. It
also lacked the central leadership needed for negotiating
political gains. Like the PLO, the Arab states did not quite
know what to do with the unexpected uprising which they did
not control. At an extraordinary summit organized to discuss
the 'intifada' in Rabat in June 1988 the Arab leaders present
did not even agree on an analysis of the new situation. All
they could do was to express full support for the uprising and
provide $600 million to help finance it through the PLO
networks in the West Bank and Gaza.

The 'intifada' showed that Israel would have to find a new
modus vivendi with the inhabitants of the occupied territories. This was no longer a problem that could be tackled as
part of the broader Arab-Israeli conflict. No Arab government could speak on behalf of the occupied territories during
direct negotiations as demanded by Israel. Many Israelis,
including part of the Labour Party leadership, understood
this strictly local aspect of the problem faced by the Jewish
state.

At the end of July 1988 King Hussein, taking into account
the new reality created by the 'intifada' announced an end to
Jordan's many special links with the occupied West Bank.
This, in effect, removed much of the ground for any future
claim of Jordanian sovereignty over the territory. This, the
king said, was a move aimed at persuading Israel that the idea
of an independent Palestinian state could no longer be
rejected in favour of a new partitition of the occupied
territories between Jordan and the Jewish state.

If the confrontation between the PLO and Israel and the

struggle of the Palestinians in the occupied territories provide two of the four sets of crises that make up the Arab-Israeli conflict, relations between Israel and its neighbours could be considered as a third crisis. Israel's embattled relations with its neighbours were originally shaped by the partition of Palestine. Since 1948, however, new sources of tension and conflict, not exclusively related to the issue of Palestine, have come into being with the result that Israel has remained in a virtual state of war with its neighbours. Even in the case of Egypt, where the Camp David accords created a theoretical framework for normal relations, Israel failed to develop anything resembling friendly ties beyond the higher echelons of the Egyptian leadership and bureaucracy.

Israel's repeated military interventions in Lebanon, although originally provoked by PLO attacks and Syrian manoeuvres, have over the years assumed a dynamic of their own. Israel has tried to intervene directly in Lebanese politics by playing the shi'ite and Maronite cards on different occasions. In 1982 the Israelis virtually chose Lebanon's president and had him sign an agreement that turned Lebanon into something of a protectorate of the Jewish state. Israel has also carved out an enclave of its own in southern Lebanon.

Israel's relations with Syria are even more complicated and tension-ridden. Israel has formally annexed the Golan Heights which it seized in 1967 without anything remotely resembling legal or even biblical justification. Syria and Israel are also locked in their rivalry for domination in Lebanon. The Israelis consider Syria as their number one Arab enemy and have over the past four decades seized virtually every opportunity for striking against Syrian military capability. Even without the all important issue of Palestine, which is used as a centrepiece in Syrian propaganda, Israel and Syria would have many bilateral problems that could keep them at daggers drawn for a long time to come.

Relations between Israel and Jordan are often considered

to be relatively free of tension. King Hussein has certainly been the one Arab leader most forthcoming in seeking a settlement with Israel since Sadat travelled to Jerusalem. Nevertheless, Jordan and Israel have bilateral quarrels of their own. These include rival demands on sharing the waters of Jordan and prospecting for oil in the Gulf of Aqaba. But more importantly, Jordan, where Palestinians form a majority of the urban population, cannot be indifferent to what happens in the Israeli-occupied West Bank. Since 1967 Israel has exercised much economic pressure on Jordan by depriving it of its natural hinterland.

The fourth and last layer of the Arab-Israeli conflict consists of the hostility that exists between the Jewish state and almost all Arab countries. Years of propaganda have portrayed Israel as the number one enemy of the Arabs regardless of the specific issue of Palestine. Most Arab elites, both on the left and the right, are genuinely persuaded that Israel has a secret agenda for the domination of the entire Middle East. Israel's behaviour has strengthened such suspicions. Israel has used military force against Saudi and North Yemeni islands in the Red Sea and has been responsible for the destruction of the Iraqi nuclear research centre near Baghdad. Such actions, taken outside the context of the Arab-Israeli conflict over Palestine, have given credence to propaganda claims by radical Arabs concerning 'Zionist plots'.

Israel has further contributed to the deterioration of its relations with Arab states not directly involved in the conflict over Palestine by using its influence in the United States and Western Europe to frustrate Arab policies. Various US administrations have had to refuse the sale of arms and equipment to Saudi Arabia, Kuwait and even tiny Bahrain as a result of Israeli pressure exercised through Congress. Considering itself to be at war with all Arab states, probably with the exception of Morocco, Israel has used its diplomatic, military and secret service resources against most members of the Arab League on countless occasions. Israel's support for Ethiopia against Somalia during the 1960s and early 1970s, and for Iran against Iraq during the Gulf War, were also seen by many Arabs as examples of 'Zionist' hostility towards the Arabs as a whole and beyond the limits of the Palestinian issue. The Arabs found Israel a tough competitor in many parts of Black Africa, Asia and Latin America. Israel's dramatic success in air-lifting thousands of Ethiopian Jews (Falashas) to the Holy Land via the Sudan, a member state of the Arab League, was seen by many Arabs as Zionist disregard for the sovereignty of other nations.

The overall tension that exists between Israel and most Arab states has a direct bearing on prospects for the solution of the Palestinian issue. This tension makes it more difficult for the Arab countries directly adjacent to Israel to advocate peace through negotiations. Just as any progress towards a solution of the Palestine issue will dramatically improve relations between Israel and the Arab League members, a reduction of tension in these relations could, in turn, facilitate the task of seeking a negotiated settlement over Palestine.

Although relations with the Arabs have been at the centre of Israeli preoccupations ever since the Jewish state came into being, Israel's governing elites have failed to achieve concensus even on the definition of the problem at hand. As a result Israel has mostly reacted to events, including going to war or making peace as was the case with Egypt, without developing a coherent analysis of the ensemble of its problems as a state that faces a hostile environment.

Broadly speaking, Israel's governing elites are divided into two camps. There are those who believe that the Arabs will, in time, tire of hitting their heads against the strong walls of a fortress Israel and that all the Jewish state needs to do is to stand firm and prevent the building up of Arab military capabilities. Partisans of this view advocate a formal annexation of the West Bank which they regard as part of 'Greater

Israel'. They also claim that the demographic domination of the West Bank by the Arabs could be broken through mass expulsions which they describe as 'population transfers'. Some supporters of these views would be prepared to pay compensation to the Arabs who would be expelled. Others, however, are convinced that the Arabs are usurpers of a land that God has given to the Jews and should, therefore, leave without any compensation.

Opponents of 'fortress Israel' advocate an end to the Israeli occupation of the West Bank and Gaza, though not of Syrian Golan, in exchange for formal peace treaties with neighbouring Arab states. But even these 'doves' are not prepared to allow the creation of an independent Palestinian state in the occupied territories.

The Israeli right, with the Likud bloc at its heart, wants direct negotiations with the Arab states in the absence of the PLO. The Israeli left, centred around the Labour Party, would accept some form of international conference with the two superpowers present to guarantee any accord that might be reached. But even Labour would not be prepared to accept the PLO as a negotiating partner. Since most Arab states, principally Syria and Jordan, were not prepared to enter into direct talks with Israel in the absence of the PLO and without any form of United Nations participation, the so-called peace process initiated by Camp David remained frozen for nearly a decade.

Israel's electoral system, based on proportional representation, accentuated the nation's political divisions and prevented the adoption of coherent policies regarding the occupied territories and relations with the Arab states. The grand coalition government formed by the Likud and the Labour Party from the mid-1980s managed to take radical measures needed to reform the economy but remained deadlocked on the Palestinian issue.

Another centre of crisis likely to remain in the headlines for some time to come is Lebanon. After 1975 Lebanon, in fact, ceased to exist as an independent nation state capable of deciding its own policies. In 1988 there were at least eight major sectarian armies in Lebanon: two Maronite, two shi'ite, three sunni and one Druze. These existed side by side with a Syrian occupation force, an Israeli mercenary army in the south, a UN peace-keeping force and 'volunteer' units from Iran and Libya. At the same time Lebanon's own national army continued to exist thanks to cash donations from the United States and tacit support from Syria. For a total population of just over three million people Lebanon counted no fewer than 150,000 armed men on its soil.

The Lebanese parliament, which also elected the president of the republic and named a prime minister and cabinet, could not be renewed through general elections for nearly a decade. Its strength was reduced as its members died or went into exile. Its moral authority had been reduced to a minimum by 1988. There was no Lebanese party or political force capable of contemplating the country's situation beyond sectarian considerations. Lebanon was divided into fiefdoms held by warlords in the name of this or that religious faith. The trouble was that the constitutional framework imposed on the country during the French mandate ran counter to the realities existing on the ground. All factions spoke of maintaining Lebanon's unity as a nation state with the proviso that they themselves should be at the centre of power.

Israel, having failed to seize control of Lebanese politics through Bechir Gemayel's Phalangists in 1982, remained determined to sabotage any attempt at creating a central government in Beirut. Syria, for its part, pursued its long-term policy of gingerly annexing Lebanon in all but name. Syria's ambitions, however, ran into opposition from both Iran and Israel as well as the PLO which succeeded in rebuilding its own armed presence in parts of Beirut and the south from 1986 onwards.

Between 1980 and 1988 the Persian Gulf region remained in the news as the scene of a major international crisis. The Gulf's importance as a source of energy for the West and Japan declined in relative terms during the 1980s as demand for crude oil lagged behind supply, especially from non-OPEC sources. Nevertheless, the seven oil-exporting countries of the Persian Gulf (Iran, Iraq, Saudi Arabia, Kuwait, Qatar, UAE and Oman) continued to control more than twelve per cent of the international market for crude. Even more important was the Gulf's vast reserves of oil and natural gas which gave it long-term strategic importance. The Gulf is destined to remain a major exporter of energy long after the oil reserves of the North Sea and the continental United States have dried up.

The development of new weapons systems and the slow but steady easing of tension between the United States and the USSR from the mid-1980s onwards meant that the Gulf was no longer regarded as a possible theatre for superpower confrontation in the immediate future. Under Mikhail Gorbachov the USSR adopted a low profile in Gulf affairs while the United States, excluded from Iran since 1979, could play only a limited role. Nevertheless, the Gulf as a whole retained much of its economic and political importance. With total imports estimated at more that $70,000 million a year the eight states of the Gulf represented a lucrative market, especially for arms and consumer goods.

Over a longer term the Persian Gulf might emerge as a major source of energy for a USSR that is expected to become a net importer of crude oil within the next decade or so. And if Soviet industry picks up as a result of Gorbachov's *perestroika*, or re-structuring, policies the Gulf might be seen as an attractive market from Moscow. The Gulf is likely to become an even more interesting theatre of East-West competition, if not actual confrontation, in the years to come. The roots of political crisis in the Gulf, however, go beyond competition among outside powers. The Gulf states have not yet succeeded in working out a basis for stable relations among themselves.

The Iran–Iraq war is the most dramatic illustration of this instability but it is not the only one. The end of the war would in no way mean an end to tension in the region. Because of its larger population and the fact that it owns the entire eastern coasts of the Persian Gulf and the adjacent Gulf of Oman, Iran considers itself as the natural leader of the region. This Iranian ambition, nurtured under the shah in the 1970s, was amplified under the revolutionary regime of the mullahs. The fact that the mullahs based the legitimacy of their regime on the claim that they alone represented 'true Islam' added a new dimension to Iran's already uncertain relations with its Arab neighbours.

Iran financed and encouraged shi'ite dissident groups, including some that had recourse to terror, in all the Arab states of the Gulf. At the same time Iran and Saudi Arabia became involved in a major quarrel regarding control of the holy shrines at Mecca and Medina. The Saudi royal family defended its position as the guardian of holy shrines and exercised its right to fix the number of pilgrims during the Haj ceremonies. Iran, however, called for the creation of an international Islamic committee to control the shrines and supervise the Haj. For the first time in history, Iran decided to boycott the Haj pilgrimage in 1988 and thus deepened the first major schism in Islam in more than five centuries.

Apart from their unsettled relations with one another, the states of the Gulf continued to suffer from internal instability also. Few enjoyed the means and traditions necessary for greater popular participation in decision-making and none enjoyed the institutions of freedom and responsibility that alone could ensure political stability in the long run. The presence of a growing middle class that included tens of thousands of people educated in the West meant that a genuine constituency for the idea of a more open society already existed in most states of the Gulf. The desire of the new middle classes for change became a potential source of conflict with the traditional rulers who accepted economic modernization but resisted political reform.

One direct consequence of the Iran–Iraq war was the gradual diversion of oil routes from the endangered Strait of Hormuz to the Red Sea. Between the 1940s and 1980 no new major oil pipelines had been constructed in the Gulf region. Between 1980 and 1988, however, four major pipelines had been completed and four more were being planned. The reason was that all the oil exporting countries of the region wished to move their oil trade routes as far from the Persian Gulf as possible. Iraq constructed two new pipelines, one to Turkey and thence to the Mediterranean and another that joined the Saudi network onto the Red Sea. Kuwait, Saudi Arabia, the UAE and Qatar also managed to reduce the volume of oil exports through the Gulf. Even Iran began planning for pipelines linking its oilfields to terminals on the Gulf of Oman.

The diversion of a good part of the Gulf's oil exports to the Red Sea region diminished the crucial importance of the Strait of Hormuz in favour of a new 'choke-point', the Bab al-Mandab – an even narrower and more vulnerable sea-route. The Strait of Hormuz was unlikely to be closed either by Iran or Oman, which jointly controlled it, for the simple reason that both countries were themselves exporters of oil. The same could be said of the Persian Gulf as a whole which remained open to shipping through more than eight years of war. None of the littoral states had an interest in seeing the Gulf turned into a sea of flames shunned by international shipping.

The situation in the Red Sea, which by the next decade will handle more oil than the Persian Gulf, was quite different. Most littoral states like South and North Yemen, the Sudan and Ethiopia were not oil exporters and thus did not have a direct interest of their own in making sure that oil routes remained secure. Furthermore, South Yemen and Ethiopia were close allies of the USSR while almost all the oil that passed through the Bab al-Mandab and the Red Sea in general was destined for the West. The new oil route could also be threatened by Israel in the case of a new major war with the Arabs. Israeli jets were capable of attacking Bab al-Mandab to stop tankers from passing through. The radical nature of the regimes in Ethiopia and South Yemen and the fragility of state authority in North Yemen and the Sudan, meant that the Red Sea could become more vulnerable to terrorist attacks than the Gulf.

Another potentially major centre of crisis was Afghanistan which, although not part of the Middle East as such, was affected by the politics of the region and, in its turn, could have an impact on developments in Iran, Pakistan and the Arab states of the Gulf. In 1988 the USSR announced that it had ended its direct military intervention in Afghanistan in accordance with an agreement signed in Geneva. But the parties to the agreement, the Soviet-sponsored government in Kabul and Pakistan, did not control the situation inside Afghanistan. By the summer of 1988 the Kabul government controlled less than twenty per cent of Afghan territory, with more than a dozen guerrilla armies controlling the rest. Financed and armed by the United States, Saudi Arabia, Iran, Egypt and the UAE, the various guerrilla forces were unable to agree on a common strategy regarding the future government of the country.

Deep divisions among the guerrilla leaders combined with the conflicting ambitions of the United States, the USSR, Pakistan, Iran and Saudi Arabia to turn Afghanistan into a veritable powder keg not far from the Persian Gulf. The country's tribal and sectarian feuds, dating back to the eighteenth century, threatened to create a Lebanon-style situation on a much larger scale.

Instability in Afghanistan would, almost by definition, extend into Pakistani Baluchistan where central authority has always been under strain. Developments in Pakistani Baluchistan could, in turn, provoke tension in Iranian Baluchistan, a vast almost empty space of rugged mountains that are difficult to control by military force alone. The presence of large numbers of Afghan refugees in the Pakistani provinces of Sind and Baluchistan was established as a source of communal conflicts that led to more than 200 riots and over 700 deaths between 1986 and 1988. In Iran Afghan refugees were better integrated and more effectively controlled. Nevertheless, Iran also felt a certain tension resulting from the presence of the refugees. In 1988 more than 8,000 Afghans were in prison in Iran mostly on charges of smuggling or activities in support of the Kabul regime.

14

BEHIND THE HEADLINES

Not all the elements in the cauldron that is the politics of the Middle East are reflected in the world headlines devoted to the region. The Arab-Israeli conflict in some of its aspects, the Iran-Iraq war and the acts of Middle Eastern terrorism against western targets are given prominence. But a great deal is left out until the simmering crisis explodes into a violent event capable of attracting instant attention.

One fact that is not sufficiently known outside the Middle East is that none of the countries in the region could be said to live under normal conditions. Turkey was under martial law between 1983 and 1985, with emergency rules still being in force in parts of eastern Anatolia in 1988. The state of emergency declared in Egypt in 1980 was extended until 1991. In Iran and Iraq the special conditions created by the war were not the sole reasons for the imposition of emergency rule on large parts of each country. In Saudi Arabia there were no formal emergency measures but parts of the kingdom, especially al-Hassa where the shi'ites formed a majority, lived under a special security regime. Syria has been living under successive regimes of martial law or emergency regulations since 1962. And South Yemen began a new era of martial law in 1986.

With the exception of Turkey and Egypt where some opposition parties were allowed to function, none of the Middle Eastern states recognized or tolerated the right of dissent. Israel, of course, remained in a category of its own as far as its Jewish citizens were concerned. The occupied territories, however, remained under military administration and were governed in accordance with emergency rules.

Another major issue seldom mentioned in headlines regarding the Middle East was the region's veritable demographic explosion. The entire population of the region was estimated to be just over 62 million in 1938. Fifty years later this was over 200 million. Registering one of the fastest rates of population growth in the world, the Middle East was projected to top the 400 million mark by the year 2010. Very few of the countries of the region had the financial and administrative resources required for providing minimum standards of education, health and gainful employment for their expanding populations.

One direct result of the demographic explosion in the region was that in most countries, especially the larger ones, the percentage of illiterates increased in the 1980s, reversing the trend of the period of 1965–75.

Formal attempts at population control have been made in Egypt, Turkey and Iran under the shah with little impact. Public opinion remains hostile to family planning which is described by both fundamentalist and nationalist elements as a 'plot' by the West to keep the region underpopulated and weak. Fundamentalist propaganda emphasizes the West's alleged fear that Muslims might turn the Mediterranean into an Islamic lake simply by altering its demographic balance. Western Europe, Mesopotamia and the relatively under-populated Sudan are portrayed in fundamentalist propaganda as natural spaces for the overspill in the populations of North Africa, Egypt and Turkey.

The Middle East's demographic explosion has led to the rapid but disorderly growth of many towns and cities. In 1938 less than twenty per cent of the region's population lived in towns with a population of more than 10,000. In 1988 that figure exceeded fifty per cent. Also in 1938 only one city in the region, Cairo, had a population approaching the one million mark. In 1988 there were seventeen such cities. Cairo, with a population of more than 12 million, and Tehran with 10 million were among the world's most populated urban centres in 1988. A further thirty Middle Eastern cities were expected to pass the one million population mark before the end of the century.

The increase in urban population was only partly due to natural demographic growth. In most cases rural migration played an even greater part in the expansion of Middle Eastern cities. This was especially true in the case of Egypt, Turkey, Iran and Iraq. As more and more cities became ringed with slums, the political weight of a rootless population consisting of ruined peasants, seasonal workers and the urban poor came to be felt in many countries of the region. It is among the slum-dwellers that the fundamentalist preachers recruit much of the muscle power they need in their struggle for domination in Egypt, Turkey, Iran, Lebanon and Iraq.

The emergence of slum megalopolises has also meant a dramatic increase in crime rates and drug addiction in the larger countries of the region. In 1986, for example, Iran announced that it had to cope with more than two million 'serious cases' of heroin and opium addiction. Extensive cultivation of opium in Iran and parts of northern Iraq, and the boom in the business of growing hashish in Lebanon, put the Middle East on the map as a major centre for the production of narcotics.

Life in the big cities also illustrates the widening gap between the rich and the poor. A certain section of the rich, even in revolutionary Iran, feels and acts in a 'foreign' manner and appears as an alien class to a majority of the population. For these rich the country of their birth is nothing more than a place in which one makes the money needed for investment or expenditure in the West. Throughout the 1970s and 1980s the Middle East, including such poor countries as South Yemen, was a major exporter of capital to the United States and Western Europe. Foreign investment made by individuals, companies and governments of the region in that period probably exceeded $100,000 million. Even Egypt, a relatively poor nation, had its own multinational investors, mostly emerging out of President Sadat's policy of 'infitah' or free enterprise.

The ostentatious style of life adopted by the new rich contrasted sharply with living conditions in the tin and cardboard districts of many large cities where lack of sanitation, pollution, overcrowding and violence created an image of hell on earth. Many of the region's larger slum-ringed cities are the scene of frequent riots leading to clashes with security forces.

Dismissing the slum-dwellers as the quintessential 'lumpenproletariat' the left in the Middle East consistently ignored the political potential of the new poor. This gave both the Islamic fundamentalist groups and right wing nationalist movements a chance to use the mass of the 'downtrodden' as an inexhaustible source of popular support for themselves. In the 1960s it was in the region's universities that the message of revolt was preached with the greatest passion. In the 1980s and probably the 1990s also it is the urban slums that serve as the cradle of revolt against the established order.

The Middle East's serious problem of terrorism in the 1970s and 1980s is directly, though not exclusively, linked with the climate of social tension provoked by the rich-poor divide. Attempts to curb terrorism through more efficient police work have proved insufficient in the absence of policies that could give hope to the poor. Even the creation of a more democratic atmosphere does not necessarily lead to an end of terrorist activities. Turkey, where an elected government was established after the referendum in 1983, continued to suffer from terrorism of both the right and the left. Between 1983 and 1988 no fewer than ninety-seven acts of terrorism were recorded, mostly in the eastern provinces. In June 1988 Prime Minister Turgot Ozal escaped an assassination attempt by a member of the pan-Turk 'Grey Wolves' organization. Egypt, which also experienced some measure of democratization, had a similar experience. In 1988 more than 700 people were in prison on charges directly related to various acts of terrorism between 1983 and 1987.

Another potentially explosive issue that is not reflected in world headlines with regard to the Middle East concerns the status of women in society. The 1980s could be described as a period of retreat for those who supported the cause of legal equality and more individual liberties for women. Under pressure from Islamic fundamentalists most Middle Eastern governments have either postponed or cancelled earlier policies in favour of more rights for women. More importantly, the number of girls attending school at all levels declined through much of the 1980s, especially in Iran, Turkey and Egypt. Ironically, it was only in the more traditionally Islamic states such as Saudi Arabia that the number of girls attending school continued to increase in both absolute and relative terms.

Political back-tracking on women's rights, however, did not reflect the true status of women in the larger countries of the region. In Iran and Iraq the continuation of the war meant that, with many men at the front, women assumed a greater role in running the economy and the bureaucracy. This was specially true in the case of Iraq where women registered an impressive advance at virtually all levels of economic and administrative life.

The absence of millions of men who worked abroad meant that women in Egypt and Turkey were able to enhance their role in the economy without securing an improvement in their legal and social status. The more traditional societies like Saudi Arabia, Kuwait, Qatar and the emirates, offered women new educational opportunities but did not follow this up by providing jobs for women graduates. Women continued to be barred from many fields of activity within the administration or in industry. Even the western-educated elites continued to believe that women were primarily destined to be wives and mothers and that education for women was more of a luxury than a necessity. None of the governments in the predominantly Muslim states of the region were prepared to consider a reform of Islamic rules and traditions regarding the status of women.

The issue of a new and more equal status for women was only part of the broader issue of human rights in the region. Some of the states in the region were signatories to various international covenants on human rights. But none could be said to abide by the internationally accepted rules. In 1988 only Israel, Turkey and Egypt could be described as more or less free societies where individual and collective political rights were recognized and respected at least in part. Israel's treatment of its Arab citizens as a separate 'millet' (religious and ethnic community) meant that they did not enjoy full equality with their Jewish fellow Israelis. Turkey continued its policy of cultural repression against the Kurdish minority and also denied more than a million of its citizens such rights

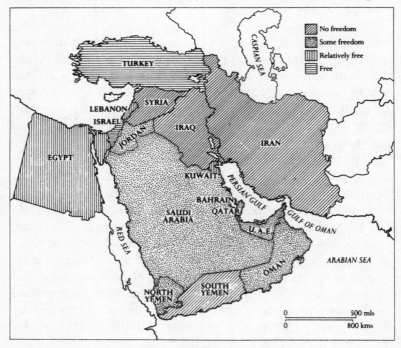

Freedom in The Middle East

as foreign travel or practising a profession of their own choosing.

Overall, the human rights situation in the Middle East showed a marked deterioration in the 1980s compared with the preceding decade. Part of this was due to the Islamic Revolution in Iran and the Gulf War, events that frightened many states of the region and wrongly persuaded them that concessions on human rights could lead to revolution. Nevertheless, a growing constituency for western-style human rights had, by 1988, become a fact of life in most countries of the region. Scores of private groups, large and small, campaigned for human rights in Iran, Iraq, Turkey, Egypt, Israel, Lebanon, Syria and the Gulf emirates. These groups carried little political weight in 1988 and many of their leaders were either in exile or frequently imprisoned. And yet they represented a potentially serious political force which few governments could afford to ignore.

The argument most often used by governments in their attempt to justify the slow progress achieved on human rights is that the Middle East must consider economic development as its top priority at least for the foreseeable future. The assumption that respect for human rights might somehow compromise a nation's economic development is general among the governing elites in the region. This is due to the absence of a coherent and comprehensive understanding of the problem of modernization in general. Few people in the region question the necessity of adopting western technology as part of an effort to improve the material conditions of life. Even Iran's revolutionary mullahs acknowledged the need to learn from the West in industrial and scientific fields. The fact that the West's technological progress and economic prosperity cannot be divorced from its political system and moral values, however, is either ignored or rejected as a colonialist illusion.

The paramount role played by the state in economic decision-making in most countries of the region has led to policy experiments often dictated by ideology. The authoritarian model of development adopted by Mehmet Ali Pasha in Egypt, Atatürk in Turkey and Reza Shah in Iran, was not seriously questioned until the 1970s. In Egypt, Nasser used a socialist vocabulary of his own but pursued a policy of state-funded and controlled development on the same lines as that of the modernizing Khediv. Under Nasser the Egyptian government took over almost the whole of the non-agricultural sector of the economy down to the level of street kiosks. The result was superficial industrialization symbolized by a series of big projects aimed at enhancing the role of the government in the economy. Sadat, who succeeded Nasser in 1970, had little difficulty in handing over part of the economy to private entrepreneurs, often chosen from among his relatives and political friends. But this did not reduce the overall domination of the economy by government bureaucracy.

Iran under the shah presented itself as a champion of free enterprise but, in fact, had a centrally-controlled economy. That part of the GNP controlled by the government through central or regional plans and budgets was more than seventy-five per cent, higher than most countries in socialist East Europe.

Turkey's economic *étatisme*, considered to be a sacred part of the kemalist heritage, was not seriously questioned until the mid-1980s. It was the government of Turgot Ozal that achieved a major, though incomplete, break with the traditional policy of state intervention at all levels of the economy. Ozal preached deregulation and monetarism and told the Turks that it was not only their right but also their duty to try to get rich. Nevertheless, Ozal made sure that the central government remained the main player in the economic game through tight and detailed budgetary control. His government also printed as much money as it could get away with.

The period 1950–1980 was marked by a general fascination with big projects aimed at strengthening the state. This was a period of white elephants - prestige projects often financed by oil windfalls or foreign loans. The aim of economic development was considered to be industrialization. And industrialization meant expensive iron and steel plants and car assembly factories. In many countries, agriculture was considered to be a source of social and economic backwardness and, therefore, largely ignored in government investment plans. One result of this lack of attention to the needs of agriculture was that by 1988 all countries of the region, with the exception of Turkey, were net importers of food. The failure of the region's agriculture to keep pace with population growth and the accumulated technical backwardness of the past four or five decades mean that the Middle East might remain dependent on food imports for the foreseeable future. As a larger slice of the region's oil income is spent on food imports the part of national income that could be invested in economic development will continue to decline.

The 1980s, nevertheless, have been marked by a growing awareness that economic development should be aimed at meeting the needs of the people through the mobilization of available resources. A number of oil-based industries, notably petrochemicals, have come into being. Housing, education, public health and the preservation of the environment have been recognized as important priorities. The ability of unscrupulous western salesmen to find customers for their white elephants in the Middle East has been dramatically reduced.

And yet many countries of the region seemed to be heading for a prolonged economic crisis in the years to come. Only four countries, Iran, Qatar, UAE and Oman had no foreign debts. In the case of Iran the main reason was that not a single major development project had been launched since 1980. Qatar, UAE and Oman either lacked the population base for major development that would need large financial resources or could still rely on their vast reserves of foreign currency accumulated during the preceding two decades. Even wealthy Saudi Arabia, however, was forced to seek foreign loans to finance its continued development in 1988.

Inflation, indebtedness, growing unemployment and the

persistent backwardness of the agricultural sector were some of the signs of the economic crisis that loomed ahead. One reason for the relative lack of success experienced by most economic development plans in the region is the limited nature of national markets in the Middle East. Where there is a sufficiently large population base, as in Egypt for example, it is the lack of purchasing power that limits demand for most goods and services. And where purchasing power exists in abundance, as is the case in Qatar or Kuwait or even Saudi Arabia, the small size of the population imposes obvious limits on demand.

Attempts at creating larger markets and co-ordinating development plans in the region have so far produced little tangible result. In the 1960s and 1970s Iran, Turkey and Pakistan tried to pool their resources through Regional Co-operation for Development (RCD) but made little progress largely because of national jealousies and conflicting ambitions. Also in the 1970s some Turkish leaders and technocrats, including Turgot Ozal, advocated the creation of a pan-Islamic common market but faced strong opposition from both Iran and Egypt. Iran, for its part, advanced the idea of an Indian Ocean common market that would include parts of the Middle East as well as the Indian subcontinent down to Indonesia and Australia.

The Gulf Co-operation Council (GCC), various pan-Arab development banks and joint development planning commissions grouping together a number of Arab states represent more modest, but also more effective, attempts at fostering regional co-operation. In 1988 the Arab states of the Gulf, with the exception of Iraq, were involved in more than 100 development projects in various parts of the Middle East notably Egypt and Turkey.

Despite more than three decades of sustained effort the Middle East as a whole remained a largely underdeveloped region. It had tremendous assets, including vast reserves of cheap labour in Egypt, Turkey and Iran with Pakistan and Afghanistan providing back-up capacity. It also enjoyed a steady flow of cash from oil exports, an income which, if converted to investment could speed up the development of the entire region. There were also important reserves of unused arable land in Turkey, Iran and Iraq, with the Sudan capable of offering even larger areas for cultivation. Development plans based on pooling the resources of the region together with its natural peripheries such as Pakistan and Afghanistan to the east and the Sudan to the southwest, could help create a new setting for economic activity in which each country would have its own role to play. But all that remained in the realm of dreams in 1988. Land, population, water and financial policies continued to be uncoordinated with no prospect of bringing them together in the context of a regional economy. The political weakness of most governments meant that they remained obsessed with the problem of their own security and survival and were not prepared to take major risks by surrendering any part of their control of their economies to supranational authorities.

The wealthier countries of the region were prepared to pay subsidies to the poorer ones but would rarely agree to enter into industrial and agricultural joint ventures. Some countries, notably Syria and North Yemen, owed their economic survival in the 1980s to subsidies and gifts from the Arab states of the Gulf and Iran. These subsidies and gifts alleviated the short-term problems of government but frustrated all serious attempts at tackling basic economic issues.

During its long history the Middle East has been a perfect illustration of the evanescence of human achievements; the rise and fall of so many civilizations is a testimony that progress is not vertical and that the battle for dignity and prosperity is a constant struggle. The oil boom of the 1970s and part of the 1980s in some countries of the Middle East gave the region a new reputation as a latter-day Eldorado. The Middle East was portrayed as a land where camels were replaced by Rolls-Royces and emirs competed with one another in acquiring the latest of frivolous gadgets that the West had to offer.

That distorted image hid a number of cruel facts, including the region's appalling economic and social underdevelopment even compared with most Asian and Latin American countries. Even in 1988 infant mortality in the Middle East remained higher than anywhere else in the world with the exception of parts of Africa. Average life expectancy was half that of most Western European countries and lower than the average for many Asian and Latin American ones. Hunger, lack of shelter, disease and poverty remained the basic problems of life for more than half of the region's population. Even in the fabulously rich oil-states, important segments of the population lived under conditions normally associated with the poor nations of the Third World.

Mounting economic problems, including indebtedness, did not prevent average military expenditure from increasing throughout the region during the 1980s. In 1988 only North Yemen, which allocated less than twelve per cent of its national budget to defence, was close to the international average for military expenditure. All other countries spent much more. Egypt, Israel, Syria, Iran, Iraq and Saudi Arabia reserved more than twenty per cent of their national budgets for defence. In most cases the real figure could have been even higher had indirect expenditure by the military sector been taken into account. The Camp David peace accords between Egypt and Israel did not lead to a reduction in military expenditure by either country but helped moderate the steady growth of their defence budgets. In the case of Syria, real expenditure on the military, including the cost of intervention in Lebanon, accounted for nearly half the national budget in 1987–1988. This was a major factor in the severe economic crisis faced by the country.

The presence of oversized military machines in almost all Middle Eastern countries was not always due to the ever present threat of war. In many countries, including Israel and Turkey each in its own specific way, the army provided the backbone of the state structure. In Egypt, Syria, Jordan, Iraq, North Yemen and South Yemen the armed forces controlled not only political power but also many sectors of the economy. They saw themselves as the guardians of state security and saw expenditure on defence as an investment in preserving the nation's integrity and independence.

From a longer-term point of view, however, excessive expenditure on the military could be regarded as a threat to internal peace and stability in many Middle Eastern countries. By giving the armed forces the lion's share in national budgets most Middle Eastern countries had to limit investment in economic development and the provision of social services. This in turn led to disaffection, especially among the poor, and helped radical movements attract the muscle power they needed for threatening the security and stability of the state. At the same time it was not at all certain that the armed forces, which consisted mostly of conscripts, would as a whole remain loyal to the established order.

In Egypt, years of infiltration into the armed forces by Muslim fundamentalists attracted world attention when President Sadat was murdered by an army lieutenant during a military parade. Between 1980 and 1988 more than 6,000 officers and NCOs were either purged or forced into early retirement in Egypt. Hundreds were imprisoned or subjected to police interrogations for their alleged links with fundamentalist groups. It was no longer possible to be sure that the Egyptian armed forces would defend the established order against any challenge to its authority.

The situation was only slightly different in Turkey where the armed forces took pride in their kemalist traditions. Between 1980 and 1988 an extensive purge of the Turkish armed forces meant that hundreds of officers and NCOs were forced into early retirement or relieved of sensitive posts of command.

In Iran the Islamic Revolutionary Guard had been created by Ayatollah Khomeini as a protector of the regime against possible hostile moves by the regular armed forces. But by

1988 the ayatollah appeared uncertain of the Guard's loyalty and, in a series of moves, brought the force under the direct control of the ruling mullahs. More than $30,000 million spent on the Guard over more than nine years had failed to ensure its complete loyalty to the theocracy.

The presence of excessively large armed forces, especially in the smaller states of the region, was a source of more instability rather than less. Few rulers ignored the fact that most political changes in the Middle East have been initiated by the armed forces. Some regimes, like the Marxist-Leninist one in South Yemen, hoped to control the armed forces and prevent them from developing political ambitions by putting many key units under direct or indirect foreign command. In 1988 the South Yemeni armed forces benefited from the services of more than 2,000 Soviet, East European and Cuban military advisers who, in reality, controlled the most sensitive parts of the machine.

In Oman and some of the emirates of the Gulf a similar role was played by British, Australian, Canadian and, more importantly, Pakistani officers and NCOs seconded to the local armies. The presence of thousands of professional soldiers from both Iranian and Pakistani Baluchistan as well as Jordan, Egypt, the Sudan and North Yemen also helped prevent the armies of Oman and the emirates from assuming an independent political role of their own. But this was at best a transitory situation and each year more and more local people assumed a greater role in the armed forces of the countries concerned.

The increasingly sophisticated nature of the weapons systems acquired by most countries of the region, together with the growing complexity of modern military organization and warfare, meant that a new highly-educated officers corps gradually came to the fore especially in Iran, Iraq, Saudi Arabia and the emirates. Compared with them the ruling elite, especially in the more traditionalist states, appeared conservative and reactionary. This emphasized the role of the armed forces as a potential ally of the progressive forces in the region.

As the 1980s draw to a close the Middle East remains both a generator and victim of insecurity and instability. Leaving aside the special case of Israel, it is only in Turkey, Egypt and, in a different context, Jordan, Kuwait and Bahrain that the established order has shown a willingness to broaden its popular base by providing some measure of public partici- pation in decision-making. In Iran the revolutionary turmoil accumulated over decades and unleashed in 1978 is likely to need more time before settling down and thus allowing the Iranians to develop the new system of government needed for tackling the nation's political, economic, social and demo- graphic problems. Syria and Iraq, despite their apparent stability under exceptionally ruthless regimes, remain in a state of suspension and thus likely to experience more violent changes in the future.

South Yemen, although unlikely to shake off its one-party system in the near future, will almost certainly move towards the political centre in the years to come. Such a move is dictated partly by changes in Soviet foreign policy that make alliance with countries like South Yemen far less attractive than was the case under Leonid Brezhnev. This means that South Yemen will have to find new sources of financial support and seek to ensure its security by creating better relations with its neighbours rather than depending on Soviet guarantees.

North Yemen, which assumed some importance during the 1960s because of its civil war, has already relapsed into its marginal role in regional politics. Faced with almost in- surmountable problems caused by poverty and under- development, North Yemen is likely to continue to depend on foreign aid for many years to come. The instability of its regime will almost certainly be as much dictated by the attitude of its foreign benefactors, notably Saudi Arabia, as by its own internal political developments.

The region's more traditionalist states, notably Saudi

Arabia and the emirates, have avoided many a political pitfall thanks to large oil incomes and the relatively small size of their populations. But there, too, the old structures do not appear flexible enough to accommodate the new political forces that had come into being during more than four decades of economic and social development. Not a single country in the region escaped from the cauldron.

BIBLIOGRAPHY

Abdallah, Umar F., *The Islamic Struggle in Syria*, Berkeley, California, 1983.

Abdel-Malek, A., *La Pensée Politique Arabe Contemporaine*, Paris, 1975

————,*Egyptian Military Society*, New York, 1967.

Abir, Mordechai, *Oil, Power and Politics: Conflicts in Arabia, the Red Sea and the Gulf*, London, 1974.

Ervand Abrahamian, *Iran between two Revolutions*, Princeton, New Jersey, 1982.

Abu Jaber, Kamel, *The Arab Baath Socialist Party*, Syracuse, New York, 1966.

Abu-Lughod, Ibrahim, *The Transformation of Palestine*, Evanston, Illinois, 1971.

Adams, Sherman, *Firsthand Report*, New York, 1961

Adamson, David, *The Kurdish War*, London, 1964.

Afkhami, Gholam-Reza, *The Iranian Revolution, Thanatos on a national scale*, Washington, DC, 1985.

Afshar, Haleh (ed.), *Iran: A Revolution in Turmoil*, London, 1985.

Ajami, Fouad, *The Arab Predicament*, Cambridge, Massachusetts, 1981.

————, *The Vanished Imam*, New York, 1986.

Al-Ahmad, Jalal, *Occidentotis : a Plague from the West*, Berkeley, California, 1984.

Algar, Hamid, *Religion and State in Iran, 1785–1906: The Role of the Ulama in the Qajar Period*, Berkeley and Los Angeles, 1969.

——, *Islam and Revolution. Writings and Declarations of Imam Khomeini*, Berkeley, California, 1981.

Ali, S. R., *Saudi Arabia and Oil Diplomacy*, New York, 1976.

Ali Jaidah, M., *An Appraisal of OPEC Oil Policies*, London, 1983.

Almana, Mohammad, *Arabia Unified: A Portrait of Ibn Saud*, London, 1980.

Al-Otaiba, M. S., *OPEC and the Petroleum Industry*, London, 1975.

Amin, Samir, *Irak et Syrie 1960–1980*, Paris, 1982.

Amir-Arjomand, Said, *The Shadow of God and the Hidden Imam: Religion, Political Order and Societal Change in Shi'ite Iran from the Beginning to 1980*, Chicago, Illinois, 1984.

Amirie, Abbas (ed.), *The Persian Gulf and Indian Ocean in International Politics*, Tehran, 1976.

—— (ed.), *Iran in the 1980s*, Tehran and Washington, DC, 1978.

Amirsadeghi, Hossein (ed.), *Twentieth Century Iran*, London, 1977.

—— (ed.) *The Security of the Persian Gulf*, New York, 1981.

Amos II, John W., *Palestinian Resistance: Organisation of a Nationalist Movement*, New York, 1980.

Anderson, Norman, *The Kingdom of Saudi Arabia*, London, 1978.

Arberry, Arthur J., *The Koran Interpreted*, Oxford, 1972.

Arkoun, Muhammad, *Pour une Critique de la Raison Islamique*, Paris, 1984.

Avery, Peter, *Modern Iran*, London, 1965.

Azari Farah, (ed.), *Women of Iran: the Conflict with Fundamentalist Islam*, London, 1983.

El-Azhar M. S., (ed.), *The Iran-Iraq War*, London, 1984.

Aziz, Philippe, *Les Sectes Secrètes de l'Islam*, Paris, 1983.

Al-Baharna, Hussein, *The Arabian Gulf States – their Legal and Political Status and their International Problems*, Beirut, 1975.

Ball, George W., *Error and Betrayal in Lebanon*, Washington, DC, 1984.

Balta, Paul, *L'Islam dans le Monde*, Paris, 1986
———, *Irak-Iran, Histoire d'une Guerre*, Paris, 1986.

Banani, Amin, *The Modernization of Iran*, Stanford, California, 1971.

Barnavi, Elie, *Israël au XXème Siècle*, Paris, 1984.
———, *Une Histoire Moderne d'Israel*, Paris, 1988.

Baron, Xavier, *Les Palestiniens, un Peuple*, Paris, 1984.

Bayne, E. A., *Persian Kingship in Transition*, New York, 1968.

Beaujeu-Garnier, J., *L'Economie du Moyen-Orient*, Paris, 1977.

Beck, L. and Keddie, N. (eds), *Women in the Muslim World*, Cambridge, Mass., 1978.

Beling, Willard, *King Faisal and the Modernization of Saudi Arabia*, Boulder, Colorado, 1980.

Ben Gurion, David, *The Jews in Their Land*, New York, 1974.

Benjelloun-Olivier, Nadia, *La Palestine: un Enjeu, Deux Stratèges, un Destin*, Paris, 1984.

Benoist-Mechin, Jacques, *Mustapha Kemal*, Paris, 1954.
———, *Un Printemps Arabe*, Paris, 1974.
———, *Faysal: Roi d'Arabie*, Paris, 1975.

Bereby, Jean-Jacques, *Le Golfe Persique*, Paris, 1959.

Berger, Monroe, *Islam in Egypt Today*, Cambridge, 1970.

Berkes, Niyazi, *The Development of Secularism in Turkey*, Montreal, Canada, 1964.

Bernard, Cheryl and Khalilzad, Zalmy, *The Government of God*, New York, 1984.

Berque, Jacques, *The Arabs: their History and Culture*, London, 1964.
———, *Normes et Valeurs dans l'Islam Contemporain*, Paris, 1966.
———, *Mahgreb, Histoire et Société*, Paris, 1974.

Bill, James A., *The Politics of Iran: Groups, Classes and Modernization*, Colombus, Ohio, 1976

——— and Leiden, Carl, *The Middle East, Politics and Power*, Boston, Mass., 1974.

Binder, Leonard, *Iran: Political Development in a Changing Society*, Berkeley and Los Angeles, 1962.

———, *In a Moment of Enthusiasm: Political Power and the Second Stratum in Egypt*, Chicago, 1978.

Bitterlin, Lucien, *Hafez el-Assad, Le parcours d'un combattant*, Paris, 1986.

Blandford, Linda, *Oil Shaikhs, Inside the supercharged World of the Petrodollar*, London, 1984.

Boissard, M., *L'Islam Aujourd'hui*, Paris, 1984.

Boulares, Habib, *L'Islam, la Peur et l'Espoir*, Paris, 1982.

Braudel, Fernand, *La Méditerranée et le Monde Méditerranéen*, Paris, 1966.

———, *La Grammaire des Civilisations*, Paris, 1987.

Briere, Claire, *Liban, Guerres Ouvertes (1920–1985)*, Paris, 1985.

——— and Olivier Carre, *L'Islam, Guerre à l'Occident, Paris, 1983*.

Brown, L. Carl, *International Politics and the Middle East: Old Rules, Dangerous Game*, London, 1985.

Brzezinski, Zbigniew, *Power and Principle: Memoirs of the National Security Adviser 1977–1981*, New York, 1983.

Bulloch, John, *The Final Conflict: The War in Lebanon*, London, 1977.

Bullard Rider, (ed.), *The Middle East*, Oxford, 1961.

Burlot, Joseph, *La civilisation islamique*, Paris, 1982.

Burrel, R. M., *The Persian Gulf*, Beverly Hills, California, 1972.

Calvocoressi, Peter, *World Politics since 1945*, London, 1987.

Cantwell-Smith, W., *Islam in Modern History*, Princeton, New Jersey, 1957.

Carrere d'Encausse, Hélène, *La Politique Soviétique au Moyen Orient 1955–1975*, Paris, 1975.

Carre, Olivier and Dumont, Paul (eds), *Radicalisme Islamique (Tomes I et II)*, Paris, 1985, 1986.

—— and Gérard Michaud, *Les Frères Musulmans*, Paris, 1983.

Caroz, Yaacov, *The Arab Secret Services*, London, 1978.

Carter, Jimmy, *Keeping Faith*, New York, 1982.

Chaliand, Gerard, *Revolution in the Third World*, New York, 1977.

——, *People without a Country: the Kurds and Kurdistan*, London, 1980.

Charles, Raymond, *Le Droit Musulman*, Paris, 1982.

Charnay, Jean-Paul, *L'Islam et la Guerre*, Paris, 1986.

Chouraqui, André, *L'Etat d'Israël*, Paris, 1984.

Cobban, Helena, *The Palestinian Liberation Organisation: People, Power and Politics*, Cambridge, 1984.

Cohen, E. J., *Turkish Economic, Social and Political Change: Development of a more Prosperous and Open Society*, London, 1970.

Cohen, Aharon, *Israel and the Arab World*, Boston, Massachussetts, 1976.

Cook, M. A. (ed.), *Studies in the Economic History of the Middle East*, London, 1970.

Copeland, R. W., *The Land and People of Jordan*, New York, 1965.

Copeland, Miles, *The Game of Nations - The Amorality of Power Politics*, London, 1970.

Corm, Georges, *Le Proche-Orient Éclate*, Paris, 1984.

Cottam, R. W., *Nationalism in Iran*, Pittsburgh, Pennsylvania, 1979.

Cotterell Alvin, (ed.), *Persian Gulf: a General Survey*, Baltimore, Maryland, 1980.

Cremeans, Charles, *The Arabs and the World – Nasser's Arab Nationalist Policy*, New York, 1963.

Curtis, Michael (ed.), *Religion and Politics in the Middle East*, Boulder, Colorado, 1981.

Da Lage, Olivier and Grzybek, Gérard *Le Jeu des Six Familles*, Paris, 1985.

Dawisha, Adeed (ed.), *Islam in Foreign Policy*, Cambridge, 1983.

De Bock, Walter and Deniau, Jean-Charles, *Des Armes pour l'Iran*, Paris, 1988.

Deeb, Marius, *The Lebanese Civil War*, New York, 1980.

De George, Gérard, *Syrie*, Paris, 1983.

Raoul Delcorde, *La Sécurité et la Stratégie dans le Golfe Arabo-Persique*, Paris, 1983.

Derriennic, Jean-Pierre, *Le Moyen-Orient au XXe Siècle*, Paris, 1983.

Desjardins, Thierry, *Cent Millions d'Arabes*, Paris, 1974.

Devlin, John, *Syria: Modern State in an Ancient Land*, Boulder, Colorado, 1983.

Dewdney, J. C., *Turkey*, London, 1971.

Dickson, Violet, *Forty Years in Kuwait*, London, 1971.

Dickson, H. R. P., *The Arabs of the Desert*, London, 1972.

Dietl, Wilhelm, *Holy War*, New York, 1984.

Djalili, Mohammad-Reza, *L'Océan Indien*, Paris, 1978.

Doughty, Charles, *Travels in Arabia Deserta*, (2 vols.), London, 1964.

Duncan, Andrew, *Moneyrush*, London, 1979.

Duncan Betts, Robert, *Christians in the Arab East, a Political Study*, London, 1979.

During, Jean, *Islam: le Combat Mystique*, Paris, 1975.

Eagleton, William Jr., *The Kurdish Republic of 1946*, New York, 1963.

El-Cherif, Kamel, *Les Frères Musulmans dans la guerre de Palestine*, Cairo, Egypt, 1948 and 1982.

Elwell-Sutton, L. P., *Persian Oil - a Study in Power Politics*, Westport, Conn., 1976.

Enayat, Hamid, *Modern Islamic Political Thought*, Austin, Texas, 1982.

Exposito, John L. (ed.), *Voice of Resurgent Islam*, Oxford, 1983.

Essaid, Abdul-Aziz, *Le Réveil de l'Islam*, Marseille, 1985.

Etienne, Bruno, *L'Islamisme Radical*, Paris, 1987.

Eveland, W. C. *Ropes of Sand: America's Failure in the Middle East*, New York, 198?.

Fadhlallah, Muhammad-Hussein, *Islam and the Logic of Force*, Beirut, 1981.

Farouk-Sluglett, Marion and Peter, *Iraq since 1958, from Revolution to Dictatorship*, London, 1987.

Fenelon, K. G., *The United Arab Emirates: an Economic and Social Survey*, London, 1973.

Fesharaki, Fereydoun, *Development of the Iranian Oil Industry: International and Domestic Aspects*, New York, 1976.

Feuillet, Claude, *Le Système Saoud*, Paris, 1983.

Fisher, W. B., *The Middle East*, London, 1978.

Fischer, Michael M., *Iran: from Religious Dispute to Revolution*, Cambridge, Massachussetts, 1982.

Frangi, Abdullah, *The PLO and Palestine*, London, 1983.

Franck, Claude and Herszlikowicz, Michel, *Le Sionisme*, Paris, 1980.

Fraser, T. G., *The Middle East, 1914–1979*, (Documents of Modern History), London, 1980.

Freedman, Robert, *Soviet Policy Toward the Middle East since 1970*, New York, 1982.

Frye, Richard, *Iran*, London, 1960.

Gabbay, Ronay, *Communism and Agrarian Reform in Iraq*, London, 1978.

Garaudy, Roger, *La promesse d'Islam*, Paris, 1981
———, *L'Affaire d'Israël*, Paris, 1983

Gardet, Louis, *L'Islam: Religion et Communauté*, Paris, 1967.

———, *Le Mystique*, Paris, 1981.

Edmond Ghareeb, *The Kurdish Question in Iraq*, Syracuse, New York, 1981.

Ghirshman, Roman, *Iran*, London, 1978.

Gibb, H. A. R., *Studies on the Civilization of Islam*, Boston, Massachussetts, 1962.

Gilmour, David, *The Dispossessed: The Ordeal of the Palestinians 1917-1980*, London, 1980.

———, *Lebanon: The Fractured Country*, New York, 1984.

Golan, Matti, *The Secret Conversations of Henry Kissinger*, New York, 1976.

Golan, Galia, *The Soviet Union and the Palestine Liberation Organization: An Uneasy Alliance*, New York, 1980.

Graham, Robert, *Iran, the Illusion of Power*, London, 1978.

Graz, Liesl, *Les Omanais, Nouveaux Gardiens du Golfe*, Paris, 1981.

Grenville, J. A. S., *A World History of the Twentieth Century*, London, 1980.

Gresh, Alain and Vidal, Dominique, *Palestine 47, un Partage Avorté*, Paris, 1988.

Grose, Peter, *Israel in the Mind of America*, New York, 1983.

Grossman, David, *Le Vent Jaune*, Paris, 1988.

Grummon, Stephen, *The Iran-Iraq War*, New York, 1982.

Gubser, Peter, *Jordan: Crossroad of Middle Eastern Events*, London, 1983.

Guerreau, A. and A., *L'Irak, Developpement et Contradictions*, Paris, 1978.

Guillaume, Alfred, *Islam*, London, 1977.

Habiby, Emile, *The Secret Life of Saeed, the Ill-fated Pessoptimist*, London, 1985.

Haddad, Wadi, *Lebanon: The Politics of Revolving Doors*, Washington, DC, 1985.

Haig, Alexander, *Caveat*, New York, 1984.

Haim, Sylvia (ed. and trans), *Arab Nationalism, an Anthology*, London, 1962.

Hajjar, Joseph, *L'Europe et les destinées du Proche-Orient*, Paris, 1977.

Hale, W. M. (ed.), *Aspects of Modern Turkey*, London, 1976.

Hall, Alan, *Arafat*, London, 1985.

Halliday, Fred, *Arabia without Sultans*, London, 1975.

―――― and Alavi, Hamza (eds), *State and Ideology in the Middle East and Pakistan*, London, 1988.

Harrison, Paul, *Inside the Third World*, New York, 1982.

Hawley, D. F., *The Trucial States*, London, 1970.

―――――, *Oman and its Renaissance*, London, 1976.

Haykal, Mohammed Husanayn, *The Road to Ramadan*, New York, 1975.

Heard-Bey, Frauke, *From Trucial States to United Arab Emirates*, London, 1982.

Heikal, Muhammad, *Autumn of Fury*, London, 1983.

Henry, Paul-Marc, *Les Jardiniers d'Enfer*, Paris, 1984.

Hershlag, Z. Y., *Economic Structures of the Middle East*, Leiden, Holland, 1975.

Hirst, David, *The Gun and the Olive Branch*, London, 1983.

———— and Beeson, Irene, *Sadat*, London, 1981.

Hobday, Peter, *Saudi Arabia Today*, London, 1978.

Hodgson, Marshall G. S., *The Order of the Assassins*, The Hague, 1955.

Hodlen, David and Johns, Richard, *The House of Saud*, New York, 1981.

Holt, P. M., Lambton, A. K. S. and Lewis, B., *The Cambridge History of Islam*, (vols. I and II), London, 1970.

Hoogland, Eric J., *Land and Revolution in Iran 1960–1980*, Austin, Texas, 1982.

Hosaini, I. M., *The Muslim Brothers*, Beirut, 1969.

Hourani, Albert, *Arabic Thought in the Liberal Age 1798–1939*, London, 1962.

Hoveyda, Fereydoun, *Les Nuits Féodales*, Paris, 1983.

Howard, H. N., *Turkey, the Straits and US Policy*, Washington, DC, 1974.

Hudson, Michael C., *Arab Politics: the Search for Legitimacy*, New Haven and London, 1977.

Hunke, S., *Le Soleil d'Allah Brille sur l'Occident*, Paris, 1985.

Hureau, Jean, *La Syrie Aujourd'hui*, Paris, 1984.

Hurewitz, J. C., *The Struggle for Palestine*, New York, 1950.

————, *Middle East Politics: the Military Dimension*, New York, 1969.

Hussein, Asaf, *Political Perspectives of the Muslim World*, New York, 1985.

Iskander, Amir, *Saddam Hussein, le Militant, le Penseur et l'Homme*, Paris, 1980.

Ismael, T. Y., *Iraq and Iran: Roots of Conflict*, Syracuse, New York, 1982.

Issawi, Charles, *The Economic History of the Middle East 1800-1914*, Chicago, 1966.

Iyad, Abu, *My House, My Land*, New York, 1981.

Jackh, Ernest, *The Rising Crescent*, New York, 1944.

Jansen, Godfrey H., *Militant Islam*, London, 1979.

Johany, Ali, *The Myth of the OPEC Cartel: The Role of Saudi Arabia*, New York, 1980.

Jazani, Bizhan, *Capitalism and Revolution in Iran*, London, 1980.

Joumblatt, Kamal, *Pour le Liban*, Paris, 1978.

Kadar, Benjamin Z., *Crusade and Mission: European Approaches towards the Muslims*, Princeton, New Jersey, 1984.

Kadhafi, Mouammar, *Je Suis un Opposant à l'Échelon Mondial*, Lausanne, Switzerland, 1984.

Kalisky, René, *Le Monde Arabe: 1) L'Essor et le Déclin d'un Empire*

———, *Le Monde Arabe: 2) Le Réveil et la Quete d'Unité*, Paris, 1963.

Kaminsky C. and Kruk, S., *La Syrie - Politiques et Stratégies*, Paris, 1987.

———, *La Stratégie/Soviétique au Moyen-Orient*, Paris, 1988.

Kayyoli, A. W., *Palestine: A Modern History*, London, 1978.

Keddie, Nikki R., *Religion and Politics in Iran*, London, 1983.

Kedourie, Elie, *Arabic Political Memoirs and Other Studies*, London, 1974.

———, *Islam and the Modern World*, London, 1980.

Kelidar Abbas, (ed.), *The Integration of Modern Iraq*, London, 1979.

Kepel, Gilles, *Le Prophète et le Pharaon*, Paris, 1984.

Kerr, Malcolm, *Islamic Reform: the Political and Legal Theories of M. Abduh and R. Rida*, Cambridge, 1966.

Kiernan, Thomas, *The Arabs*, London, 1978.

Kimche, David and Bawly, Dan, *The Sandstorm: the Arab-Israeli War of 1967*, London, 1968.

Kinross, Lord, *Atatürk: The Re-birth of a Nation*, London, 1964.

Kirk, G. E., *A Short History of the Middle East*, London, 1964.

Kissinger, Henry, *White House Years*, New York, 1979.

———, *Years of Upheaval*, New York, 1982.

Khadduri, Majid, *Socialist Iraq: a Study in Iraqi Politics since 1968*, Washington, DC, 1978.

Khalidi, Walid, *Conflict and Violence in Lebanon*, London, 1983.

Khalidi, Rashid, *Under Siege: PLO Decision-making during the 1982 War*, New York, 198?.

Khalili, Nader, *Racing Alone*, San Francisco, 1983.

Khayat-Bennai, G., *Le Monde Arabe au Féminin*, Paris, 1985.

Khomeini, Ruhollah, *Islamic Government*, Rome, 1984.

Khouja, M. W. and Sadler, P. G., *The Economy of Kuwait, Development and Role in International Finance*, London, 1979.

Kutschera, Chris, *Le Mouvement National Kurde*, Paris, 1979.

Lacey, Robert, *The Kingdom*, London, 1983.

Lacouture, Jean, *Nasser*, Paris, 1971.

Laffin, John, *Fedayeen*, London, 1973.

———, *The Arab Mind*, London, 1978.

———, *The Dagger of Islam*, London, 1981.

Lambton, A. K. S., *Landlord and Peasant in Persia*, London, 1953.

———, *The Persian Land Reform 1962–1966*, Oxford, 1969.

Landau, J. M., *The Arabs in Israel*, Oxford, 1969.

Landen, R. G., *The Emergence of the Modern Middle East (Selected readings)*, New York, 1970.

Laoust, Henri, *Les Schismes dans l'Islam*, Paris, 1965.

Laqueur Walter, (ed.), *The Middle East in Transition, New York, 1958.*

Laqueur Walter, (ed.), *The Struggle for the Middle East. The Soviet Union and the Middle East*, London, 1969.

—— (ed.), *A History of Zionism*, New York, 1972.

—— and Rubin, Barry (ed.), *The Israeli-Arab Reader*, London, 1984.

Laraoui, Abdallah, *L'Idéologie Arabe Contemporaine*, Paris, 1982.

Laurent, Annie and Basbous, Antoine, *Guerres Ouvertes au Liban*, Paris, 1987.

Ledeen, M. and Lewis, W., *Débâcle: the American Failure in Iran*, New York, 1981.

Lenczowski, George, *Russia and the West in Iran*, New York, 1949.

——, *Iran under the Pahlavis*, Stanford, California, 1978.

Levy, Reuben, *The Social Structure of Islam*, Cambridge, 1962.

Lewis, Bernard, *The Emergence of Modern Turkey*, Oxford, 1961.

——, *The Middle East and the West*, New York, 1964.

——, *The Arabs in History*, London, 1977.

——, *The Assassins*, London, 1982.

Long, David E., *The United States and Saudi Arabia, Ambivalent Allies*

Lutfiyya, A. M. and Churchill, C. W. (eds), *Readings in Arab Middle Eastern Society and Culture*, Paris and the Hague, 1970.

Luttwak, Edward, *Coup d'État, a Practical Handbook*, London, 1979.

Mabro, Robert, *The Egyptian Economy 1952–1972*, Oxford, 1974.

Malfray, Marie-Ange, *L'Islam*, Paris, 1980.

Mangold, Peter, *Superpower Intervention in the Middle East*, London, 1978.

Mansfield, Peter (ed.), *The Ottoman Empire and its Successors*, London, 1973.

——, *The Middle East: A Political and Economic Survey*, London, 1973.

Mantran, R., *Histoire de la Turquie*, Paris, 1977.

Maoz, Moshe and Yaniv, Avner, (eds), *Syria under Assad*, London, 1986.

Marr, Phebe, *The Modern History of Iraq*, Boulder, Colorado, 1985.

Marshall, G. S. Hodgson, *The Venture of Islam*, 3 vols, Chicago, 1974.

Masse, Henri, *L'Islam*, Paris, 1948.

Massignon, Louis, *Parole donnée*, Paris, 1962.

Mawdoodi, Abul-Ala, *Islamic Law and Constitution*, Rome, 1984.

Mclaurin, Ronald D., *The Political Role of Minority Groups in the Middle East*, New York, 1979.

Merad, Ali, *L'Islam Contemporain*, Paris, 1984.

Mernissi, F., *Sexe, Idéologie, Islam*, Paris, 1983.

Migdal Joel S. (ed.), *Palestinian Society and Politics*, Princeton, New Jersey, 1986.

Mihailovitch, Lijoubomir and Pluchart, Jean-Jacques, *L'OPEP*, Paris, 1980.

Miles, S. B., *The Country and Tribes of the Persian Gulf*, London, 1966.

Miller, Aaron David, *The PLO and the Politics of Survival*, New York, 1983.

Miquel, André, *L'Islam et sa civilisation*, Paris, 1977.

Mitchell, Richard, *The Society of Muslim Brothers*, London, 1969.

Monteil, Vincent, *Clefs sur la pensée Arabe*, Paris, 1974.

———, *Dossier secret sur Israël: le Terrorisme*, Paris, 1979.

More, Christiane, *Les Kurdes aujourd'hui, mouvement National et partis politiques*, Paris, 1984.

Morris, James, *The Hashemite Kings*, London, 1959.

Mortimer, Edward, *Faith and Power, the Politics of Islam*, London, 1981.

Moss Helms, Christine, *The Cohesion of Saudi Arabia*, London, 1980.

Mosley, Leonard, *Power-Play: Oil in the Middle East*, New York, 1973.

Nakhleh, Emil, *The Persian Gulf and American Policy*, New York, 1982.

Nantet, Jacques, *Histoire du Liban*, Paris, 1986.

Nasr, S. H., *Ideals and Realities of Islam*, London, 1966.

Nasser, Gamal Abdul, *The Philosophy of the Revolution*, Cairo, 1964.

Niblock, Tim, *Iraq: the Contemporary State*, London, 1982.

Nizan, Paul, *Aden, Arabie*, Paris, 1967.

Nuseibeh, Hatim, *The Ideas of Arab Nationalism*, Princeton, New Jersey, 1956.

Nutting, Anthony, *The Arabs*, New York, 1965

————, *Nasser*, London, 1972.

Olson, Robert W., *The Ba'th and Syria 1947–82*, Princeton, New Jersey, 1982.

Owen, Roger, *The Middle East in the World Economy 1800–1914*, London, 1981.

Pakradouni, Karim, *La Paix Manquée*, Paris, 1984.

Patai, Raphael, *The Arab Mind*, New York, 1976.

Peroncel-Hugoz, Jean-Pierre, *Une Croix sur le Liban*, Paris, 1984.

Peterson, J. E., *Yemen: The Search for a Modern State*, Baltimore, Maryland, 1982.

Piscatori J. (ed.), *Islam in the Political Process*, Cambridge, 1983.

Poliakov, Léon, *De Moscou à Beyrouth*, Paris, 1983.

Popovic A. and Veinstein, G. (eds.), *Les Ordres Mystiques dans l'Islam*, Paris, 1966.

Poulton, Michel and Robin, *L'Afghanistan*, Paris, 1981.

Purser, B. H., *The Persian Gulf*, Berlin, 1973.

Quandt, William *et al*, *The Politics of Palestinian Nationalism*, Berkeley, California, 1973.

Qutb, Muhammad, *Islam - the Misunderstood Religion*, Rome, 1984.

Raban, Jonathan, *Arabia Through the Looking Glass*, London, 1979.

Rabinovich, Itamar, *The War for Lebanon 1970–1982*, New York, 1984.

Rahman, Fazlur, *Islam*, Chicago, Illinois, 1984.

Rahnema, Z., *Mahomet, le Prophète*, Rome, 1984.

Raouf, Wafik, *Nouveau regard sur le Nationalisme Arabe*, Paris, 1984.

——, *Irak-Iran, des Vérités Inavouées*, Paris, 1985.

Raymond André, (ed.), *La Syrie d'Aujourd'hui*, Paris, 1980.

Richard, Yann, *Le Shi'isme en Iran*, Paris, 1980.

Richmond, J. C. B., *Egypt 1798–1952*, London, 1967.

Rizk, Charles, *Entre l'Islam et l'Arabisme, les Arabes jusqu'en 1945*, Paris, 1983.

Rodinson, Maxime, *Israël et le Refus Arabe*, Paris, 1968.

——, *Marxisme et Monde Musulman*, Paris, 1972.

——, *Mohammad*, London, 1973.

——, *Islam and Capitalism*, London, 1977.

Rondot, Philippe, *La Syrie*, Paris, 1977.

——, *L'Irak*, Paris, 1979.

Rouhani, Fouad, *A History of OPEC*, New York, 1971.

Rouleau, Eric, *Les Palestiniens*, Paris, 1984.

Roy, Olivier, *L'Afghanistan: l'Islam et Modernité Politique*, Paris, 1985.

Rubin, Barry, *The Arab States and the Palestine Conflict*, Syracuse, New York, 1981.

Rubinstein, Alvin Z. (ed.), *The Arab-Israeli Conflict: Perspectives*, New York, 198?.

al-Rumaihi, Muhammad, *Bahrain, Social and Political Change*, London, 1977.

Rustow, Dankwart, *Oil and Turmoil*, New York, 1982.

Ruthven, Malise, *Islam in the World*, London, 1984.

Saadoui, N., *La Face Cachée d'Eve, les Femmes dans le Monde Arabe*, Paris, 1982.

Sablier, Edouard, *Iran: La Poudrière*, Paris, 1980.

Sachs, Ignacy, *The Discovery of the Third World*, Cambridge, Massachussetts, 1976.

al-Sadat, Anwar, *In Search of Identity*, New York, 1978.

Safran, Nadav, *Saudi Arabia: the Ceaseless Quest for Security*, Cambridge, Massachussetts and London, 1985.

Said, Edward W., *The Question of Palestine*, New York, 1979.

Salibi, Kamal S., *Crossroad to Civil War: Lebanon 1958– 1976*, New York, 1976.

Sampson, Anthony, *The Seven Sisters*, New York, 1975.

Sanger, Richard H., *The Arabian Peninsula*, New York, 1970.

Savory, R. M. (ed.), *Introduction to Islamic Civilization*, Cambridge, 1976.

Sayigh, Y. A., *The Economies of the Arab World*, London, 1978.

Schacht, Joseph and Bosworth, C. E., *The Legacy of Islam*, Oxford, 1974.

Scholl-Latour, Peter, *Les Guerriers d'Allah*, Paris, 1986.

Seale, Patrick, *The Struggle for Syria*, Oxford, 1965.

Seymour, Ian, *OPEC, Instrument of Change*, London, 1980.

Sharif, Faruq, *A Guide to the Contents of the Qur'an*, London, 1986.

Shiff, Zeev and Yarl, Ehoud, *Israel's Lebanon War*, New York, 1984.

Shlaim, Avi, *Collusion Across the Jordan*, London, 1988.

Sourdel, Dominique, *L'Islam*, Paris, 1986.

Spencer-Trinigham, J., *The Sufi Orders in Islam*, London, 1971.

Stephens, Robert, *Nasser: A Political Biography*, London, 1971.

Stookey, Robert, *Yemen: The Politics of the Yemen Arab Republic*, Boulder, Colorado, 1978.

Tabataba'i, S. Mohammad Hussein, *Shi'ite Islam*, Albany, New York, 1975.

Taheri, Amir, *The Spirit of Allah, Khomeini and the Islamic Revolution*, London, 1985.

Taheri, Amir, *Holy Terror, the Inside Story of Islamic Terrorism*, London, 1987.

Taher-Kheli, Shirin and Ayubi, Shaheen (eds), *The Iran-Iraq War: New Weapons, Old Conflicts*, New York, 1983.

Tarab-Zamzani, Abdel-Majid, *La Guerre Iran-Irak*, Paris, 1985.

Tavernier, René, *Tentation de l'Orient*, Paris, 1977.

Taylor, Alan, *The Arab Balance of Power*, Syracuse, New York, 1982.

Terzian, Pierre, *L'Étonnante Histoire de l'OPEP*, Paris, 1983.

Thesiger, Alfred, *Arabian Sands*, New York, 1959.

————, *The Marsh Arabs*, London, 1978.

Thomas, Hugh, *Suez Affair*, New York, 1966.

Tillman, Seth, *The United States in the Middle East*, Bloomington, Indiana, 1982.

Tueni, Ghassan, *La Guerre pour les Autres*, Paris, 1985.

Tuval, Saadia, *The Peacemakers: Mediators in the Arab-Israeli Conflict 1948–1979*, Princeton, New Jersey, 1982.

Upton, John, *History of Modern Iran: An Interpretation*, Cambridge, Massachusetts, 1961.

Vadney, T. E., *The World since 1945*, London, 1987.

Vance, Cyrus, *Hard Choices: Critical Years in American Foreign Policy*, New York, 1983.

Van Dam, Nikolaos, *The Struggle for Power in Syria*, London, 1979, 1981.

Valland, Pierre, *Le Liban au bout de fusil*, Paris, 1976.

Vatikiotis P. J. (ed.), *Egypt since the Revolution*, London, 1968.

———— (ed.), *Nasser and His Generation*, London, 1978.

Vital, David, *The Origins of Zionism*, Oxford, 1975.

Vocke, Harald, *The Lebanese War*, London, 1984.

INDEX

Compiled by Gordon Robinson